Edward Barnsley and h

Arts and Crafts in the Twentieth Century

After studying History of Art followed by Museum Studies at the University of Manchester, Annette Carruthers worked at Leicestershire Museums, where the collection of Gimson–Barnsley furniture inspired her interest in the Arts and Crafts Movement. This was further developed at Cheltenham Art Gallery and Museums where she was involved in creating new displays of the rich Arts and Crafts collections.

Annette Carruthers is currently a Leverhulme Research Fellow at the University of St Andrews and the National Museums of Scotland. She is married to an archaeologist and lives in Edinburgh.

Edward Barnsley and his Workshop
Arts and Crafts in the Twentieth Century

Annette Carruthers

Published by

White Cockade Publishing
71 Lonsdale Road
Oxford OX2 7ES

British Library Cataloguing-in-Publication Data

A catalogue record for this book is available from the British Library

ISBN 1 873487 03 7 paperback

The publisher gratefully acknowledges generous support for the original
production costs of this book from The Guild of St George, The Paul Mellon
Centre for Studies in British Art, and Southern Arts.

Opposite title page
1. Edward Barnsley in his workshop, 1945.

Cover design by Gerald Cinamon
Text design by Perilla Kinchin
Typeset in 10 on 12.5 Photina at the Oxford University Computing Service
Printed in Great Britain by The Bath Press

For Alan

2. The workshop in 1980: George Taylor, Oskar Dawson, Tania Barnsley and
Mark Nicholas in the 'top shop'.

CONTENTS

PREFACE AND ACKNOWLEDGEMENTS

For many years Edward Barnsley thought that he would write his own book. This was to be not an autobiography, but an accurate record of the lives and work of his father, Sidney Barnsley, his uncle Ernest, and their colleague Ernest Gimson, as well as a practical work on design for the use of handicraft teachers in schools and colleges, and a convincing argument for the value of craft skills and small workshops in the twentieth century. In 1959 and 1960 he made a determined attempt to work out his ideas on paper but he found the process extremely frustrating and eventually gave up in despair, contenting himself over the next twenty years with writing long and detailed letters in an attempt to put the record straight. I first met Edward when I was researching a catalogue of the Leicestershire Museums furniture collection and I found his comments invaluable because he was not simply concerned with factual matters, but also with inference and understanding.

The picture that I can give of Edward Barnsley and his work is clearly not the one he would have presented himself, but I have included as much as possible in his own words because these give a vivid impression of his character and concerns. 'How I delight in writing reames [sic] of old rubbish. And spell so many words wrong', he wrote to David Leach in 1967, in a typically self-deprecating phrase. Most of his letters were typed and I have worked mainly from the uncorrected carbon copies, though I have also seen some originals. His spelling and punctuation were always individual and the actual letters, with amendments and small drawings, have an immediacy which is not present in transcripts. For many of Barnsley's correspondents, this was one of the great pleasures of hearing from him, but to save confusion between his practice of pausing mid-sentence with several dots, and my cuts to his text, I have tidied up his punctuation. Obvious typing errors have been corrected but spelling mistakes I have left.

The research for this book has been made pleasurable by the kindness of the many people I have met in my search for information and the friendships I have made. I thank them all for their help.

For their unfailing interest, hospitality, and patience, I am particularly grateful to all the Barnsley family, especially Karin Antonini, Eva, Jon, and Tania Barnsley, and Anthony and Rochelle Davies.

The book would not have been started without the encouragement and practical help of Margaret and the late Max Burrough, and it has only been finished with the aid of Mary Greensted, Alan Peters, and Alan Saville, whose comments on the typescript have been invaluable.

For information about the running of the workshop and issues affecting twentieth-century furniture makers, I am indebted to Hugh Birkett, Chris and Louise Butler, Lou and Richard Elderton, Pat Kirkham, Penny Laughton, Graham Leake, Morris Lupton, Mike McGrath, Oliver Morel, Alan Morrall,

Mark Nicholas, Vera Simpson, George Taylor, Robert Townshend, and the late Herbert Upton. Rod Herdman kindly explained the workshop finances and accounts to me, and William Inman has provided insight into the timber trade.

Clients and friends of Barnsley and owners of his furniture have been immensely helpful and enthusiastic, and my thanks go to Jane Bailey, John Barnfield, John Beer, the late Mrs Mary Biddulph, Mr and Mrs Davey Cole, Alfred Gimson, the late Nina Griggs, Nigel Grimwood, Lawrence Mitchell, Rosemary Mulholland, the late Roger Powell, Peyton Skipwith, and Gonda Stamford.

Barnsley's work at Loughborough and the educational questions involved have been illuminated for me by Godfrey Beaton, Idris Cleaver, Arthur Dearden, the late Bill Elloway, Elisabeth Gemmill, Cecil Gough, Joe Maslin, Don Porter, John Purdy, Ken Rosewarne, John Tuck, John Warburton, and Ashley Wiffen. Information about the Rural Industries Bureau has come from Brian Baxter, Liane Bradbrook, Bill Carter, and Arnold Pentelow.

For discussion of the Arts and Crafts background and issues affecting the crafts, I am grateful to Janet Barnes, Alan Crawford, Ann Hartree, David and Lida Kindersley, Fiona MacCarthy, Sir George Trevelyan, and Barbara Van Dyke.

The production of this book has been made possible by the generous financial assistance of The Guild of St George, The Paul Mellon Centre for Studies in British Art, and Southern Arts. I am very grateful to Anthony Harris, David Jones, David Kay, Professor Michael Kitson, Mrs Evelyn Newby, Mr Douglas Smith, and Clive Wainwright for their help and advice. My thanks are due to Perilla Kinchin for her commitment to the book, her editorial advice, which has greatly improved the text, and her inspired arrangement of text and illustrations.

Illustration Acknowledgements

Most of the illustrations are from the archive of the Edward Barnsley Educational Trust. For help in obtaining additional photographs I am very grateful to John Barnfield, Bedales School Library, Cheltenham Art Gallery and Museums, Cecil Gough, David Kindersley, Ian Larner, James Noel White, John Purdy, Vera Simpson, and George Taylor.

For permission to reproduce copyright photographs thanks are due to Pamela J. Barnsley *58, 74*; British Steel *84*; Bromhead (Bristol) Ltd *81*; Cheltenham Art Gallery and Museums, Woodley and Quick photograph *36*; Prudence Cuming Associates Ltd *75*; Department of the Environment *85*; Srdja Djukanovic *65*; Brian Donnan *67*; Donald C. Eades *2, 55, 100, 101*; Hulton Deutsch *1, 43, 44*; Harold Lowenstein *62, 73, 83, 89, 92, 94, 95, 99*; John Manners *68*; P.J.E. Photos *102*; Rural Development Commission *49, 50, 51*; Vanessa Stamford *26, 32, 37, 80, 93*; O. W. Wilmot *63, 66, 86, 90, 91*.

THE EDWARD BARNSLEY ARCHIVE

Edward Barnsley's designs, sketches, photographs, letters, and business records are preserved and available for study by appointment in the cottage in which he spent most of his life. The archive is not a completely comprehensive collection, since few copies of letters survive from before 1938 and some drawings are known to have been given to clients, but it is a remarkable resource for the study of furniture making and the history of the craft movement in the twentieth century.

The archive is still growing and the Edward Barnsley Educational Trust would be pleased to hear from anyone with letters from Barnsley, or similar material of which there may not be copies in the collection. The Trust can be contacted via the Barnsley Workshop, Cockshott Lane, Froxfield, Petersfield, Hampshire, GU32 1BB.

Funding from the Leverhulme Trust made possible the cataloguing of the collection, which was carried out under the aegis of the History Department at Loughborough University through Dr Marylyn Palmer. It was supervised by Bill Elloway until his death in 1984 and thereafter by Dr Godfrey Beaton, and the work was done by Robert Walker in 1984 and by Penny Laughton from 1984 to 1987. Conservation work was undertaken by Lou Elderton, and invaluable advice on storage, indexing, repairs, and conservation was received from the Hampshire Archives Trust. Racks and shelving were made by the craftsmen in the workshop. The small-scale drawings have been microfilmed by World Microfilms, London, and details of these can be obtained from the Trust. A catalogue of the designs was typed by Avril Turner.

Barnsley's vast correspondence has been indexed and filed under the supervision of Karin Antonini, Penny Laughton, and Lou Taylor by members of the Petersfield Branch of the National Association of Decorative and Fine Art Societies: Mrs Jane Burstall, Mrs Jane Coward, Mrs Phylis Dacam, Mrs Ros Hamilton, Mrs Jane James, Mrs Julia Kerr, Mrs Penny Rose, Mrs Rosemary Ryder, and Mrs Phillida Wedderburn-Ogilvy. N.A.D.F.A.S. members have also assisted Karin Antonini and Lou Elderton with fund-raising for the project.

Donations to the archival project were received from the following grant-giving bodies and from individual donors: Antique Dealers' Association; Chase Charity; Crafts Council; East Hampshire District Council (for decorating the archives room); Gane Trust; Godinton Trust; Hampshire Archives Trust; Hampshire County Council; I.B.M., Hursley Park; Sir Cyril Kleinwort Charitable Settlement; National Association of Decorative and Fine Art Societies; Petersfield Decorative and Fine Art Society; Sotheby's, Billingshurst; T.V.S. Trust (for drawings catalogue).

June 24th 1974

My Dear Vera,

First to ask how you both are,and to say how much I hope that (things' are
well.   I no longer attend for therapy for my hand, and though little if
any change has happened in the last few months, I hardly notice the trouble
and am reconciled to having it only 8o per cent right. Hard to get hold of
tools in some pisitions.   I forget if I told you that I was walking
with a stick about five months ago, but all that has settled down and I
feel nothing; until the next small crumble?.!
There is a possibility that a visit will be made to the Lakes,in October.
I for a few weeks,Tania for say two weeks. No definite plans, and depends
upon a talk I hope to fit in at Loughborough..which would be on my way up,
and which I do hope to fit in with another talk at another college.(The
costs of things being as they are this arrangement has a certain financial
interest and would ease my mind regarding travelling expences.! to the
Lakes I mean.   *But I did!!*
I'd better not start on money. As you well know its a constant obsession,
and the most recent example may interest you,as illustrating the extraordinary
increases.   In the 50s we used to make some ather pleasant delicate mirrors
on stand of three drawers,mirror frame all delicate curves, carcase serpentine,
inlay;selling price £40. Present cost in region of £370 for the same thing.
Our whole way of working has to change,things must (generally) be batched up
and made in small repeats. Lately finished seven dining tables, various woods
and slight modifications of detail, in fact four elliptical and three restangle
but all so planned that the same mould used for all,to make the curved laminated
stretchers.   Very considerable saving. Two men working cooperatively,all the
laminates,all venerring and others details done at the same time of course.
And to go with tables there are a few over 90 chairs...so you will imagine that
these changes are both interesting,effective,and surprising. Foreman,Upton is a
most inventive practical chap with powered tools and processes. His latest
success is to made a fitting for spindle moulding machine,(which carries out a
great number of different jobs,includingof course simple grooves for inlay etc,)
which allows grooves for our inlay to be made with a saw, instead of the laborious
job of a scratch stock.   A saw is always used, of course, where lines are
straight and dimensions suitable, but this fitting allows the saw to be used on
chair backs,where inlay runs as shown, and is on a piece of wood that has no
right angled edges..... in about one day the grooves can be cut on backs of 37
chairs.Imagine the time,the dullness,the manual strain doing this 'by hand'..
might take over two weeks.   That's how we go
To finish with costs,client calling today to see a
kneehole writing desk,a special one at a time job,
and may be startled at the cost which should be made,
just under £1200.   Enough enough..but the crises for us may
come sometime next spring,when present orders run out. They come in
very intermittently lately. But I've always assumed, periodically,
that the firm was coming to an end.!

But now for more pleasant thoughts. Birds. Lately I have been reading Early
Grey's Falloden Papers..talks he gave in period 1919-1924..and they were talks
and not prepared lectures because his sight was failing and he had to speak
extemporary. One talk abou birds includes surprising information.. did you know
certain drakes have an "eclipse"? This happnes with the most brilliant plumaged
drakes. The Mandarin.or Carolina Drake. "Females of this species are quite sober
and dull-coloured birds,so that anyone,in the breeding season who knew nothing

3. Part of a typical Barnsley letter, to Vera Simpson, herself a cabinet-maker.
Barnsley's long letters are a mine of information for the history of the workshop
and of the crafts at large.

INTRODUCTION

Edward Barnsley's lifetime spanned a period of great change for the crafts in Britain. When he was born in 1900, the Arts and Crafts Movement was at its height and seemed to offer some workable solutions to the problems of poor design and social injustice caused by rapid industrialization in the nineteenth century. By the 1920s, when Barnsley began to run his own workshop, many saw the Arts and Crafts as a joke, and then in the hard financial climate of the 1930s the idea of making things by hand rather than by machine began to seem simply immoral. A reassessment of the role of the craftworker took place during the Second World War and since then there has been a slow but steady growth of appreciation for the value of the crafts. An increasing number of people have come to recognize both quality in well-made things and the quality of life that makers can gain from their work, though it is clear that there are still many misunderstandings about the nature of craftwork, especially in tourist areas and at Craft Fairs, where mass-produced goods of purely ornamental value have 'craft' as a selling slogan.

Since 1971, substantial government funds have financed a national body, originally known as the Crafts Advisory Committee and now the Crafts Council. This promotes standards, supports and encourages craftspeople and publicizes the results of their activities. New workshops start up every year and in 1992 there are 183 furniture-making craft workshops listed as established in the English countryside.[1] Now cabinet-making has risen so far above its humble 'trade' origins as to be considered a suitable occupation for members of the royal family. In the 1990s, the crafts combine the appeal of contemporary art and design with the all-pervasive nostalgia for the past which seems to have swept away the 1960s enthusiasm for the white-heat of the technological revolution. Craftwork can now be made to pay.

This apparently healthy state of the crafts today perhaps makes it difficult for us to appreciate the contribution made to twentieth-century cabinet-making by Edward Barnsley, but before the current resurgence of interest in individually made work, there was a much less optimistic attitude, and many people felt that quality handwork was in danger of extinction. After the First World War, Sidney Barnsley advised his son not to go into furniture making because he would never be able to make a living from this type of work. Writing during the Second War on the crafts of the countryside, Freda Derrick, an early champion of William Morris and his ideals, lamented the disappearance of traditional knowledge and skills, and quoted Eric Gill haranguing an audience thus, hurling the word 'museum' like a stone: ' "You can have art in your daily life if you want it, but you don't. You prefer fountain-pens and motor cars." (It was so he summed up the convenience and comfort that machinery and mass-production give us.) "The only place for art today is in a museum." '[2]

Some twenty years later, David Pye in *The Nature and Art of Workmanship* also looked pessimistically at the survival of the crafts and made a strong argument in favour of a return to what he termed 'the workmanship of risk' involved in craft production, in order to provide diversity and the unique aesthetic qualities of handwork which were absent from the machine-produced 'workmanship of certainty'. By 1978, however, when his book was reprinted in paperback, Pye was clearly heartened by the increasing interest in the crafts and was encouraged to feel that it might be possible for craftspeople to make a living from their work. Today, although the luxuries described by Gill are considered essential by most of us, and have been augmented by a long list of new consumer goods, and although most people are prepared to spend much more on mass-produced fitted kitchen cabinets than they are on a hand-made dining table, nevertheless, there is now a much wider market for craftwork than in the past, and a larger number of craftspeople are able to make enough to live on from their work, without the backing of teaching salaries or private incomes.

Four years after he retired from a part-time advisory post at Loughborough Training College in 1965, Edward Barnsley was able to say for the first time that he made an adequate income from his workshop alone. His father, Sidney Barnsley, who was in at the beginning of the craft revival in the nineteenth century, had always been supported by a private income, and was one of the middle-class working craftsmen, like William Morris, who influenced hitherto rigid notions about the social status of those who worked with their hands. For a variety of reasons this movement came to be seen as an entirely backward-looking rearguard action rather than as a proposal for changed values in life, and the better-argued ideas of modernism and mass-production were triumphant in the middle years of the twentieth century. The precarious survival during this period of the Barnsley workshop, and the few others like it, mainly in the fields of ceramics, metalwork, and textiles, has been essential to the survival, growth, and recent blossoming of the craft movement. For without the example of the highest standards of design and execution, represented in the production of over seven thousand pieces of furniture by the workshop, and without the accumulation and transfer of traditional skills to younger people through the training of apprentices and pupils, there would be no foundation for the present craft revival.

There are many aspects of this revival of which Barnsley would not approve, but that is part of the interest of the story. In the absence of the socialist revolution promoted by William Morris, the crafts have to find their own compromises with capitalism. Craftwork offers an attractive way of life for those brave enough to try an uncertain path, and it is to be hoped that this account of one of the twentieth-century pioneers will be of interest to those 'doing and making' today.

The aim of this book is to chart the development of Edward Barnsley's work over more than sixty years and to describe the furniture and woodwork made in his workshop, the craftsmen who carried out his designs, and the clients for whom pieces were made. It will look also at the clichés and misunderstandings associated with the image of the craftworker in the twentieth century and the problems involved in running a commercial business while trying to maintain the highest standards of work. For Barnsley the problems were legion, and the survival of the workshop was a triumph of dogged determination in the face of both unfavourable external conditions and facets of Barnsley's character which militated against him. He was a contradictory man: his credo was 'doing and making', he enjoyed physical labour, and he despised the idea of 'design' as an activity of higher intellectual value separate from practical work; but within the workshop his time was largely spent in the drawing office and after he started teaching in 1938 he did little benchwork. He believed that the maker of things was more important than the thing made; but he was uncomfortable with employees and had little understanding of or interest in them as individuals. He felt awkward with strangers and was not liked by all; but within his family and a wide circle of friends he was a source of comfort and wisdom, a willing listener with whom they could talk about anything, a man generous with his time.

Barnsley also believed in 'work not words' but had a well-deserved reputation among friends and colleagues as a prodigious letter writer. He was in some ways a modest man and his correspondence reveals a realistic attitude to his own achievements and faults, a concern for fairness in what has been written about his own and his father's work, and a real desire that the craftsmen who carried out his designs in the workshop should be properly credited for their work. Because of his dislike of self-publicity, the workshop is not as well known as it could be, and I hope that this account will help to balance the picture. I hope, too, that it gives adequate credit to the superb craftsmen without whose dedication the Barnsley workshop could not have survived: each made his own contribution to the standard of work produced, and to the training of younger makers. In most cases the craftsman's role was not simply that of executant of Barnsley's designs. In particular, the relationship over fifty-five years between Barnsley and Herbert Upton, who became the workshop foreman in 1938, was a mutual partnership, with two sets of ideas and ideals combining in a common purpose, each man bringing his own skills and standards to the work in hand. This involved compromises on both sides, led to clashes of opinion and reassessment of values, and changed the nature of the work that each would have done on his own, but it was a fruitful collaboration, and gave the furniture made in the Barnsley workshop its particular character.

From the late 1970s, Edward Barnsley began to retire gradually from the running of the business and in 1980 an Educational Trust was formed by some long-standing friends and clients with the agreement of the Barnsley family: the aim was to ensure the survival of the workshop and the continuation of the valuable tradition of training offered to apprentices. New ways of solving the practical problems of running a workshop are being evolved to suit the changed circumstances of the 1990s and the different personalities involved. It is to be hoped that a further book to chronicle this new phase in the history of the workshop will be required in perhaps twenty years' time, and that the centenary in 2023 will see the Barnsley tradition still flourishing.

1. BARNSLEY'S BACKGROUND AND EARLY LIFE

Gimson and the Barnsleys – Arts and Crafts in the Cotswolds – the birth of Edward, 1900 – village life and family tensions – school at Bedales – training with Geoffrey Lupton – building Bedales library – an episode in London – the Barnsley workshop begins, 1923

Edward Barnsley's career as a furniture maker, and his rather remarkable adherence to a way of life and methods of work which many would think uncomfortable and even eccentric in the twentieth century, stem from his family background and his upbringing among people dedicated to the ideal of making beautiful things in pleasant surroundings.

His father, Sidney Barnsley, his uncle Ernest, and their friend and colleague Ernest Gimson, were key figures in the Arts and Crafts Movement based in the Cotswolds and were probably the most significant and influential of all the Arts and Crafts furniture designers. Sidney was the youngest son in a Birmingham family which owned a large building firm that had profited from the enormous urban expansion of Victorian Britain. Following his elder brother, Ernest, Sidney Barnsley had attended classes in drawing, architecture, and building construction at Birmingham School of Art and then spent some years working in London as an 'improver' for the eminent architect, Norman Shaw, while Ernest joined the office of John Dando Sedding. Also with Sedding was Ernest Gimson, who came from a similar skilled and prosperous background in Leicester. Like the Barnsleys, he was a younger son and was able to look beyond the family business for a career, and he was influenced in his choice by the growing awareness among the new middle classes of the social problems brought by the Industrial Revolution. The Gimsons were noted for their free-thinking attitudes, were stalwarts of the Leicester Secular Society, and in their own factory had experimented, unsuccessfully, with co-operative working.[1]

As a student of architecture, Ernest Gimson responded eagerly to William Morris's ideas on how to change the conditions under which people worked and his direct contact with this great idealist and reformer is documented,[2] though whether or not the Barnsleys met Morris before they went to London is not clear. They certainly found they had much else in common with Gimson, and their years in London proved to be of great importance for them, involved as they were in the inspiring and influential, though rather separate, circles around Morris and round Norman Shaw, at the forefront of the movement to reform British architecture and design. Long and heated discussions took place in the architects' offices, at the Art Workers' Guild, at the Society for the Protection of Ancient Buildings, and in other such recently-formed groups. Talk ranged over the principles of building and design, the need for honesty in the use of materials and construction techniques, and the importance of a return to traditional ways of making things.

The ideas expressed by Pugin and Ruskin, and elaborated by Morris into a socialist theory, are now well known, and the history of the Arts and Crafts Movement and its many ramifications has been well documented and interpreted in recent years. It was a broadly-based movement encompassing a range of different attitudes and ideas, many of which were first expressed and defined during these discussions among small groups of architects in London in the 1880s, often in the convivial surroundings of Gatti's restaurant with Morris and Philip Webb after meetings of 'Anti-Scrape', as the Society for the Protection of Ancient Buildings became known. Gimson's letters from this period[3] tell of his enthusiasm for this new world in which he had become involved, and it is clear that the principles expounded, questioned, and absorbed here by the Barnsleys and Gimson influenced their work throughout their lives, and later formed the basis for Edward Barnsley's own philosophy of life and work.

In 1888, Sidney Barnsley and a colleague, Robert Weir Schultz, travelled to Greece to make a study of Byzantine churches, part of which, an account of the Monastery of St Luke of Stiris in Phocis, was later published.[4] On his return, Sidney Barnsley received his first architectural commission, from Dr Edwin Freshfield whom he had met in Greece, for a church at Lower Kingswood in Surrey. With its patterned brick exterior and marble-sheathed walls, this lovely small church shows clearly the influence of Barnsley's Byzantine studies, and the richness of the interior reflects an interest in painted flower decoration which can be seen later in some of his furniture designs.[5]

The church at Lower Kingswood also contains some remarkably sophisticated furniture, which must have been made by Kenton and Company,[6] the firm set up by William Lethaby, Gimson, and a group of friends, which Sidney Barnsley had been persuaded to join. This business was short-lived but was of great importance in showing Barnsley and Gimson what they wished to do with their lives; it lasted only from 1890 to 1892, and in the following year the two men decided to leave London to live in the country. Edward Barnsley believed they were prompted to this step by William Morris himself, who told them that if they wanted to be real architects they must understand the art of building, and that to understand the arts and crafts they must be practising craftsmen and makers. This they could not achieve in London, so he suggested that they should find a suitable place in the country and 'go away and do it'.[7]

Both had travelled widely in the past ten years, visiting country houses and churches all over England and Europe and filling sketchbooks with meticulous drawings of buildings and details of furniture and fittings. It is not known why they chose to settle in the Cotswold area in particular, though Morris had his country retreat at nearby Kelmscott and others, such as Guy Dawber, had arrived in Gloucestershire before them. Their main aim seems to have been to live in an area where craftwork was carried out as an ordinary part of everyday life, not as something special and exclusive, and this was true of Gloucestershire, where traditional methods of building, preparing stone slates, wheelwrighting, fencing, and other such basic crafts were still in evidence. The Cotswolds were well served by the railway and so the area was easily accessible from London, but it had not changed as much as the countryside closer to the capital, and the local building vernacular must also have appealed to them.

In 1893 Barnsley and Gimson found temporary accommodation at Ewen, near Cirencester, while looking for somewhere more suitable. From the beginning they had some idea of establishing a rural community of craftsmen, forming a nucleus around which others would gather, and to a certain extent this is what they eventually achieved, though Edward Barnsley recalled a certain wistful jealousy on his father's part towards C. R. Ashbee's endeavours in Chipping Campden.[8] Though ultimately unsuccessful in many ways, the Guild of Handicraft in Campden was on a far larger and more ambitious scale than the little group near Cirencester.[9] Gimson's plans involved starting a craft village and he was still working to bring this to reality at the time of his early death in 1919.[10]

Ernest Gimson and Sidney Barnsley were both extremely diffident characters: they felt that they needed the impetus of the more expansive and sociable nature of Sidney's brother Ernest to help them form the community they envisaged, so they persuaded him to join them. Ernest had set up his own architectural practice in Birmingham, had married in 1887 and by now had two daughters. His wife, Alice, was not at all enthusiastic about leaving her friends and the house Ernest had built for her in favour of the unsure prospect of life in the country, though according to Edward Barnsley, 'Alice would not have been consulted, and probably not much considered either'. However, the three men soon found a suitable centre for their work at Pinbury Park, a decaying Elizabethan house in its own grounds, which Sidney Barnsley came across on one of his long exploratory walks in the neighbourhood. Eagerly he persuaded the others to come and have a look, and reluctantly, because each had wanted to be the one to find *the* place, they agreed that it was ideal.[11]

Pinbury belonged to Earl Bathurst who granted a repairing lease at a low rent and proved to be a valuable patron of the enterprise.[12] Ernest Barnsley's family moved into the house, while Gimson and Sidney had quarters in the converted outbuildings, but they soon experienced the common difficulties of town-people living in the country and bachelors looking after themselves, so Gimson suggested that they should ask his cousin Lucy Morley, with whose family in Lincolnshire he had often stayed as a boy, to act as housekeeper for them. A photograph taken at Pinbury shows the group in about 1895, and as Edward Barnsley commented later, 'The camera is very misleading at times, but this picture does show you who was, at least in the earlier days, the leader. Neither the sombre figure

4. At Pinbury, about 1895. From left to right are Sidney Barnsley, Lucy
Morley, Ernest Gimson, Alice, Mary, Ernest Barnsley, and Ethel Barnsley.

sitting looking at his beloved dog, or the shy figure sitting away by himself
sheltered by the wall and supported by HIS beloved dogs...'.[13] Ernest
Barnsley, standing at ease, smiling at the camera and showing off his
daughters, was in these early years very much the driving force and
business leader, the negotiator of leases and hirer of assistants. While the
other two would suddenly find that their dogs needed walking in the woods
as visitors approached Pinbury, Ernest Barnsley enjoyed social contact and
'it was on him that "the county" left their cards'.[14] The extensive and
careful renovation of Pinbury occupied much of his time in the first few
years, and all three men were busy in their shared workshop, practising
their chosen crafts and learning new skills.

Kenton and Company had employed trained cabinet-makers to execute
the partners' designs, but the Barnsleys wanted to be able to make furniture
themselves and they set about learning the skills of joinery and cabinet-
making, often the hard way, by trial and error. Edward later said his father
had told him that they didn't know the professional methods at this time,
and in making chests of drawers would construct the drawers and then
make a 'box' to put them in.[15] They were remarkably observant people,
however, and their practice of making detailed drawings had given them a
theoretical knowledge of techniques which now had to be applied to real

5. The shared workshop at Pinbury, about 1895, showing furniture by the Barnsleys under construction, and plasterwork and turned chairs by Gimson.

materials. Another photograph from this period shows work being carried out at Pinbury; heavy pieces of furniture in solid timber by the Barnsleys, and light turned chairs and modelled plasterwork by Gimson. Like Ernest Barnsley, Gimson also spent some of his time on architectural commissions, but they both seem to have approached their work in a somewhat dilettante fashion and Edward remembered his mother telling him of the scene as she often saw it, in the workshop at Pinbury before her marriage.

> She would make the cakes for the mid-morning break, and the drinks, and taking them in find SHB hard at work at the bench, the other two standing by, often hands in pockets, whistling Gilbert and Sullivan tunes. This story does fit. It fits the characters. Ernest B. was never a persistent hard worker. Gimson was not a maker of furniture, only of the rush seated chairs & plaster work, and his strength lay more in planning for others to carry out. His talent, amounting to genious, in knowing how things could and should be made, in wood and metal, in spite of the fact that he did not use the tools himself, is remarkable to a high degree. Of the three father was the crafts-man-maker in essence. He loved the work itself, and the making was his joy.[16]

While some have accused the group of escapism, Edward Barnsley likened their actions to those of a 'research scientist, who shut himself off from the harrassments and the interuptions of the "big world", and carried out his work in circumstances and under conditions suitable and essential to its success'.[17] Sidney Barnsley's application to his work resulted in a number of assured and impressive pieces made in these years. The main elements were the use of English woods, generally in solid planks, and the frank and decorative expression of the construction of the piece through exposed tenons and dovetails. Throughout his life, Sidney Barnsley worked on his own, planning his furniture, sawing the timber, constructing and finishing, occasionally making a light and delicate piece as a rest from the heavy labour of making dressers and tables.[18] His decision to work alone, far from being an ideological stand on the principle that the designer and maker should be one and the same, was mainly a consequence of the London experiment and clearly caused him some feelings of guilt: 'I remember when Kenton's closed down', he wrote in 1926, 'how Hall our famous foreman rejoiced to make some furniture for himself in the shop we lent him until our lease was up — overmantels of bevelled plate glass & turned balusters glued on — Oh! such things as you've never seen & it was that that made me decide never to employ men — a stupid selfish decision I know — but that was how I was made! Gimmy stuck at it & in Waals' case at any rate he reaped a harvest.'[19] Occasionally he made the attempt to work with an assistant but he was shy and uneasy in company, though he covered his nervousness with a bright and smiling manner. Malcolm Powell joined him for a short period early on and they found an arrangement that suited them, each man working separately at his own bench on his own piece, but two later assistants stayed for only a very short time.[20]

This habit of solitude and quiet was perhaps increased rather than lessened by Sidney Barnsley's marriage in 1895 to Lucy Morley, who had gone deaf at the age of nineteen because of a congenital problem which had also afflicted five of her six sisters. A letter from Lucy to her friend, Jeannie, who was married to Gimson's brother, Sydney, shows that she had considered carefully whether she was right to marry with this handicap, and was encouraged by the fact that none of her friends had suggested that she should not. She was able to lip-read Sidney easily, she said, and her sense of humour shows itself in the hope that she and Jeannie 'will never fight each other as to who has got the best Sidney!'[21]

Lucy Barnsley was a woman of some character, described by her son much later as 'one of the sweetest natures of that day and age. And at the same time practical, efficient and to a high degree competent, and with her disability holding her back, advanced for her generation. In the physical ways I mean, the first lady cyclist of the district, a rider to hounds of no uncertain quality (Lincolnshire). She had a bigness, deep kindliness, & thoughts, unexpressed in the main, long ahead of the majority of women at the time'.[22] She also recognized the value of the work at Pinbury and supported Sidney Barnsley wholeheartedly in his chosen way of life.[23]

Sidney and Lucy's first child, Grace, was born in 1896 and was followed four years later by a son, William Edward, born on 7th February 1900 at

6. The Barnsley family at Pinbury, 26 November 1900: Lucy, the young Edward staring keenly at the camera, Sidney, and Grace.

Pinbury. In later life, Edward attributed his robust good health to the fact that Pinbury was surrounded by deep snow at the time of his birth and he had therefore not suffered the interference of doctors at this early age. He was certainly a strong infant and only ten months later his father described him breaking the 'stick which keeps him in his chair — a stick one would have thought too strong for a 4 year old boy to break'.[24]

This year also saw the marriage of Ernest Gimson to Emily Thompson and it soon became clear to all that Pinbury was no longer big enough to accommodate three families. Coincidentally, their landlord, Earl Bathurst, was looking for a suitable summer home for his own use and was contemplating building near Pinbury, until Ernest Barnsley suggested that he should take back the house, which by now had been extensively renovated, largely at the group's own expense.[25] In return for the unexpired lease, and on payment of the same combined rent, each of the men would have some land at nearby Sapperton and money with which to build his own house, and the use of another of Bathurst's properties, Daneway House, for workshops and showrooms.[26] Daneway provided ideal accommodation for the business started by Gimson and Ernest Barnsley in 1900, a workshop temporarily housed in the yard of a Cirencester hotel. Several cabinet-makers were taken on to execute the two partners' designs, including Harry Davoll from Liverpool, Tom Smith, who was a Scotsman,[27] Percy Burchett and Ernest Smith from London, and as foreman, Peter van der Waals, a Dutchman of wide practical experience, who had an immediate influence on the quality of craftsmanship of the group.

Sidney Barnsley stood apart from this scheme, feeling that friends and relations should avoid business partnerships, and he designed his new house on the edge of Sapperton with its own workshop in the garden. From 1902 or 1903, family life here was very settled; Barnsley's uncompromising attitude to his work extended, as did Gimson's, into his home life, and Edward and Grace were brought up in a simply furnished, even spartan, household, surrounded by the beauty of the Cotswolds. The house, with its whitewashed walls, oak floors, bookshelves between the ceiling beams, Japanese prints, and mixture of antiques and examples of Sidney's own design, was clearly a source of some pride to their mother, who sent a photograph of the interior to her own mother at Christmas 1903, and

7. Sidney Barnsley 's workshop was on the upper floor of this small building in his garden at Sapperton. His house was tiled, so the choice of thatch for the workshop roof is unexpected, though Gimson's cottage just down the road was also thatched.

8. Beechanger, Sidney and Lucy Barnsley's house at Sapperton, Gloucestershire, probably photographed in 1904. Most of the furniture was by Sidney Barnsley himself. The chair and firedogs were from Gimson's workshop.

another to 'Allie' in January 1905 of the same room rearranged.[28] Tania Barnsley however later recalled both the lack of hot water and the planning of the kitchen as extremely inconvenient.

At the Daneway workshop on occasional visits, Edward marvelled at the work of Gimson's assistants and absorbed naturally from them how to handle tools, while from their father the children learned the importance not just of the final product of work — beautifully made and individual furniture — but also the satisfaction to be gained both from skilled craftwork and from hard physical labour, in the workshop and in the garden. Edward in later years remembered that none of the family talked much. His mother's deafness proved a barrier to a close relationship, for 'To be unable to communicate or to "be near" one's own mother when born and when quite young, must effect all one's life'. He also felt very separate from his sister, Grace: 'I was always alone, when little, and shall always remain so, in nearly all ways. I'm the only human being with whom I can be comfortable for any length of time, and the only times when I really completely feel at one, is when in the lake district, walking alone on the fells and tops'.[29]

Through necessity Edward developed the ability to be alone and then found solitariness the easier situation.

Sidney Barnsley was clearly proud of his children and committed to family life, but like many fathers and sons, he and Edward had little discussion even about their mutual interest in their work, let alone more personal matters, much to Edward's later regret. His father's teasing 'was the only thing about him which I did not like, and the only thing of which I know about him which leads me to qualify my thinking him the sweetest man I've known', wrote Edward in 1968, but he recognized that the cruel teasing was the result of Sidney's own treatment in childhood.[30]

Within the village community, the Gimson–Barnsley group was something of an enigma; clearly of the 'gentry', they made things with their hands, to the puzzlement of their neighbours, who were not used to gentleman-workers. Sidney Barnsley took his family to the local church on Sundays, sometimes attending twice, and later shocked his son by telling him that they went to 'set a good example in the village'.[31] Ernest Barnsley, however, rarely attended and Norman Jewson recorded a rather cool relationship with Mr Cropper, the Rector, though this was perhaps connected with a proposal of marriage from the elderly Vicar to one of Ernest's daughters.[32] The group did, however, take part in village life. They knew and admired the work of the local craftsmen such as Richard Harrison, the wheelwright, and Arthur Gardiner, the carpenter and builder, and they were interested in the history and traditions of the area. After Lady Bathurst paid for a new village hall in 1912, designed by Ernest Barnsley and furnished by Gimson's workshop, they joined in with village shows and productions of Gilbert and Sullivan operas, and encouraged the revival of local songs and country dances, in accordance with the aims of Cecil Sharp, who was an occasional visitor.[33]

Social contact also came through the many other artists and craftspeople who came to live in the area, such as Alfred and Louise Powell, best-known for their painted pottery, the artist William Rothenstein and his family, Norman Jewson, who became Gimson's architectural assistant, and later, the Geres, the Paynes, Fred and Nina Griggs, and William and Eve Simmonds. Members of the Gimson and Barnsley families also came on frequent visits from the Midlands to enjoy the hospitality of Pinbury, and Herbert Barnsley, Ernest and Sidney's older brother, took many fine photographs at Pinbury and Sapperton.[34]

Less happily, a disagreement over business between Ernest Gimson and Ernest Barnsley, exacerbated by a lack of sympathy between Emily Gimson and the two Mrs Barnsleys,[35] led to their estrangement and caused some social difficulty for Sidney Barnsley and Gimson, who remained on good terms but were only able to meet on neutral territory outside their homes. This must have been particularly distressing for Sidney Barnsley, whose friendship with Gimson was of long standing. They often shared designs and 'shared many things including loans from time to time, depending on who was short of cash',[36] and they would appear to have had a much more comfortable and equal relationship than that between Sidney and his brother. Norman Jewson described Ernest Barnsley as referring always to Sidney as 'the Boy', and taking for granted 'that his extra years gave him a permanent superiority'.[37] 'How I wish and wish that we had been able to remain close to him', wrote Edward of Ernest Gimson, for his sister, Grace, had early childhood memories of being in and out of Gimson's cottage and of his 'kindnesses and easy ways'. '"Big Uncle" as Gimson was known to all of us, was in certain ways a big man, not only in his height. Whereas there was something 'little' about my Dad, if comparisons must be made'.[38] Edward felt, without filial bias he said, that Sidney Barnsley was more successful than the two Ernests at planning buildings, but he was sorry that his father's private personality made it impossible for him to attain the wider range of work achieved by Gimson, who, though himself a quiet man, had a tenacity of purpose that enabled him to get more done.[39]

In his father's workshop as a child, Edward Barnsley absorbed the principles of Arts and Crafts work and learned to use woodworking tools, making a small table or stool with his father's help when he was only five. More formal education was provided by a governess, Hilda Eames, who, with her sister, a general maid, lived in. A letter from Sidney Barnsley to Philip Webb gives a glimpse of family life in 1904: 'We still live the same life that you knew at Pinbury, cooking and eating in the kitchen with the added luxury of a retiring room now, where we sit in the evenings and the children have their lessons, and in this way we have a sunny room all day'.[40]

This life was disrupted for a while in 1909, when Edward went to school at Cirencester Grammar and Sidney Barnsley rented a house in the town for the family, cycling over to Sapperton every day to work; but the school did not suit Edward, who was 'given up as a bad job', he said,[41] and in the following year he and Grace were both sent to Bedales School in Hampshire. This may have been suggested by Alfred Powell, whose brother, Oswald was a co-founder and an important influence in the school. Another brother, Malcolm, had also taught there from 1898 to 1902, before a period of working with Sidney Barnsley.[42] In addition, several of Gimson's nephews attended as pupils between 1894 and 1907, one of them, Basil Gimson, later becoming a teacher there; and Geoffrey Lupton, Gimson's pupil-apprentice in 1905, was also an Old Bedalian. It must have seemed the obvious choice.

Bedales suited Edward very well. Founded in 1893 by J. H. Badley, who had been involved in the beginnings of Abbotsholme School in Derbyshire and who left to put into practice more of his own ideas, it was a progressive, co-educational establishment. Badley himself had received a traditional classical education at Rugby and Cambridge, and one term of teaching classics in a similar environment at Bedford School had confirmed his doubts about his suitability for this kind of career. His misgivings began with a realization of the narrow, second-hand 'bookishness' of his own education, and were fostered at Cambridge by his friendship with Lowes Dickinson, Roger Fry, and Nathaniel Wedd, all of whom were interested in ideas expressed by Walt Whitman, John Ruskin, William Morris, and particularly

Edward Carpenter, on the need for social change in industrial Britain. In 1889, Badley heard about a new school being set up by Cecil Reddie with the backing of Carpenter, and he hurried back to England from Germany to see how he could take part in what seemed to him a most sympathetic scheme.[43]

Reddie's purpose was to broaden the scope of education in schools to cover a wider range than the usual public school model of training for the life of a 'gentleman'. Teaching at Abbotsholme involved farming and outdoor work as well as academic study, with considerable emphasis on healthy 'comradeship'. Badley appreciated the value of his two and a half years of teaching at Abbotsholme, though he regretted that Edward Carpenter's involvement ceased almost immediately, and he found Reddie autocratic, as did everybody else who came into contact with him. He felt that greater democracy in the running of a school would bring a more congenial atmosphere and better results, and he believed that the purpose of education was to stimulate others to develop their own activities and to form their own opinions, a view he thought Reddie did not share.

Badley was by now engaged to Amy Garrett, a music teacher and feminist, and he believed, unlike Reddie, that women could have a beneficial effect on the education of both girls and boys, and that there were considerable advantages to co-education. In order to practise his own ideas and to spread the influence of the 'new school movement', Badley decided to leave Abbotsholme to start his own school, a course of action which Reddie, perhaps with some justification, regarded as rivalry and betrayal.

Bedales was thus founded as a school for boys aged 9 to 15 in January 1893 in a house of that name near Lindfield in Sussex, and it moved to Steep in Hampshire in 1900, when expansion became urgent. Accounts of its earliest years suggest that much more emphasis was given to outdoor activities and unpaid labour, such as levelling the cricket pitch, cleaning the lake for use as a swimming pool, and hay-making in the fields, than to academic study.[44] Such work was intended to lead both to an understanding of some basic crafts and to a recognition of the interdependence of the human community.[45] By 1910, when Edward Barnsley started, the school was better established and the curriculum had benefited from the advice of external school inspectors. The interest in physical activities, such as gardening and a range of sports, was retained, and the children were encouraged to develop leisure interests of their own, including Swedish wood carving and bird stuffing,[46] but there was also a more defined programme of study towards the School Certificate examinations. Bedales was 'recognized as efficient' by His Majesty's Inspectors in 1911.[47]

The 'family' atmosphere idealized by Badley (who liked to be known as 'the Chief') and his wife, made real by Oswald Powell and his family, and enhanced by the admission of girls from 1898, encouraged the social development of the pupils and fostered a strong school spirit, and many retained close links with Bedales long after they left. Some, like Edward's friend, John Rothenstein, found it all too earnest. He was not impressed by the vegetarian, sandal-wearing older boys he encountered, remnants of Bedales' pioneering past, nor by the headmaster's perhaps heavy-handed attitude to what was termed 'silliness' between boys and girls,[48] a criticism also made by Julia Strachey, who was suffocated by this intense, unimaginative, and repressive good sense.[49] Rothenstein, an incipient Roman Catholic convert, was also critical of Badley's lack of religious belief and he felt that Bedales was unable to supply the shortcomings in his previous education since, he said, the teaching was not very good and knowledge was never tested by exams. In his view, he already possessed the qualities of tolerance, appreciation of craftsmanship, and the ability to form independent judgements which Bedales aimed to instill in its pupils, but what he needed was intellectual discipline.[50]

Edward Barnsley, brought up to feel the importance of doing and making, within a background of considered, principled behaviour, found the whole experience very congenial once he got over the initial humiliation of being nick-named 'bum-bags', the result of his mother's devotion in making him trousers of a particularly hard-wearing brown fabric, which was quite different from anything worn by the others and proved virtually indestructible. The school's wide range of activities suited him and he eagerly took part in singing, practical lessons, summer camps in the countryside, and sports, though he baulked at piano lessons and decisively and unseen crossed his name off the list. Somehow he got away with this.[51] Although quiet and shy, his prowess at football and cricket gave him distinction, and in 1917 he was made Head Boy, a role which earned him high praise in the Headmaster's report. His mother showed her pleasure at this success by transcribing Badley's comments and Sidney Barnsley recorded his satisfaction that Bedales had proved so successful, in a letter to his son of December 1917, when Edward was about to leave.[52]

Edward had stayed on for an extra term to take over the woodwork classes when the teacher was called up, an experience he found rather depressing since he simply followed the pattern of instruction which he had himself found rather dull as a pupil, and only realized later that he could have done it differently.[53] His school-teaching career was short-lived, however, for his own call-up arrived in winter 1917. He trained as an officer cadet with the Inns of Court Officers' Training Battalion in Berkhamsted and at New College, Oxford, but just missed being sent to France as the war came to an end. The only aspect of his military career which he thought worth mentioning in later life was a debate in which he participated, on the subject of whether brothels should be legalized. According to his own account, he caused some mirth with his naïve opinions, based on ignorance and the 'Bedales spirit', but in spite of getting muddled and embarrassed he stuck to his views.[54]

Now that the war was over, what was he to do with his life? He spent the spring and summer in his father's workshop in 1919, but Sidney Barnsley advised him against becoming a furniture maker on the grounds that he would never make a living at it, so for a while he seriously thought about taking up farming, and in later years sometimes regretted that he did not do so. He was then offered a teaching post at Bedales, which he accepted, but was persuaded by Alfred Powell that he should first gain some real experience of woodworking. Gimson's workshop seemed the obvious place in which to train, but Sidney Barnsley again advised against this because of the close relationship (he probably also knew how ill Gimson was), and Alfred Powell once more came up with the solution, that Edward should train with Geoffrey Lupton, at Froxfield, near Petersfield in Hampshire.

Lupton was an interesting and unusual man, a forthright Yorkshireman who rejected a career in his family's engineering firm, Hathorne, Davy and Company of Leeds, after a curtailed apprenticeship there on leaving Bedales in 1901, and went to Gimson's workshop as a pupil for a year in 1905-6.[55] He had built his own modest cottage and workshop in Froxfield, just a few miles from Bedales, as well as a number of other houses around the area, often in collaboration with Theodore Crompton, another Old Bedalian, a fruitgrower and farmer who had studied architecture as an articled pupil from 1901-5 and then attended agricultural college.[56] In 1911 Lupton had donated to his old school a new assembly hall designed by Ernest Gimson and built by himself and his employees. He was extremely energetic and hard-working, rather in the same mould as Sidney Barnsley, though an incident recalled by Edward Barnsley from his childhood suggests that he could be austere to the point of eccentricity. On this occasion, Lupton was visiting the Barnsleys at Sapperton and having refused an offer of a bowl of soup produced a knife and some raw cabbage and began to eat.[57] The explanation could be that Lupton was vegetarian and the soup was not, but Roger Powell also remembered staying with Lupton for a week while his parents were away and finding that his host ate only one meal a day, of stewed rhubarb and ginger cake.

When Edward joined him in 1919 as a pupil-apprentice, there were several craftsmen working at Froxfield, mainly on joinery and construction work, though a number of pieces of furniture were also made, usually for clients who were having houses built. The most exciting prospect was the construction of Bedales School library, designed by Gimson as part of a larger scheme for a quadrangle of buildings, including a gymnasium and laboratories, to be raised as a memorial to those from the school who had died during the war. A vivid picture of the building of the library emerges from a series of photographs taken on the site, and from Edward's own account, written in a letter in 1972.[58]

> Gimson's designs were completed before he died (August 1919) and Lupton had already had them for study. And all was set to get down to the work by January 1920. I was the first assistant on the site, in January '20, when I was sent down with employed labourer, Spiers, to sort out and stack up the rafters, joists and other smaller timbers.
>
> A certain myth grew up about the oak for the building, arising from the wish to have as much as possible cut on the estate. There were some trees felled, in the Butts Field, and up near the old football ground, (where the

9. Geoffrey Lupton at work on Bedales library, 1920: a graphic illustration of his practical approach to building.

sand pit is now), but only some smaller items of the building did come off the estate, all the main large items were supplied by Hall and Company of Waterlooville. All the oak arrived on the site in the January, having been fresh sawn, and work started at once on this wood. There are mixed opinions about the ways in which the building of earlier times were carried out, I myself believing that trees were felled in the dead of winter, always, ideally between about December 20th and January 10th, that's what I consider is the dead of winter when the sap is truely at its lowest. Then, usually I fancy, these trees were left for long periods before conversion. But, I don't bet on this because it is much easier to work fresh sawn timber, and oak can become extremely hard with time. One factor which applies is that the old barns were alternatively dry and wet, with the changing seasons, whereas heating was put in the library at once after completion. An early job was to lay deep re-inforced concrete over the whole site. Onto this the main timbers were laid, according to need, and the actual constructional work went on, under foremanship of Old Bill as we called him, Bill Grant, with his main assistant Phil Burgess.

Barnsley's respect for his fellow workers is clear, while they soon dis–covered that he was not quite what they expected.

I have a clear memory of arriving down on the job on my first morning, and starting straight away planing some beam or other, and Bill Grant looking quizzically across and making some remark to Burgess about this young toff coming amongst them, and I have the happy recollection of some surprise showing on his face, on both faces in fact, as the shavings came sweetly from the jack plane. Working green oak can be a joy in those respects. And I had had years already of the simple use of basic tools and enjoyed using them. Grant and Burgess were of the old school especially Grant, and their work was always excellent. Lupton himself was a remarkable craftsman, and in respect of this particular type of work, I would think him unique in this time, and his practical intelligence was most impressive. One memory of the early time of the building was his sending down from Froxfield a large straight fir, which he had used as main vertical post when building the Hall, which was placed in a large barrel of sand, and acted as the main structure from which the pulleys and ropes raised up the large braces, which we fitted together complete on the ground and then raised into position, ropes being taken to the surrounding pine trees on both ends of the building, to take the strain as the truss arrived vertical. But to come back to 1920, Lupton sent this tree down and then set it up on stools, and sawed it from end to end with a rip saw. Then the two pieces formed the main sides of the adjustable arm of a home-made crane, used to raise the Library timbers.

The structure of the library was in two parts, with the construction of the beams, posts, ties, and braces independent of the brickwork shell.

The main posts were set out on the concrete floor, marked out as to positions of joints, the joints cut and the pairs of posts fitted to beams in the three dimensions. Then starting at the Hall end, the woodwork was raised and fitted, bay by bay. It was here, especially when at the main tie beam level (above the gallery) that Lupton's knowledge and intelligence was so remark-able to watch. The flooring material came over from Pinbury, part of Gimson's stock.[59] The oak of the main 'nave' of the building was 2" stuff, the rest 1", and all the gallery floor (laid by me) is Chestnut wood. There are times when I seem to hear some mythology about my contribution to this building, and suggestions that I was in some ways responsible. Not at all, I was a pupil apprentice, and did what I was instructed to do. My main pleasure was the fitting up of all the roof timbers above the level of the main cross tie beams, on this I had the labour help of Spieres and another man. Wish I could remember the name of the foreman bricklayer, who was a skilled responsible charming man, one of his assistants was Harry Varnes, who was an older man, an example of what we call the 'old school', worked for many years for Lupton.

Metal fittings for the library were made at Froxfield, where Lupton had a blacksmith's forge next to the workshop.

Steve Mustoe was the smith, and he came over from Gimson's smithy in Sapperton, and worked for Lupton for a number of years, making hinges, latches, casements etc for a number of the buildings in Cockshott Lane,

10. Edward Barnsley on the roof beams of Bedales library, 1920. The supervision of this part of the building was his main pleasure.

which were built between 1919 and 1925. The first set of hanging lampcases were of ironwork. All the catches for cupboard doors are also Mustoe's work. The double-sided gallery bookcases were made in the Froxfield workshop by Berry. All the other bookcases and shelves either made on site, or up in Froxfield. Seats and panelling of bays on ground level were made by Grant & Burgess, and those above on the gallery by other assistants (one year later approximately) including Charles Bray, and I was put in charge of this and assembled it all on site. With exception of the South East bay window fittings I managed a fair job, but that first octagonal bay was, in some ways a dire mess of a job. Careful looking at the way in which the seats and their backs, and the uprights of the panelling fit to the splayed woodwork of the windows should be of some interest constructionally.

Once the building was completed, it was furnished with chairs and tables to Sidney Barnsley's design, made by Lupton's craftsmen at Froxfield. Edward Gardiner, who had made turned ash chairs for Gimson but had stopped during the war, was persuaded to get out his tools again to make sixty chairs for the library and soon found that he had so many orders for more that he had to start up his business again properly.[60] At first the library was very spartan in appearance, but more furniture was provided by the Barnsley workshop in later years and Neville Neal, Gardiner's assistant and successor, now working at Stockton, near Rugby in Warwickshire, has been able to keep it well stocked with appropriate chairs.

The building of Bedales library gave Edward experience of a wide range of constructional problems on a variety of scales and incidentally changed his mind about teaching, since he visited the staff room for tea while working there and knew he could not face it. 'Chief "let me off"!', he said.[61]

While working at Froxfield he lodged with family friends, Oswald and Winifred Powell, the parents of Roger and Oliver, whom he had first met in

11. Interior of Bedales Library in the early 1920s. Sidney Barnsley designed the library tables and chairs in oak, and they were made in Edward's workshop. The turned chairs in ash were made to Gimson's designs by Edward Gardiner.

Gloucestershire in about 1907. He always claimed that Oliver had punched him on the nose within minutes of their meeting, and they became friends for life. Edward and Roger had met again at Bedales and shared an enthusiasm for cricket, which prompted them to form a team of Old Bedalians to play against the school after the war. In the early 1920s, Roger Powell tried poultry farming in Sussex for some years until he took up bookbinding, the craft in which he later excelled, becoming one of the foremost British binders and a specialist in conservation techniques. The two remained close and were able to collaborate on several occasions, with Edward designing pieces of furniture to house important books, or Powell providing tooled leatherwork to decorate items of furniture.

At the age of 22, in search of further stimulus for ideas on design and wider experience than he was gaining in the workshop, Edward went to London in 1922 to study at the Central School of Arts and Crafts, then under the direction of F. V. Burridge, who aimed to continue the principles established by his predecessor, W. R. Lethaby, that 'Tuition should be to further the highest development of the artistic handicrafts, their application to manufacture, and their commercial usefulness'.[62] The Central had been started with Lethaby as its first Principal in 1896 to give apprentices and assistants in London firms the opportunity to acquire some training in design, primarily as related to their own trade, though they were encouraged to take an interest in other crafts. Part of the aim was to improve the awareness of design within industry instead of trying to apply fine art training to industry from the outside, as previous colleges had done. In the beginning, classes were held in the evenings only, but the workshops were also open during the day for use by the students and Lethaby gathered together an inspiring collection of objects, books, and photographs for study. To implement his policies, he had appointed a distinguished staff of practising craftsmen and women as teachers in the Central School, including Halsey Ricardo on architecture, Christopher Whall for stained glass, Francis Troup for leadwork, Edward Johnston on calligraphy, and May Morris on embroidery.

Charles Spooner, the teacher of cabinet-making appointed around 1900, and still at the Central when Edward arrived, was a contemporary of Gimson and the Barnsleys and had been a pupil of Sir Arthur Blomfield in the mid 1880s when they also had been training in London. His ideas on architecture and furniture making were very close to Sidney Barnsley's, and he seems to have felt that he had little to teach Edward beyond advising him to study old furniture in the Geffrye Museum and the Victoria and Albert.[63] In the 1930s, Edward showed his drawings from this period to Oliver Morel and complained at the waste of his time as a student in producing them, but it seems likely that they had beneficial effects on his own sense of proportion and design, though he was unaware of this at the time.

It is perhaps surprising that Edward felt so uncertain about 'design' at this stage. Norman Jewson in *By Chance I Did Rove* described his own training by Gimson in drawing and design, and Grace Barnsley was advised by Alfred and Louise Powell to study nature as a basis for pattern design for painting pottery. In the furniture workshops, however, design was rarely mentioned either by Sidney Barnsley or by Lupton, and work was explained in more architectural terms as 'plans'. Like Lethaby they believed that 'design is only a matter of arranging how things shall be done'.[64] Edward felt that architecture required a wider approach, for which he did not have the capacity, and it was perhaps this perceived inadequacy that made him uncertain and hesitant about his own work. He was on more familiar ground when it came to practical work and developed considerable respect for Brandt, who was in charge of the Central School's workshop, and for Minihane, who taught full-size drawing.[65]

While in London, Edward stayed at the Gray's Inn Square chambers of his father's friend, Robert Schultz Weir, who was known to him and other friends as 'Uncle Daddy', while his colleague Francis Troup for reasons unknown was always 'Aunt Francis'.[66] He went to tea with Lethaby himself on at least one occasion and was impressed and a little disconcerted by Lethaby's humility towards a callow student after he arrived late, apologizing profusely for keeping Edward waiting, having been unable to bring himself to use the telephone.[67] Barnsley later realized how fortunate he had been to have met so many of the leaders of the Arts and Crafts Movement, but life in the capital does not seem to have made any great impression on him and he rarely referred to anything he had done there.

In 1923 Geoffrey Lupton decided that he wished to give up his workshop, and he offered a tenancy to Edward, who came back from London to take over. He was 23, still a shy and awkward young man with a deep-seated and continuing lack of faith in his intellectual abilities, but a straightforward delight in his athletic prowess, which for many years he would show off by performing party tricks. One involved seating himself on one of two dining chairs placed facing each other, launching himself into the air, twisting in mid leap and landing seated, facing the other way on the second chair. As well as pure muscle-power he also rejoiced in a natural co-ordination of hand and eye, which clearly contributed to his enjoyment of cricket and gave him another trick, described by Bill Inman, a friend in the timber trade: 'he rather endeared himself to the sawmill staff by offering to pay for a pint of beer to anyone who could split with an axe a matchstick which he wedged upright in a log of oak lying in front of the sawmill. Several tried and failed and then naturally challenged Edward to do it. Establishing a steady stance, he stood for a moment weighing matters up like a golfer attempting a long putt, then swung the axe and cleft the match. After a moment's silence there were cries of "cor, guvnor, do it again!" but he, perhaps wisely, declined'.[68]

Such skills were, perhaps, of little use to someone about to embark on the running of a business, but his health and strength, along with his years of practical experience and his brief training at the Central School, provided a good foundation for the beginning of Edward Barnsley's own workshop.

2. THE WORKSHOP AND BUSINESS PRE-WAR

The range of work and clients — early help from father and the Bedales connection — the first apprentice — marriage of Edward with Tania Kellgren — problems of profitable furniture making — financial crisis in the 1930s — rescue — work at Loughborough — wartime hits the workshop, 1941

The Froxfield workshop in 1923 was a low, rectangular building of white-painted brick with small, wood-framed windows and a red-tiled roof. It had an office at the back overlooking the garden and woods, a central work area where the benches and saw-pit were situated, and a blacksmith's shop fronting on to the lane. Lupton retained use of the smithy for making metal fittings: he was still building houses in the area, and continued to live in the cottage next door and to use the garages at the side of the workshop.

Along with the building, Edward Barnsley also took over responsibility for Lupton's team of craftsmen. Walter Berry, the foreman, had been with Gimson at Daneway before joining Lupton in 1911 to help build Bedales School hall. Though he worked for Barnsley until 1936, he was reportedly unreliable and was replaced as foreman in 1924 by Charles Bray, a local man who had attended a short retraining course at the Central School, having been invalided out of the army after the First World War. The others were Tom Barnet, Jack Harfield, William Patrick, Luff, and Cutter.

12. The young 'Guvnor' with Charlie Bray and Bob Etherington, outside the workshop in Froxfield, about 1933.

The workshop job record book, started in July 1923,[1] shows no shortage of work in the first few years. Although Lupton had designed and made some furniture, his workshop was primarily concerned with building and joinery work, and for some years the joinery side of the business was very important to Barnsley. He 'undertook any form of woodwork, excluding only reproduction of antiques',[2] though this was not a completely firm rule and very occasionally he would take on a job which was virtually a reproduction. In 1932, for instance, Charterhouse School ordered six Chippendale chairs for a Common Room (pl. 39), and later, in 1974, the workshop made an arm–chair in yew to complete a set of ten eighteenth-century chairs owned by Lansing Bagnall and Company. In special circumstances Barnsley would also carry out repairs to antiques, and in 1937 the workshop repaired and re-upholstered fifteen eighteenth-century mahogany dining chairs from Uppark, a nearby country house.

Some of the early joinery work was carried out for local people within a fairly small radius of Froxfield, but most was commissioned by Lupton and the records show that he provided more than thirty-seven weeks of work in the first eighteen months. This varied from windows and door-frames, to cedar shelves, to 'body to car', 'windscreen', and 'lorry body'. Lupton's son, Morris, recalled the cannibalization of several ex-army model-T Fords and their reconstruction into two sound vehicles with elegant estate-type bodies shortly after the First World War. One of these was used to carry Morris to school on wet days, fruit to Petersfield station for Covent Garden, and pigs to market.[3] Before the war, Lupton had been a generous friend to the poet Edward Thomas and his family, and it seems likely that he now gave much of this work to Edward in a similar spirit, to help him to get started.

In later years Edward would have been pleased to have more of this type of joinery to do and in 1949 when Alan Peters joined as an apprentice, the oak workshop sign still advertised building and joinery work as well as cabinet-making.[4] But by then Barnsley's reputation as a furniture designer was such that few clients would think of coming to him for mere 'fittings' and this remained only a small percentage of the production, although some of the local customers who had patronized the workshop from the beginning continued to ask for work of this kind, just as local customers, friends, and people involved in the Arts and Crafts Movement continued to order simple

---

FURNITURE & JOINERY.

EDWARD BARNSLEY.   FROXFIELD, PETERSFIELD.

Sidney H. Barnsley,
Sapperton, Cirencester.

Edward Barnsley.

                         March 1927

---

13. Letterhead from a bill of 1927 indicating the early connection of Sidney Barnsley with his son's business: his name is crossed out as he died in 1926.

and inexpensive items of furniture. In 1952, for instance, the workshop repaired and renewed oak doors, screens, and pillars for Mrs Blow at Hilles in Gloucestershire, the magnificent house built by Detmar Blow between 1914 and 1939.

Sidney Barnsley gave up making furniture in about 1924 because he had a lot of architectural work to look after and increasingly found the physical effort of woodworking too much for him. He gradually cleared his workshop and gave Edward stocks of timber and a number of tools, including the hand- and foot-powered circular saw which for a long time was the only machine-tool in the workshop.[5] He nevertheless continued to receive commissions and to design furniture; according to Edward Barnsley, the last piece his father made himself was a dresser for Ambrose Heal in early 1923, but the collection of his drawings in Cheltenham Art Gallery and Museum includes sixteen furniture designs dated between 1923 and 1926.[6] A few of these were for use by the estate workers at Rodmarton Manor, and some were for Bedales library furniture, but most were for individual pieces which were made in the Froxfield workshop.

Sidney Barnsley's late designs were generally for established clients who had previously commissioned work from him and from Gimson, and who continued to buy from Edward and from Peter Waals. These included the Biddulphs at Rodmarton Manor, who were furnishing their house with work suited to Ernest Barnsley's architecture, Victor Smith, who lived in Gimson's

14. The dining room at Rodmarton Manor in 1928 with furniture designed by Sidney Barnsley. The built-in dresser was made in the Rodmarton estate workshop, and Edward Barnsley's workshop made one of the tables.

White House in Leicester, and Francis Dodd, the artist.[7] The Murrays of Painswick Lodge, a house altered by Sidney Barnsley in 1926, also began to acquire furniture and amassed a very substantial collection over the years that followed, and members of the Gimson and Barnsley families continued their support for the crafts.

As well as passing on clients, Sidney Barnsley was also able to help his son by advising him in letters about specific queries in relation to working with an architect on fittings for a house, on the construction of mouldings for panelling, and on the design of furniture. In August 1926 he suggested that Edward would probably have to turn one of the sheds into a shop for rougher jobs because the workshop was too crowded and he counselled against the expense of running a car, having recently acquired one himself.[8]

The other main source of work was Bedales School, where the furnishing of the library was still to be completed, and individuals, both staff and pupils, began to commission pieces. The houses of the staff at Bedales were depicted in Helen Thomas's *World Without End*, where she described the 'Bedales people' as she knew them from 1907 onwards: 'Their houses were in faultless taste outside and in. Their simple oak furniture was made by skilful craftsmen and their curtains were hand-woven'.[9] Presumably she was referring to the houses of members of the Powell and Gimson families, but staff appointed later soon absorbed the craft ethos, and Dr Laurin Zilliacus, who came to the school in 1917, ordered several pieces from Barnsley in the early twenties. Contemporaries of Edward, such as Roger Powell, Vyv Trubshawe, Robert Best, and Myers Salaman were also among his earliest customers; no doubt they were encouraged by their schooling to appreciate hand-craftsmanship and also wished to support their former schoolfellow in his new venture. Edward in turn, bought several of Best's stylish 'Best-Lites'. As time went on, and many of these friends married, orders also came in for wedding gifts and furnishings for new homes.

Not all the furniture was for individual clients though, and from the very beginning the workshop was also involved in large-scale architectural projects, such as items for Schultz Weir's St Andrew's Chapel at Westminster Cathedral in 1924-5 and doors for Khartoum Cathedral in 1929. Seventy-four weeks of work in 1926-7 were spent on making and fitting panelling, doors, lintels, and a staircase at a house in Southwold for Miss Peskett and Miss Corns, clients of the architect Alister Gladstone MacDonald, who was a couple of years older than Barnsley and had preceded him at Bedales. Their collaboration on this project gave Sidney Barnsley something to talk about when he met Alister's father, Ramsay MacDonald, the Labour M.P. and briefly in 1924, Prime Minister, at Rodmarton in September 1926, a visit which he suggested rather gleefully to Edward would 'stir up the Conservative Dovecot in Ciceter!'. His next letter reported a strenuous time 'helping to entertain R. M.', who was interested to hear that Edward was assisting his son and also seemed pleased to see the cottages Sidney Barnsley had designed for the Rodmarton Estate, 'though of course such cottages don't help the ordinary housing problem'.[10]

15. Woodwork in a house in Southwold designed by Alister MacDonald. Oak ceilings, doors, panelling, beams, lintels and staircase were carried out by the Barnsley workshop in 1926-7 at a cost of £698.

The initial burst of work must have been very encouraging for Edward, and in 1924 he decided to take on his first apprentice, a local boy named Herbert Upton, who was then 14. Upton's father was a general builder and architectural carpenter in nearby Steep and young Bert had always been interested in working with wood, both at school in Petersfield and at home, where he had his own workbench. He already knew Barnsley, who was lodging next door to the Upton family in Steep, and the Froxfield workshop must have seemed the obvious place to acquire a proper training in cabinet-making.[11]

His apprenticeship was a thoroughly formal and traditional arrangement, with proper indenture papers which set out the conditions of his training, which was to last five years, at a starting pay of four shillings per week, rising to 4/6d after six months and increasing thereafter at six-monthly intervals. This was rather less than apprentices were paid at Waals's workshop in Chalford and at Gordon Russell's in Broadway, though at Chalford the new boy worked unpaid for the first three months so the annual wage in the beginning was less than at Froxfield. All three of these Arts and Crafts workshops paid meagre sums in comparison with the general cabinet-maker and undertaker in Sidmouth, Devon, where Max Burrough started in 1928 on 7/6d a week, in spite of the fact that the trade was in difficulties and Max was told by a fellow worker on his first day that there was 'no future in cabinet-making'. 7/6d per week was also the figure mentioned by T. R. Dennis, who started an apprenticeship in Preston in 1924.[12] In most parts of the furniture trade except at the top end, however, apprenticeships were by now a rarity, especially in London and the big cities, where it was necessary for workers to specialize in one small part of the production in order to be able to make fast enough to compete in price.[13]

In trying to preserve the best aspects of an almost vanished system of skilled working, the earliest Arts and Crafts workshops had to employ people who had been trained in the trade because there was no-one else available, with the sort of results described by Sidney Barnsley (p. 22). Some fine craftsmen proved to have no understanding of the type of work they were being asked to produce, though others, such as Waals and Davoll and Smith, became fully absorbed and made a great contribution to the work. All those who were serious about the social meaning of the Arts and Crafts Movement, like C. R. Ashbee, Arthur Simpson, and Ernest Gimson, and were not simply concerned to have their own designs executed by a competent workshop, began a scheme of training, often partly as a means of providing useful work for youths in the country.

Gimson and Waals, and now Edward Barnsley, provided this training in the form of an indentured apprenticeship. In a way this seems unexpectedly formal, but it may have been necessary as the recognized method of doing things in a rural area, or a symptom of the respect that Gimson and the Barnsleys had for the skilled cabinet-maker as a species, or simply the easiest, because tried and tested, way to organize a contract.

The apprentice's training gave a very thorough grounding in the practical aspects of the trade and its importance lay in the fact that skills acquired over decades of work could be transferred from the older craftsmen in the shop to the apprentice, by-passing the element of trial and error which Gimson and the Barnsleys experienced in the 1890s. The idea was that apprentices could be taught the skills which were felt to be particularly relevant to the type of work that was being done, and since their whole experience would be in the one place, they would absorb ideas about design as they went on. Bert Upton was a quick and willing worker and soon proved his usefulness.

Once Edward was settled in and established in the workshop, he began to send his work to exhibitions, starting on a rather grand note with the British Empire Exhibition at Wembley in 1924-5. The British display was organized by Sir Lawrence Weaver, whose books and articles on contemporary architecture and interiors had done much to publicize and foster appreciation of Arts and Crafts work and who planned a book on Gimson and the Barnsleys, unfortunately not completed by the time of his death.[14] The British Pavilion was not well received by the art press and *The Studio's* reviewer described a first impression of 'solidity, not to say stolidity'.[15] To this display Edward contributed a lovely glazed cabinet in walnut and ebony which he had made himself and which he subsequently gave to his wife as a wedding present, since it did not sell (pl. 28).

More ambitiously, in the following year he sent an oak dresser and display rack to the 1925 Paris Exhibition, where it was displayed with work by Ambrose Heal and Gordon Russell in a show which was overshadowed by the dazzling 'Deco' elegance and exoticism of the French contribution.

16. Oak dresser made in 1924 and sent to the 1925 *Exposition Internationale des Arts Décoratifs et Industriels Modernes* in Paris. With its panelled doors, stepped feet, handmade metal handles and chamfered shelf supports, this is a typical Cotswold-style piece.

The architecture of the British section was generally considered very poor in relation to the others but some reviewers thought the British work could stand comparison with anything else there, and one particularly noticed Barnsley's sideboard. 'Perhaps one of the outstanding exhibits in the Pavilion is a very fine dresser of English oak designed by Edward Barnsley ... It is a really fine example of twentieth century furniture, and occupies the centre of the left flank of the foyer, attracting a considerable amount of attention'.[16] Unfortunately this writer's next comments suggest that the publicity value of the exhibition was limited for Barnsley, since his piece was not clearly labelled, unlike all the other furniture.

Since 1922 Edward had been engaged to Tatiana Hedvig Kellgren, whom he had met at Bedales when he was working on the library and she was still a pupil. In 1925 she was in Paris, having gone there to improve her French at the École Pigier, Sorbonne, and École Polyglote, and to 'finish' her education. This she did by working at a variety of jobs ranging from teaching English and making and selling stylish appliqué leatherwork with Margarita Classon-Smith, to secretarial work for a linoleum importer whose accountant turned out to be a swindler and absconded, leaving Tania to take over the books.

While Tania was still in France, Edward was offered the chance to acquire the workshop at Froxfield permanently, when Geoffrey Lupton decided to sell up and emigrate to South Africa, where he bought 2000 acres of raw veld which he transformed over the next ten years into a flourishing fruit farm.[17] In 1925 he offered the whole of his property for sale and Sidney Barnsley decided to buy it.

This property comprised a large area along the south side of Cockshott Lane running along the ridge of Stoner Hill above the village of Steep to the north of Petersfield. As one turns into the lane from the road running up from Steep, there is a natural wooded area on the right and then the timber-sheds and workshop. Next is the cottage which Lupton built for himself in 1909, camping out in the workshop while construction work went on. This is a brick and tile house of modest size, with entrance porch, kitchen, larder, and living room on the ground floor, two bedrooms above, and originally a large open landing, which was later filled in to provide another bedroom, probably when Lupton married. From the road, the cottage is very private and although the garden front is more open and welcoming, it still has no pretensions about it and the tiny entrance porch leads straight in to the living room. It is the kind of house that might have been erected at any time in the eighteenth or nineteenth centuries, using unchanged methods of construction and stylistic features common in this part of the country. By 1909 there were few people working in this way and certainly fewer who used hand-cut oak floorboards, fifteen and more inches wide, and latches and nails which were handmade in Gimson's and Lupton's workshops.[18]

In accordance with the Arts and Crafts man's usual unconcern for bodily comfort, the earth closet was outside and Lupton built no bathroom, but had made a concrete bath under a removable floorboard in front of the fireplace in the sitting room. In a letter about the Bedales School hall, Edward Barnsley commented on Lupton's attitude to comfort in a passing reference to the seats: '... certainly their extreme torment fits in well with Lupton's belief in the efficacy of subduing the flesh. Once I sat next my father at some performance, with Tania's brother on my knee, and made some remark about comfort, and Lupton leant across my dad and said, "Yes, you wouldn't wish to subdue the flesh would you". As far as I know, the only sharp remark he ever made about me ...'[19] When he married in 1911, Lupton built on a bathroom like an oasthouse with a conical roof, tucked in next to the cottage and half underground. This original construction is now, unfortunately, gone, replaced in 1964 by a more conventional bathroom above a cloakroom and small entrance hall at the side of the house.

Before moving in, Edward added a small window in the east wall to improve the light in the sitting room and over the years he made a few other changes to the building, such as installing electricity in 1955 and a wood-burning stove in the 1980s. In the beginning there was no running water supply and rain water was collected from the roof and stored in tanks under the kitchen.

Surrounding the house are gardens of three-quarters of an acre, provid-ing ample space for vegetable plots and fruit trees, and disappearing dra-matically down the slope to a steeply wooded area, giving a stunning view of the Hampshire countryside stretching towards the South Downs. 'The beauty is beyond expression at times,' wrote Edward in 1968, 'and the privilege of such a home almost embarassing'.[20] Throughout his life, he took enormous pleasure from working in the garden, particularly at the heavy jobs such as digging. He often did some hours' work in the garden before breakfast and then was able to appreciate the beauty of the place while seated at his typewriter, as in this letter of 1963: 'The sun slowly comes up over the trees. I've had one of my earlier starts, and this garden is something beyond description, all the grass scintillating, the flowers bowed a little over with the weight of water, sparkling and flashing in great variety.'[21]

The property also included a small building known as the Bee House because Lupton kept his bee-keeping equipment in one of the two tiny unconnecting rooms. The second room had been used as a study by the poet Edward Thomas and was afterwards enlarged as a play room for Lupton's son. Edward carried out these alterations, raising the roof, widening the rooms, and making a communicating door.

17. Aerial view of the workshop and cottage at Froxfield taken after 1948 when the garage next to the house was converted into more workshop space. The Bee House is in the foreground on the right.

Further along the lane on a separate plot of land was a pair of small cottages which Edward was able to rent out to bring in some income. These were altered in 1983 for occupation by Edward's son Jon and his family and are still known as Lupton Cottage.

Sidney Barnsley bought the whole property in 1925 for £2550, a sum which represented about a quarter of his own capital. His house in Sapperton belonged to the Bathurst Estate and so could not be passed on in the family, but he had money in stocks and also a half-share with his brother in leasehold properties in Birmingham.[22] In March 1926, perhaps prompted by the recent death of his brother Ernest, Sidney Barnsley mentioned the need to have a proper agreement with his son, 'in case I depart this life suddenly'.[23] Initially Edward paid rent to his father, calculated at 5 per cent of the purchase price (£127/10/- per annum), and he was clearly eager to begin payment since in August 1926 Sidney Barnsley wrote to him, 'When you settle accounts you do so in a very lordly way!!! A Tenant doesn't pay rent in advance as you have done. You should have sent 65£ only up to June 24 & another 65£ at Christmas, so if your banking account is low shall I return you this amount?'[24]

With the future of the workshop now more secure, this seemed to Edward and Tania a good time to marry. Tania had enjoyed her years in Paris but felt ready to return to the new experience of setting up home and learning domestic skills, and the wedding was arranged for 12th December 1925. The service took place at the church in Hartley Wintney in Hampshire and it was snowing as the bride and groom left under an archway of hand-saws. At the celebrations afterwards in Robert Schultz Weir's house, The Barn at Hartley Wintney, Tania sat in the chair made in Gimson's workshop as a prototype for the seven ebony and ivory clergy stalls in St Andrew's Chapel at Westminster Cathedral, one of Schultz Weir's projects for the Marquess of Bute.[25]

A memorable feature of the service was the singing of hymns in the Bedales versions and the fact that Edward and Tania joined in with the singing, in true Bedales spirit. The school remained a focal point of their social life in years to come, giving them contact with congenial, like-minded people, such as Biff Barker the woodwork teacher, with whom Edward played darts in the pub in Steep, walking the mile and a half down the hill and back again. Through school camps Edward discovered the glories of Snowdonia and the Lake District, and he enjoyed other group activities, such as musical productions, especially of Gilbert and Sullivan operas. He had a good tenor voice and was playing Giuseppe in *The Gondoliers*, along with Basil Gimson as the second gondolier, at the time of his marriage and put off moving into the cottage until the performances were over since it was more convenient to stay in Steep. He and Tania were both involved for many years in the Bedales Society, which keeps in touch with Old Bedalians.

Tania was the daughter of Russian-born Vera Kellgren and Dr Harry (Jonas Henrik) Kellgren, a Swedish physician whose father had developed a successful system of manipulative treatment for arthritis, involving active and passive movements combined with massage. Harry Kellgren had become a successful society doctor in London: he lived in Eaton Square, moved in the right circles, and played golf with the Prince of Wales, but he died leaving large debts. Because the children were already at school at Bedales (a younger one paid for by an uncle), Mrs Kellgren had come to Steep after the death of her husband. She was, according to J. H. Badley,[26] a vivid, stimulating and outspoken character, with a keenly analytic mind and a frankness of speech which could be overwhelming, especially for children. Her granddaughter, Karin, later found her loud voice and startling remarks acutely embarrassing, but adored her. She had strong socialist views and lived a rootless existence, oblivious to her surroundings as long as she had a typewriter and paper. In her early married life she had been used to a staff of nursemaids and governesses and had neglected Tania and her elder sister because she was more interested in her intellectual and social life.

Tania inherited her intellectual acuteness, and also became a socialist, though she says she was less influenced by her mother, whose politics were anyway purely theoretical, than by the injustices she saw in country life, especially during the depression of 1929. Edward always maintained, half-joking, that he would have inherited Schultz Weir's property had Weir not disapproved of Tania's views: 'though Uncle Daddy ... took kindly to Tania, he later found out that she held most unsuitable socialist, not to say traitorous views, and that I was far from being the authodox responsible young man he had hoped for'.[27] Edward was anyway doubtful about the limitations it would have imposed on him had he moved his workshop to The Barn, and Schultz Weir had relatives to whom the property was eventually bequeathed and who looked after it 'with great affection and care.'[28] Tania could appear a little fearsome, but her straightforward manner was a great asset to the workshop in later years.

18 and 19. Edward and Tania Barnsley in the living room at Froxfield, about 1926.

Their personalities were very different. Edward was warm, emotional, good fun, adored by children, and thoroughly naïve. He was and remained a romantic, with a tendency to fall adoringly in love with beauty, and even at his engagement party he embarrassed himself by gazing at Anne Wilson (the wife of Stuart Wilson, a musician), entranced by her loveliness. He claimed to be shy, and in some circumstances, particularly with his employees and with anyone he found intellectually intimidating, he felt awkward and unhappy, but on the whole, he blossomed in company and thoroughly enjoyed being the centre of attention at any gathering.

Tania was also inexperienced in human relationships but more worldly-wise, more rigorously intellectual, and defensively self-contained. She had (and has) a streak of exoticism from her background, which contrasted with the solid Englishness of the Barnsleys' world. At a Christmas party in Edward's parents' cottage shortly after her return from Paris she wore a cerise-coloured décolleté evening dress which was made for her by Margarita Classon-Smith for a *Beaux-Arts* Ball in Paris, and she contributed arias from *Carmen* to the music making of the evening. During her stay in Paris she had been attracted to the free intellectual life around her, and under the influence of Margarita Classon-Smith, who was against marriage, had attempted to break the engagement with Edward, but had been won back when he hurried over to see her. Theirs was not an easy marriage and its survival owed much to sheer will-power on both sides, as well as to Edward's admiration of his wife: 'Always I thought her a person of quality. For many years I judged the sense and awareness of others by the extent to which they saw in her what I saw. Always I shall remember the disapproval of nearly everybody in Steep of this intention and alliance of mine. Well my dear Oliver, I would venture to say that you know, now, that Tania is a person of quality. Compared with me — well comparisons are not happy.'[29]

On occasion, Edward said that he was spoilt and cushioned in privilege,[30] and it is true that few craftsmen have their own workshop well established by the age of 25. Business so far had been good, but there were also problems. Some of them were the difficulties which continue to face furniture makers today, and others were caused by the general economic situation in the 1920s and 1930s.

Furniture is almost inevitably an expensive commodity, and handmade cabinet-furniture cannot be produced cheaply for a wide market. The high cost of skilled labour makes it difficult for craft furniture makers to compete with manufacturers who cut costs by the use of machinery and batch production, and antique dealers who can ignore the initial labour costs entirely. Potential customers are, therefore, a small group: only those with money beyond what is needed for everyday living; those who appreciate the particular aesthetic qualities of fine handwork; and those who believe in the value of supporting someone to work by hand.

Even if they find such clients, furniture makers face practical problems on a rather different scale from most other craftworkers. In particular, their materials are fairly expensive and timber needs to be seasoned over a long period, so money can be tied up in stocks for many years. One solution found by Alan Peters in the early 1960s, at the beginning of his career, was to buy seasoned timber in small quantities direct from the timber merchants, but this is relatively expensive and gives little control of quality.[31] In order to establish a reputation and to prove the ability to execute their designs to a good standard, cabinet-makers also need to make speculative pieces for display and exhibitions, which may bring no immediate financial return to the workshop.

A further and vitally important problem in a workshop employing a number of people, especially at a time of high unemployment, is that jobs must be found for them even when commissions are scarce. This usually

20. 'Potboilers' from the Barnsley workshop, 1930s. The photograph is inscribed 'Set of trays £9.9.0, single trays from £3.3.0, turned fruit bowls in figured walnut 17/6 20/- 30/- & 35/-'.

involves making 'bread and butter' items, potboilers such as boxes, candlesticks, trays, lampstands, and small tables, designed to sell in small craft shops or to tempt the casual visitor to buy direct from the workshop. With the security of his own money and orders from a clientele built up over many years, Ernest Gimson had managed to achieve a balance at the Daneway workshops, and between 1914 and 1919 about 60 per cent of his designs were made to commission and 40 per cent for 'stock', though at his death in 1919 there were still some items in stock which had been made at least twelve years before.[32] C. R. Ashbee in Chipping Campden, struggling to find work for a larger number of craftsmen and supporting administrative staff, failed to get the balance right, and when the Guild of Handicraft Limited Company collapsed in 1907, it was left with a storeroom crammed with furniture and other work, made to keep the craftsmen employed.[33]

Edward Barnsley had to face this challenge, and the workshop record shows that he was fairly successful at first: of about seventy jobs carried out in 1925, only thirteen were made for stock and most of these sold quickly, often through small galleries such as No.1 The Square in Petersfield, Pan in Church Street, Kensington, and the Little Gallery in Chelsea, and through regular exhibitions like the Cotswold Craft shows at Chipping Campden and Cheltenham, and more local displays in Alton, Haslemere, and Bournemouth.[34] The craftsmen were fully employed, and Edward himself spent more than thirty-seven weeks working at the bench.

His lack of experience in these early years shows in the too frequent entries of 'Loss!' against his calculations of prices, since he often found that

Prices of Writing Desks.

Small desks in oak, from,	18	0	0
Small walnut desks,	22	0	0
Oak bureau, selected wood and with panelled construction,	25	0	0
Walnut bureau, inlaid, from,	33	0	0
Walnut & Ebony bureau, No 9	65	0	0
Knee-hole writing desks, from,	20	0	0

No 7. Walnut Chest inlaid with Ebony.
Handles of Brass, on Ebony Plates.

21. Two pages from Barnsley's earliest surviving catalogue, late 1920s. This consists simply of photographs attached to typed sheets within a card cover.

the price he had quoted was inadequate to cover the hours taken in making the piece.[35] He also had an unbusinesslike tendency to follow the practice of his father, who would look at a piece and decide what would be a suitable price for it, almost in spite of the actual cost of making, but in a way this was inevitable since he had to compete with other furniture makers.

Comparison of prices of individual handmade pieces is extremely difficult because variations in timber and decorative details can make a very big difference to the cost of apparently similar items, but limited research suggests that Barnsley's prices were much the same as those charged by Waals, and for smaller things at least, only slightly higher than Heal's and Russell's. John and Rotha Barnfield, who began to furnish their house with Gordon Russell furniture in the 1930s, ordered a piece from Barnsley in 1938 and then found themselves hooked, since the quality of his work gave them so much pleasure that they felt it was worthwhile to pay the small amount extra.[36]

In the late 1930s Barnsley explained that he arrived at the selling price of most items by looking in an album of photographs of past pieces, in which the prices were recorded, and then estimating how much labour and material costs had risen since.[37] Years later he wrote that a fundamental problem was that the craftsmen worked at different rates and it was difficult to estimate how long each would take to make a version of something previously made by another, especially since different woods added another factor to the equation. 'One of our special shape fronted china cabinets is listed as taking 379 hours in walnut, 451 hours in Yew and 467 hours in Rosewood', he told Vera Simpson, writing of his costing troubles.[38] This was a cause of friction in the workshop for many years and was presumably one of the problems of coming from a background of 'gentleman' workers removed from the normal conditions of trade. There were few similar craftsmen with whom to compare prices and the personal nature of the design element introduced the factor of modesty about the value of the work. Edward's father admitted to being a 'poor bargainer' and when Grace ran her own pottery she felt unable to ask realistic prices for her work, even just after the war when decorated wares were scarce, so Edward's own difficulties are not surprising.[39]

To compound this problem over pricing, the market for good-quality modern furniture was not healthy at this time anyway because of a continuing interest in antiques, which had peaked in price during the First World War and were still popular enough to evoke comment from several writers in the 1920s and 1930s. Lethaby lamented the fashion for antiques, which had of course been much encouraged by the Arts and Crafts Movement. J. C. Rogers, in *Modern English Furniture* published in 1930, felt the need to argue on behalf of contemporary makers for truly modern work 'that would be recognised frankly as a product of its age, perfectly suited to the requirements of its day, reflecting without affectation the habits of life, not of one but of all classes',[40] and he illustrated his book with a considerable number of pieces by Barnsley and Waals, along with work by others in the Gimson–Barnsley tradition, such as Frances Dagley, John Stark, Gordon Russell, and Ambrose Heal, most of them producing cheaper goods by the use of machine tools and batch production. He also included modernist pieces by Chermayeff and others, but the largest number of photographs are of more traditional work.

Likewise, John Gloag in 1934 made a scathing attack on antique fakers, retail furnishers, and buyers of mock period furniture, but he had less sympathy than Rogers for the English artist-craftsmen, describing them as disgruntled hermits with no business sense who relied on the chance patronage of the rich.[41] Gloag was a buyer for Heal's and a friend of Gordon Russell and he advocated a partnership of designers and manufacturers as the way forward, but even this was a struggle in the thirties against the prevailing public taste for safe, traditional, antique-reproduction design and the furniture manufacturers' willingness to supply the goods. The conservative taste of the retailers' buyers and their pressure upon the makers to keep prices down had been noticed as early as the 1850s: it had a continuing effect which drew comment in the 1946 Furniture Working Party Report and still brought criticism in the 1980s from Ray Leigh, then Managing Director of Gordon Russell.[42] The customer got used to a kind of style that was fashionable in the shops, did not know enough about quality to recognize when it had been sacrificed, but could easily see the difference in price.

In the 1920s there were still clients who wanted the best and were prepared to pay for it, or who would have a plain oak piece rather than a decorated mahogany one in order to have quality craftsmanship, but along with everybody else these people were affected by the Depression of the late twenties and early thirties. In uncertain times the purchase of furniture was something that would be deferred if possible.[43]

The furniture makers reacted in different ways. Russell and Sons in Broadway, started by Gordon Russell in 1919 and joined by his brother Dick in 1928, abandoned the idea of having pieces made entirely by hand, in favour of batch-production methods using new materials and machinery. For Gordon Russell it became more important to produce well designed and competitively priced furniture for a wide market than to provide interesting and useful work for the maker, along the lines proposed by Morris and practised by, among others, Ernest Gimson, whose work was initially of great influence on Russell and whose workshop arrangements must have been familiar. At Gordon Russell Ltd, mechanization was introduced in the 1920s to assist the cabinet-makers and to enable them to make small batches of some designs. Edward Barnsley later recalled going in 1928 to the opening of Russell's showrooms at Wigmore Street, where handmade furniture was displayed at the front, work on which machine tools had been used was at the back of the room, and in the basement were pieces on which machinery had been employed to its full extent. Barnsley asked Gordon and Dick Russell if they thought that the machine work would take over from making by hand and they rejected the idea, but by the early thirties the firm had turned to mass-production and it survived the Depression largely through its pioneering work for Murphy Radios, making tens of thousands of the more popular models. The firm also occasionally laid off staff.[44]

In contrast, Peter Waals, who was Gimson's foreman from 1901 to 1919 and then ran his own workshop in Chalford until 1937, was committed to the methods of working practised in the Daneway workshop. In a business sense he was probably considerably hampered by the very idealism of the Gimson–Barnsley group, since their commitment to the principles of handwork at all costs was such that Ernest Gimson and Sidney Barnsley took only a very small percentage for themselves and their prices were, therefore, kept artificially low. In a letter, Edward mentioned that his father sorted out Gimson's affairs after his death and found no evidence that Gimson made any money from the furniture business.[45] For them, the purpose of the work was the practice of the craft and all parts of the process were valuable experience, for even the most tedious jobs can teach the maker more about the nature of materials. Because they had private incomes they were able to operate outside the rules of normal trade, but without the backing of independent money, Waals was only able to survive in business with the help of a few regular and reliable clients, such as the Goddards in Leicester,

Arthur Mitchell in Cheltenham, and the Biddulphs at Rodmarton Manor, and by introducing a few machine tools to speed up production. According to Owen Scrubey, there were a treadle saw and a saw bench driven by petrol motor in 1921 when he joined as an apprentice, and these were later augmented by a large circular saw, a band-saw, and a second-hand mortising machine. Waals had to compromise in this matter, though he always retained the principle of one man, one job. He, too, occasionally had to lay off workers in the early thirties.[46]

Edward Barnsley, instilled from birth with uncompromising Arts and Crafts principles, resisted for thirty years the strong pressure to bring in powered tools to make the work faster and therefore cheaper, and anyway had little choice since there was no electricity at Froxfield and a private generator would have been beyond his means. As the economic depression worsened in the late twenties many of his customers found they could no longer afford the luxury of handmade furniture. Orders were very slow, and retaining a staff of seven was a great financial burden, but it was also a responsibility which Edward felt he had a duty to sustain, partly because to give up was to fail, and partly because he knew that there were very few other jobs available for the craftsmen to go to. By 1931 the number of items made for 'stock' had increased considerably, but even accounting for the many table lamps, trays, bookends, boxes, and tea caddies, there was hardly enough work to keep the craftsmen occupied for half their time, and Edward spent less than eight weeks of that year working at the bench. Fearing that they would otherwise have to lay off staff, Tania went out to work as a secretary for a local builder and joiner for a year, leaving their two young children, Karin and Jon, aged four and one, in the care of Annie Sawkins, the maid.

Financial worries were complicated at this time by the fact that Edward's mother had decided to move house. After Sidney Barnsley died in September 1926, Edward and Tania had been concerned about her future, and when the Red House just up the road from their cottage came up for sale, Edward had persuaded her to move from Sapperton. The house had been built for Edward Thomas by Geoffrey Lupton to a design by Alfred Powell, and was a substantial six-bedroomed brick and tile cottage, with a garden laid out by Helen Thomas. Edward's sister, Grace, came with her mother, since she was by then married to a merchant seaman, Oscar Davies, whose work made it difficult to set up a proper home of their own.

Lucy and Grace moved to Froxfield early in 1927, but only three years later Lucy wrote to Edward from a visit in Letchworth that she really wanted to leave. The house had been a great disappointment, she said; it was impossible to find a suitable girl for a maid, she felt unable to be independent and to cope with the hill, and it was not fair on Grace to be so reliant upon her. Grace herself, though a loving daughter, clearly found the situation intolerably inconvenient and stressful and railed at Edward in a series of long letters for his thoughtlessness about the consequences of the move. Property at Letchworth was inspected and bought, and then in 1934 Lucy

Barnsley moved again to Rainham in Kent, where Grace and Oscar took over the Upchurch Pottery, renaming it the Roeginga Pottery. Lucy named both her houses, first in Letchworth and then at Rainham, 'Pinbury', in honour of her first married home.[47]

These moves and the setting up of the pottery were paid for from the estate of Sidney Barnsley, which was administered by Edward and his cousin as trustees. Such trusts were a popular way of arranging family finances at this date to protect the interests of the widow while avoiding death duties. After his father's death Edward continued to pay rent to his mother and to pay interest on loans he had received from Sidney Barnsley.[48] Unfortunately, each move became a drain on the finances of the estate when both houses proved difficult to sell or to let, and since Grace felt she had not been properly consulted about either purchase, she was understandably resentful about the value of the estate diminishing and about her mother having to worry about money. Then when she wanted to take on the pottery, Edward was very cautious about the idea and whether she should have a loan from the estate. This was probably partly because his own business was going through such hard times and prospects for the crafts still looked dim, but to Grace it appeared as selfishness, and more acrimonious correspondence ensued.

Edward often worried in his letters of later years about whether he could justly be accused of having done better out of the estate than his sister, since the property at Froxfield increased in value very considerably, but he appears to have been very scrupulous about the division of assets.[49] He clearly acted with the best intentions, but Grace felt that it was Edward's tendency to rush decisions that led to the reduction of the value of the estate, and certainly when their mother died, the Froxfield property and Edward's loans represented just over half the value of the whole inheritance instead of a third, as in 1926.[50] How much this was due to the difficult financial climate and how much to Edward's actions is almost impossible to know, especially since the laws governing family trusts were restrictive and they were always likely to depreciate in value at a time of low inflation like the 1930s; but while he had a clear conscience about the money arrangements, he did later on acknowledge his mistake in not consulting properly with his sister.[51]

These domestic worries came at the time when the business was at its lowest ebb, and 1931 might have seen the closure of the workshop had Edward not received timely help and encouragement at the Arts and Crafts Exhibition Society's exhibition at the Royal Academy.

Edward had been elected to the Arts and Crafts Exhibition Society in 1926, at the same time as A. Romney Green,[52] and had shown some work at the exhibitions of that year and 1928. This last he found disappointing because there was little new work he liked and he thought the tribute to his father and Ernest Barnsley, which was arranged as a memorial, was hung badly and displayed with all the wrong colours.[53] The Royal Academy shared his view and informed the executive committee of the Society that

22. Oak sideboard purchased by Mrs Ida Neale at the Arts and Crafts Exhibition Society exhibition in 1931, when the workshop finances were at their lowest ebb. Made by Barnsley and Fred Eastlake in 556 hours.

their last exhibition was not up to the standard required at Burlington House.[54]

At the 1931 show, encouragement for Edward came from Mrs Ida Neale, an established client who had already commissioned several pieces, including bedroom furniture and one or two writing cabinets, and who purchased from the exhibition an oak sideboard and a burr oak desk. In a letter to Mrs Neale, he wrote, 'I am left without words to thank you. I found your wire when I arrived at the RA after a day's job hunting — and it cheered me greatly and I am encouraged and helped far beyond the mere facts of a sale.'[55] His anxiety about the future of the workshop had clearly been intense, since he wrote again on the same day apologizing for his inability to 'let go', and again a few days later to explain himself in greater detail.

> My Dear Mrs Neale,
>
> I hardly know how to answer your letter satisfactorily without telling you all the exact details & the conditions under which I am working & financial position etc etc. And this I find hard to write; and am wondering if you are to be at Bedales again this term & if we could have a talk.
>
> But the position at present is that I am trying to avoid either bankruptcy or voluntary liquidation by getting all the work I can in the shop & at the same time applying for work as designer; to augment. (The Waals combination has

definitely fallen through I fear & I see no other partner at present) And though I have decided that I must aim at a new line of work — and close up here — I can't see likelihood of this being possible <u>immediately</u> and I must therefore earn what I can, while I can, in this shop. And for this I need hardly say your help makes a great difference, & for the moment, saves me. But I am really much upset by this — because I feel how much you are doing it (buying my things) only to help me out of a hole — & that they are things you do not really need — or want at present.

For any new work; I am definitely hunting for it — because as I say I can see no possibility of securing a full pay job just now — & my liabilities are mounting up in a way that terrifies me.

And I am carrying on solely on the strength of loans and guarantees — all of which increase rapidly — and are due to come to an end in the near future unless I can turn the tide. There being also an added liability in relation to this property and my mother's position in relation to it; and to my continuing to pay my rents. But this I would prefer to leave over hoping to see you again — and I so hate to bother you with my difficulties — and to feel I can't get over them without that which comes very close to charity. I know you will understand what I mean, & am unable to express clearly.'[56]

The reference to a combination with Waals is of particular interest. Waals was also experiencing difficulties and in May 1930 had written in similar vein, though less open manner, to a member of the Goddard family in Leicester.[57] In the late twenties, Barnsley had suggested that he and Waals might form a partnership; Waals had declined at the time but himself revived the idea later, though nothing came of it. In fact, Bert Upton remembered that on the rare occasions he visited Waals's workshop, during the fitting of a reredos at Chalford Church, he had the decided feeling that he was regarded as a spy. This would not be unnatural, given that the workshops were producing similar furniture and must have been in competition for a limited number of commissions.

Mrs Neale's purchases kept the workshop going for a while, and further commissions came from Tania's mother and from her sister, Dr Nina Kellgren, who was practising her grandfather's manipulation treatment and who had some unusually modernist pieces made for her consulting room (pl. 29). But the financial situation was saved in 1935 when Edward received an unexpected legacy from his aunts, Alice and Florence Morley, of around £830.[58] This just put the bank account back into the black and later in the year Edward was able to report to his mother some optimism about orders.[59]

Money had also begun to come in from fee-paying pupils, young people who were perhaps too old for an apprenticeship, who needed practical work for therapeutic purposes, or, most commonly, who already had some woodworking experience but needed time in a workshop to improve their skills before setting up on their own. Miss S. Arnhold, who came as a pupil in September 1935, was a refugee from Germany and the only woman ever trained in the workshop. Edward referred to her very matter-of-factly in a letter to his mother: 'New pupil turned up early on Thursday. She is a keen worker and I hope it will go well',[60] but she seems to have been at Froxfield for only about six months and her later career is not recorded.

Most pupils stayed for a year or so. Often they arrived with a specific aim and left when they felt they had learned as much as they could (or could afford financially). Some came for very short periods, like Donald Kelly and Leo Cullen, young handicraft teachers who were allowed to work in the workshop for two weeks in 1932, made a bookcase cabinet, and were inspired to emulate the standards they saw there. They camped in a tent in the garden and Edward lent them his gun to shoot the rats which stole their food.[61] Occasionally the workshop also took on pupils who had health or educational problems and Barnsley was proud of the fact that the experience often 'made' them, by providing interesting work and giving them self-respect through growing skill.[62]

In the early and mid thirties, the workshop must occasionally have seemed very crowded with these pupils working alongside the craftsmen; in the period 1932 to 1939 there were twelve pupils, usually four at any one time in the workshop, at an average fee of about £60 a year each. Their day-to-day training was under the guidance of the foreman, and also in the early 1940s of Oliver Morel, who had himself been a pupil in 1934-6. Barnsley would occasionally take pupils out to timber merchants to learn about choosing and purchasing wood and they helped him in the drawing office, where they also received advice on design, unlike the apprentices, who had no formal design training.

23. This crowded workshop scene of about 1935-7 was probably set up for the camera. From left to right are Bob Etherington, Ron Bonner, Les Mundy, and Charlie Bray, with Rupert Woods in the foreground.

Several more apprentices had been taken on in the twenties after Herbert Upton: Goodwin left after only six months in 1926 (his first name is not recorded); Lesley Mundy started in the following year; and George Brown in 1929. They were essential to the running of this workshop and others like it because of the need for highly-skilled makers familiar with the particular ways of the designer and foreman, but the economics of apprenticeships were difficult even by this date and few London firms provided them. Apprentices were paid in the beginning only four shillings a week, less than a tenth of a trained craftsman's wages, and for two-and-a-half days of the five-and-a-half-day week they did all the 'dogsbody' work such as boiling glue, oiling the flywheel of the circular saw, sweeping the workshop, and running errands, releasing the more experienced men to get on with the job, while themselves learning the fundamentals of their craft.

The records show that apprentices were also put to general tasks around the workshop and garden, building woodsheds and repairing roofs, and some of them felt that they were being exploited as cheap labour, though since Edward himself enjoyed this type of work and Bedales School had virtually been built on this basis, it is doubtful if he saw it in the same light. An arduous task for the apprentices that was certainly a legacy of Bedales was the emptying of the workshop earth closets, a form of sanitation favoured at the school on the principled grounds that it preserved the natural cycle,[63] and typical of the facilities at Froxfield at this date, the area being remote from any main centres of population and situated at the top of a hill. There was no running water, no gas, and no electricity; heat when needed came from coke stoves, while more heat than light was given by pump-up paraffin lanterns which hung above the benches, singeing the hair of those who got too close. Once a year the workshop was cleared and the walls were whitewashed to maximize the reflected light.

In the 1930s a new batch of apprentices joined the workshop: Robert Etherington in 1931; Ronald Bonner in 1934; Rupert Woods in 1935; Jim Bray, the son of Charles Bray, in 1936; and George Taylor in 1937.

George Taylor's experience, once he started, was perhaps typical. He was a local boy who had been to school in Liss, where he was taught woodwork by Mr Burbage on half a day per week. Since he enjoyed these classes, his mother's employer suggested that George should try for an apprenticeship at the Barnsley workshop: he went for an interview and was told that he would have to wait for a while because a new apprentice had only just been taken on. Having seen the work in progress in the shop, he was very keen to work there and was prepared to be patient, but after eighteen months of waiting he felt that he was too much of a financial burden on his widowed mother, so he attended another interview, for an apprenticeship in estate carpentry at Bedales School. Realizing that he was about to lose a most promising trainee, Barnsley at last took him on in May 1937, when George was nearly 16, rather older than the usual age to begin an apprenticeship at this date.

His first few days did not go smoothly. On day one, he missed his dinner break because he had no watch, so the next day his mother lent him hers, a special one for which he knew she had had to save. On this day George was required to help Barnsley move timber in the outdoor sheds, and, concerned about the safety of the watch, he frequently took it from his pocket just to make sure it was still there and going. Barnsley told him he had no room for clockwatchers and George felt that they had got off on the wrong foot.[64]

As was normal practice, he was generally supervised by the foreman, Charlie Bray, whose bench backed on to his own so that he could keep an eye on him and demonstrate methods of working. Bray had been a regular soldier at the beginning of the First World War and was a disciplinarian, but George liked him and his training progressed satisfactorily from simple jobs to more complex work. Bray also kept the workshop running smoothly while Edward met clients or worked at the drawing board. It was as well that he was strict since Edward was known as something of a Tartar, ensuring that everyone worked their full fifty hours, from 7 a.m. to 5 p.m. on weekdays and 7 to 12 on Saturdays.[65] Edward's personal shyness with his staff added to the normal difficulties of the employer–employee relationship, which he kept on a formal basis; he was always known as 'Mister' Barnsley or 'the Guvnor' to everyone in the shop, even later on in the sixties and seventies when social mores had changed, though this was partly because his foreman (then Bert Upton) also favoured the traditional approach to working relationships.

As well as discussing commissions with clients, often visiting their houses to see where the new item was to fit, and making designs, Edward also purchased the timber and took great pleasure in assessing standing trees for their potential. He discussed the designs, which were generally drawn in one-eighth scale, with the foreman, who then allocated the work to particular craftsmen and gave them instructions and cutting lists. Each man then drew up his own full-size details if necessary, chose his own wood from the stock, and worked on one piece of furniture at a time, sometimes in collaboration with another craftsman if the piece were particularly large or complicated. This meant that each man was fully responsible for his own work and in the opinion of several of the craftsmen it had a very important effect on the atmosphere in the workshop.[66]

The business was still functioning on a very tight budget and the accounts for 1936 and 1937 show that on sales each year of just over £2500 the official net profit was £440 and £382. Analysis of these accounts and study of the cash books indicate a different story, however, of continuing overdrafts at the bank, the repayment of loans from Schultz Weir and others, and consistent spending by Barnsley of more than he was earning. 1936 was the first year in which he had proper accounts prepared by Thomas H. Casey and Son and before this time he probably sent only a simple statement to the tax inspectors. The initial Statement of Affairs shows that the value of the stock of timber was very high in relation to the invoiced work, and it seems that Barnsley's passion for wood and his desire to maintain his stocks, along with a certain carelessness about receipts for items bought for business, were major factors in his precarious financial situation.[67] His own income was nominally the wage he paid himself for hours at the bench and part of the profits, though the overdraft was generally higher than his wage. From 1932 Barnsley had occasionally added a figure for 'shop', as well as a very variable percentage for his design work, to his calculations of prices, but 1936 was the first year in which overheads were allowed for as business expenses, and it would seem that much of the worry over the workshop's financial state in the thirties would have been spared had he received better advice early on.

His innocence in financial matters is hardly surprising given that his father worked alone and needed little paperwork and his prices had rarely reflected the value of the hours put into the work. At this time the idea of buying craftwork as an investment for the future had not emerged (and furniture is still a risky and long-term investment today), so prices were calculated on the basis of cost of materials and labour, balanced against how much customers were prepared to pay, bearing in mind that they were likely to make comparisons with goods in the shops. Competition within the furniture trade and a lack of consumer protection laws against iniquitous hire purchase agreements ensured that these prices were often very low, to the despair of the quality makers.[68] Stanley Davies, writing to Barnsley in 1942, said he had worked out his average income over nineteen years in his similar workshop and found it was £115 per year, 'hardly a "living"'.[69]

Ernest Gimson, with his larger workshop and paid employees, kept a job record book on which Edward modelled his own,[70] but Gimson added only about 10 per cent to the cost of wages and materials and was, therefore, effectively subsidizing the furniture business from his architectural practice and private income. Lupton too had little interest in costing and profits since he told Edward at some time around 1925, 'the trouble with me is I've had too much money'.[71]

The trouble for Edward was that he never had enough, and the difficulties that he experienced as a young man in these first, uncertain years of running the workshop almost certainly damaged his health and affected, and perhaps exaggerated, his attitude thereafter. This meant that he earned less than he thought he should throughout his working life, while his employees also felt that they were receiving less than the usual rate and found discussions of their six-monthly pay-rise very difficult. Craftsmen who were dissatisfied left the workshop for better-paid jobs elsewhere, and those who stayed usually did so because family circumstances made it possible for them to live on low wages, and because they loved the work, which they recognized as being of a type and quality which was, and still is, very rare.[72] They perhaps also realized that Edward's own modest way of life was not entirely a matter of choice. It should also be said that cabinet-making was not a well-paid trade in the twenties and thirties and craftsmen who worked for Peter Waals, for Gordon Russell, for H. H. Martyn in Cheltenham and for a small cabinet-maker and undertaker in Sidmouth have made the same complaint.[73] Those who could got out of the trade and into teaching, often taking on loans to pay college fees, or attending part-time City and Guild classes followed by six months' uncertificated teaching at low pay, to get away from the trap of badly-paid, low-status work and the threat of unemployment.

After the first fifteen years of struggle, Edward's problems were greatly alleviated in 1938 by the offer of work at the East Midlands Training College in Loughborough, where Peter Waals had been Design Adviser from 1935 until his death in 1937. This not only brought an income of nearly £150 a year, rising occasionally to more than £300,[74] and some security, but also proved important for Edward in crystallizing ideas about his work and his philosophy of design. He found that in advising younger people he was having to question and justify his own long-held beliefs. He also now had colleagues with whom he could discuss ideas, such as John Bridgeman, the head of the department, and Frank Ockenden, who joined later on in 1946.

The college at Loughborough had begun as a training institution for engineers and had introduced its two-year course for teachers of handicraft in association with Nottingham University in 1930. John Bridgeman, who was the first head of department, was later described by members of his staff as a brilliant administrator with a clear vision and the courage to implement his ideas. His aim was to solve a current problem, that teachers of handicraft were usually either trained teachers with inadequate practical skills, or experienced craftsmen with minimum teaching qualifications and too little education to be well regarded by other teachers. The college was to provide a thorough training in both craft skills and teaching techniques, with an emphasis on first-class craftsmanship.[75]

It took some time to achieve these aims and one early student has described his training from 1931-3 as a disaster.[76] This must have been related to the national financial crisis at this time, which put paid to plans for the expansion of the college in preparation for the raising of the school-leaving age to 15, and meant that intakes had to be reduced.[77] The Principal, Dr Herbert Schofield, had developed the college largely on the basis of self-help by training on production, and each student spent one day per week in the workshops making furniture and fittings for college buildings or working on engineering production jobs, which the college undertook because they were uneconomic for local businesses. This was apparently the most useful part of the course in its earliest days, since woodwork in the cabinet shop involved making furniture copied from poor quality magazines, using low-grade materials and the techniques of cheap commercial cabinet-makers. A visiting H.M.I., Bright, was horrified by the low quality of the results and measures were taken to improve the situation.[78]

First, Cecil Gough was appointed to supervise the students' practical woodwork. A highly skilled craftsman with years of experience at Gordon Russell's in Broadway, Gough was very keen on the idea of teaching and had an enormously beneficial effect in the department, where he worked until his retirement in 1971.

The next step, with funding from the Board of Trade, was the appointment as Design Adviser in 1935 of Peter Waals. He was inclined to be dogmatic and somewhat formal with the students, but he raised the stand-ard of design of their work by introducing them to the principles of the Cotswold Group. Solid hardwoods were preferred, even for the backs of cabinets where plywood might have been used before, and emphasis was placed upon quality of construction, with the grain of the wood revealed by natural wax finish without the use of stains and varnishes. The students' production work now consisted of suites of sturdy oak furniture for their halls of residence and glazed bookcases for the library, while their coursework also produced fine walnut furniture for Bridgeman's office, library chairs, and refectory furniture, all in the Cotswold style.

This was the department which Barnsley joined in 1938. It had seven-teen members of staff, including four dedicated to handicraft, and about forty students in each year of a two-year course. In the beginning he travelled to Loughborough once a month during term-time and stayed overnight so that he could advise on two days of the week, increasing later to three or four days per fortnight.

Edward had had very little experience of teaching so he asked the advice of Gigi Meo, head of the arts department at Bedales, who dismissed his worries about how to advise on design and directed him to the Propositions in Owen Jones's *The Grammar of Ornament*. Two of these struck Barnsley as particularly relevant and he often used them to illustrate his talks. They were: 'As Architecture, so all works of the Decorative Arts, should possess fitness, proportion, harmony, the result of all which is repose', and 'True beauty results from that repose which the mind feels when the eye, the intellect, and the affections, are satisfied from the absence of any want.'[79] Repose was not a word often applied to furniture, he said, or at least not in the sense implied by Jones, but it was a good one, meaning restfulness of form, dignity, a lack of unnecessary detail or ornament, no clashing of

24. The Teachers' Training Department at Loughborough College, 1937-9. Barnsley is fifth from left in the second row, John Bridgeman ninth from left , and Cecil Gough, third from right.

colour, texture, or grain of material. The meaning of 'fitness for purpose' and the use of materials fitting to the design were obvious; proportion implied a rhythm and order in the various parts making up the whole leading to harmony throughout; and to attain true beauty he advised that one should always look closely at any piece to see if anything could be added or anything taken away. Simplicity was a desirable aim and taking away was usually preferable to adding. Good judgement would come through experience, both of making and of observing.[80]

In April 1938, Barnsley gave an introductory talk to the students he would be advising, in which he made it clear that he did not expect them to go out into the world and turn all their pupils into skilled craftworkers and designers. Their job would be to make handicraft rewarding for their pupils, so that each child understood the satisfaction to be had from making things and gained some appreciation of the importance of standards of design and craftsmanship, even if these were only to be exercised as a consumer rather than a maker, for the makers of craftwork needed the support of an informed and appreciative public. He wanted to continue the tradition of fine crafts-manship and design built up by Peter Waals at Loughborough, but more he wanted to instill some understanding and appreciation of the importance of creative manual work, both for the benefit of the individual and for the future of civilization.

He was aware that this sounded a little dramatic, but it was his fervent belief that 'some form of creative expression is essential to a healthy balanced life'. Teachers could have a vital role to play in changing attitudes within society to the importance of the arts and crafts and to some of the narrowing effects on the human brain and spirit of working within the industrial system.[81] This belief informed all aspects of Barnsley's work and it was often the intensity of his views and his attention to minute details which impressed others most, and which left a lasting effect.

As well as such philosophical sermons he also occasionally gave lectures on the nature of materials, timber conversion, and the use of tools, but such formal talks were infrequent and most of Barnsley's time was spent in the woodwork and metalwork shops, where he looked at students' work, questioned them about their aims, and suggested improvements to their designs, often drawing over their own sketches to illustrate what he meant. He pointed out the need to plan for the unexpected, for instance to design a table so that it would not tip over if someone sat on the edge; and he encouraged them to visualize the piece in the round and to make accurate eighth-scale drawings and models of items of finished furniture. This was to develop their powers of observation and discernment, and he also suggested that they give their pupils memory games to play for the same purpose.

Working at Loughborough fitted in well with running the workshop and provided financial backing which enabled Barnsley to carry on, but he did not see this work as an alternative, and when in 1938 he was also asked to take over the woodwork classes at the Central School in London after the death of Charles Spooner, he declined the offer.

25. The workshop arranged for the 'reorganization sale' of 1938.

While he was away in Loughborough, much of the running of the workshop fell on Tania, who worked closely with the foreman, entertained clients, and took over the book-keeping, receiving for the first time in 1939 a salary of £52 per year, the maximum allowed to wives by the Inland Revenue. She also enjoyed driving and often delivered small items of furniture in the family car, usually a large open tourer bought second-hand.

There were some changes at Froxfield in the late 1930s, and a 'reorganization sale' was held in 1938 and alterations made to the buildings. The number of people in the workshop had always been fairly flexible and some of the craftsmen would come and go as work was available elsewhere. In 1939, Bert Upton and Lesley Mundy returned to the shop after completing a job on a house altered by Basil Gimson in Petersfield, and were told by Edward, who was worried about the small number of orders on the books, that if they knew of work elsewhere they should take it. Both found alternative jobs, as carpenters building for the local militia at Bordon Camp, but did not much care for the work, and in the meantime all was not well in the workshop. Edward therefore asked Bert Upton to return and appointed him foreman, while Charles Bray got work with a local farmer.[82]

Further and more extensive disruption came with the outbreak of war: all the younger men were called up and the skills of the older ones were deployed in aircraft production. Upton joined Airspeed, a branch of De Havilland making aircraft near Portsmouth, where Lesley Mundy and Bob Etherington also found work, and for a while George Taylor carried on alone in Froxfield. Edward Barnsley tried to persuade George to join the others at Airspeed, but he was keen to see active service and in 1941 joined the R.A.F., so the workshop now virtually closed down.

3. THE EARLY FURNITURE AND CLIENTS

The 'Cotswold' style – characteristics of the furniture of the 1920s and 1930s – ventures into the modernist idiom – Barnsley's general tenets of design – preoccupation with proportion – domestic pieces – relationships with clients – architectural commissions and first jobs for companies and schools

The 'Cotswold' style of furniture was developed by Ernest Gimson and Sidney and Ernest Barnsley working closely together as friends and receiving ideas and encouragement from other colleagues, such as W. R. Lethaby and Philip Webb, especially during the period when they were sharing the Pinbury workshop in the 1890s. Each brought individual features to the work, which, in its mature form, was a synthesis of ideas and motifs from a wide range of sources, including architectural carpentry and rural crafts such as waggon-building and tool-making, as well as English and foreign historic furniture and the work of contemporary designers. The fusion of these diverse enthusiasms into a distinctive and original style which suited a full range of types of household and ecclesiastical furniture, except upholstered pieces, was a significant achievement and one which influenced the production of many of their contemporaries and the next generation. It provided the starting point for all of Edward Barnsley's work and it did not occur to him to question anything about it until his formidable mother-in-law commented adversely on the black and white inlay which is one of its most distinctive features. A bed designed for Herbert Gimson in 1930 is decorated with an ebony and olive inlay in a much finer line than Sidney Barnsley used, presumably as a result of this criticism.[1] Inevitably there were some differences between the work of Gimson and Sidney Barnsley, mainly in the decoration and in a different emphasis in proportion, and not surprisingly Edward was more in tune with his father's work, which tends to appear solidly rooted to the floor, sometimes even over-weighted towards the base and awkward in the feet (though this is a matter of opinion).

For the son of a furniture maker, Edward Barnsley seems to have made surprisingly little in his youth, although he often said his first piece was a small stand to support a soap dish next to the pump in the yard at home, which he made under Sidney Barnsley's supervision when he was between 5 and 7 years old.[2] From about 1909, small boxes with dovetailed corners were made, and he referred to an oak hanging bookcase of about 1914,[3] but his earliest known substantial piece, from when he was sixteen, is a chest of drawers at Rodmarton Manor.[4] This is an attractive chest in solid walnut with ebony stringing, but the timber has moved very badly and the construction is faulty, with overlarge dovetails weakening the structure of the drawers. Whether his father was letting him make his own mistakes, or whether Edward disregarded the voice of experience is not recorded.

26. Cupboard of English oak, made by Edward for his mother in 1919 and used by her in the kitchen. The exposed dovetails, octagonal fielded panels, and stepped feet are typical of Gimson–Barnsley furniture.

An oak cupboard of 1919, made by Edward for his mother in Sidney Barnsley's workshop in Sapperton, is a more typical Cotswold-style piece, both in design and workmanship, solid and rectangular, with rows of neat dovetails holding the carcase together, and a heavy stand with stepped feet. The octagonal fielded panels on the doors are like those on Sidney Barnsley's late pieces, such as the sideboard made for Mrs Edge in 1924,[5] and it seems certain that the cupboard was designed by Edward's father. Lucy Barnsley always scrubbed the surface instead of polishing it, giving it a very different appearance from its present waxed finish.

Another piece which is virtually indistinguishable from the work of Sidney Barnsley or Waals is a bookcase of 1919,[6] made in Sapperton for Basil Gimson's house in Steep, and Edward's first commission from someone outside the family. Made in solid oak, it has stepped feet, cupboards in the base with fielded panels on the doors, and open shelves above, with uprights curving back in typical 'Cotswold' fashion. Barnsley was paid £6 for this piece, a remarkably low price which must have discounted the cost of the wood, or made allowances for inexperienced workmanship.[7]

Sidney Barnsley's influence was strengthened by the fact that Edward relied on his father's designs at the beginning of his career. Many of the earliest pieces made at Froxfield, such as furniture made for Rodmarton (pl. 14), were commissions which came via Sidney Barnsley, and he provided all the drawings. Edward also traced and copied his father's designs over the next decade and his year at the Central School seems not to have influenced him in any way. He did not develop his own style of drawing until the early thirties.

The furniture of the first ten years of Barnsley's Froxfield workshop was, therefore, almost entirely in 'Cotswold' style. It relied for its effect on well-chosen woods, usually native English species such as oak and walnut, though Japanese oak was also used; on decorative treatments of woodworking techniques — dovetailing, chamfering, inlaid beading, and fielded panels; on distinctive handmade handles and fittings in metal or wood; and on considered shapes and proportions, based on a combination of tradition and utility. It was usually finished with beeswax mixed with turps applied directly onto the wood (unlike the furniture of Waals, who put white spirit under the wax), though oak was sometimes treated with hot quick-lime, which gave it a lovely colour for a time but nearly always turned yellow and none too pleasant according to Barnsley's own account.[8] Oak tables and kitchen furniture were sometimes left bare and were scrubbed to a silvery whiteness by those close enough to the Gimson–Barnsley group to take handmade furniture for granted.

In construction it was a little variable, probably because Lupton's workshop was set up primarily for building work, for which a different standard was required, and because simple practical problems sometimes defeated Edward.[9] So the quality ranged from the good solid workmanship evident in the oak dresser for Victor Smith of 1924,[10] to the less than perfect effort later described by Barnsley himself: 'In 1924 I made a walnut dressing

27. The Barnsleys' cottage, arranged for the photograph to show furniture available for sale, about 1930. The burr oak writing cabinet was bought by Mrs Neale in 1931 and the armchair by Sydney Wales in 1935.

table for a Mrs Biddulph which was designed by my father. Many drawers, and all except one had solid oak bottoms. One had (still has) a bottom of oak faced plywood. I presume I ran out of thin oak and just put the plywood in as a quick solution. My father wrote to tell me that Mrs Biddulph was delighted with the piece, but surprised to find one drawer bottom in plywood. And I never did anything about it! This really does indicate something pretty doubtful about me. Stems from anxiety over costs, partly, but was a crime. Drawer bottom riddled with woodworm, and I've promised to replace it!'[11]

It was not that he was undiscriminating: indeed he criticized other furniture at Rodmarton to his father as being not of the quality they would have made and was reminded by Sidney Barnsley of the great improvements that had taken place in the 'Crafts & Arts' over the past thirty-five years, and of Mrs Biddulph's generosity in providing opportunities to carry out this work.[12] But the practicalities of quality-control and supervision had not yet been overcome and the problem of finances was ever present, resulting in the piecing of oddments of timber on the underside of even small items, such as an amboyna and ebony glove box for Charles Hawkins of 1929. The lack of 'perfection' does not always mar the piece, however, and sometimes gives a pleasing quality of idiosyncrasy, as in the walnut and ebony cabinet given to Tania Barnsley in 1925, in which the small size, good proportions, and attractive colour distract attention from the unevenly spaced dowels and badly cut tenons. This was intended to be of walnut alone but Barnsley had used all he had in stock and had to introduce the macassar ebony details to

28. Walnut and ebony cabinet made by Edward Barnsley in 1924 and given to Tania as a wedding present. The small crescent-shaped handles came from Gimson's workshop and were usually made by the silversmith, John Paul Cooper.

make up the quantity of wood. He also made a mistake with the measurements so the glazing bars were not as originally planned.[13]

Towards the end of the twenties, Barnsley began to make slight changes, noticeable, for instance, in a sideboard of 1927 for Mrs Lennox Murray, which is very similar to one made in 1924 but has extra panels in the doors and curved stretchers between the stepped feet, adding movement and variety.[14] His response to the wishes of clients occasionally had disappointing results, as he later wrote himself of a wardrobe made in 1928 'with regrettable inlay of a rising sun, on a plinth base, with some fine timber, not completely unworthy ... I went [to a sale view] expecting that it was made here because the catalogue mentioned the rising sun and I remembered giving in to client's request for its inclusion.'[15]

He also ventured into a spare modernist idiom for his sister-in-law, Nina Kellgren, who was a doctor, and for Charles Hawkins, his dentist. Furniture for their surgeries was made in an unornamented, geometric, clean-edged style (though Hawkins's desk still had stepped feet) which seems very suitable for its purpose. This was also, perhaps, a reaction to work produced by Gordon Russell Ltd to designs by R. D. Russell for batch-production, which Barnsley would have seen in Russell's London showroom in the early 1930s, or to pieces illustrated in Rogers' *Modern English Furniture* of 1930.

29. Desk and chair in walnut made for Dr Nina Kellgren, 1932, and standard lamp of 1929.
30. Walnut-veneered cabinet made in 1933 for Charles Hawkins' dental tools, in the clean-lined, unornamented style that was fashionable in the thirties.

He was also interested in Betty Joel's furniture, which has similar features, and went to her first exhibition. Laying the veneer on these smooth-lined modern pieces was very difficult by the traditional methods of hot Scotch glue, veneer hammer, hot iron and wet cloth, and was later described by Bert Upton as 'a ghastly process' which was not attempted very often.[16]

The modernist phase was quite short-lived and it may have been the interest of the clients in contemporary style or the financial necessity to accept any work offered which prompted the experiment, for this was the period of greatest difficulty for the workshop; but it is interesting to see that Edward was beginning to depart from the practice of his father, and that the change was more distinctive than he usually acknowledged later on. It was also at this date that he began to formulate a drawing style of his own. Up to the early thirties he had drawn out his designs on a variety of different types of paper, usually following the rather loose and fluid line quality of Sidney Barnsley's work, but then he changed to a very white tracing paper and a much tighter, more ordered style, bounded by double ruled lines. He sometimes used one-twelfth scale or one-sixteenth, though he usually favoured eighth-scale with full-size details, as did Sidney Barnsley and Gimson, because it is a size at which it is easy to visualize the finished object as if seen from a distance of about fifteen feet.[17] Like his father, he sometimes included a small perspective sketch of the finished piece along with the front and side elevations, and in the late thirties developed in collaboration with his friend Biff Barker, the woodwork teacher at Bedales, a device for drawing

31. A typical Barnsley design of the 1930s, in ink and wash on tracing paper, the sixty/thirty-degree view bounded by double-ruled lines. The chair was for Dr Williams's School, Dolgellau (see pl. 40).

them with tee-squares and set-squares on a drawing board to produce impressive and accurate diagonal views at sixty/thirty-degree angles. He was clearly never entirely happy with this because in 1963 he asked Cyril Wood if he could recommend someone to make attractive sketches so that he could secure a commission he wanted.[18]

Joe Maslin, who came to the workshop as a pupil with a Board of Education Studentship in 1939, recalled that at this date Barnsley was preoccupied with an attempt to devise a formula for proportion in furniture design, experimenting with the ratio between the dimensions of the sides and base of a piece in the effort to find a rule which could be generally applied. The diagonal of a square would be used to create the longer length of a rectangle, and the diagonal of the resulting rectangle would again be used to add length; or the height of a piece would be determined by the intersection of lines drawn at an angle of sixty degrees from the ends of the base length. Maslin also became interested in this and made copies of drawings by Barnsley and his father, but found that although there was a tendency towards a ratio of eight to five for rectangular pieces, most items approximated to a formula but did not exactly conform. His conclusion was that an original designer knows by instinct when the proportions are right and that Barnsley did not need rules but perhaps needed reassurance.[19] Barnsley may have been exploring this because of his recent reading of Owen Jones's *The Grammar of Ornament* for his teaching work at Loughborough[20] or because of questions from a student, rather than an interest of his own in the matter. Or it may have been John Rogers' small book on *Furniture and Furnishing* (1932), which inspired his interest. This described the use of such theories in seventeenth- and eighteenth-century furniture and illustrated a modern cabinet proportioned with the aid of a sixty/thirty-degree set square.[21]

Some general guidelines were absorbed by Maslin, however, since his main purpose in coming to the workshop was to learn about design and he was quick to pick up on things he heard Barnsley discussing. The main things he remembered after forty years were that the dominant form could be emphasized by the shadow from a band of stringing, moulding, or chamfering; that an allowance should be made for foreshortening in any area above or below eye level and that a square should therefore have greater height than width; that the base of an article should appear more robust than the upper parts in order to look as if it is capable of supporting the rest; that long horizontal lines should be lifted in the middle, especially at the base of an object; and that knobs, handles, and keyplates should be arranged slightly above centre.[22] These general rules were applied instinctively to everything designed in the Froxfield workshop, at this period and later.

From the early 1920s until the late 1940s, then, Barnsley's furniture generally continued in the Cotswold tradition. While Waals in this period made a fair number of pieces in the more elaborate and showy manner developed by Gimson from about 1910, using ebony in combination with other rich-coloured woods, Edward still worked mainly in solid oak and walnut, and occasionally in mahogany or rosewood. This may have suited his own taste, or it may just have been that Waals was better able to produce more complex work because he employed the most highly skilled of the cabinet-makers who had worked for Gimson for many years. Oliver Morel certainly had the impression during his time as a pupil at Froxfield in the 1930s that Edward was trying to raise the standards of making.[23]

32. Sir Adrian Boult's music stand. Made of walnut by Herbert Upton in 73 hours in 1934, it cost £7/15/-. The mechanism for adjusting the height was copied from a Gimson mirror design.

Most of the furniture was domestic. Straightforward articles such as sideboards, tables, desks, and chairs, were made for individual clients, and more specialized items, like music stands, for those with specialist needs. Adrian Boult had one of these in 1923 (at £5/14/-) and another in 1934 with a three-footed base, hexagonal column and adjustable mechanism based on a mirror designed by Gimson, and three others were made within the next year, two for clients and one for stock. Stock items were generally quite small and simple so that they could be sold cheaply, but occasionally large and elaborate pieces, such as a writing cabinet of 1929, were made to send to exhibitions. This was intended to rank with a large piece by 'Heal's most sensitive designer', but Barnsley later felt that it was not a happy design.[24]

On the whole, the types of piece made before the war were similar to those produced by Sidney Barnsley; plain items for those who shared a taste for simplicity or had a similarly meagre income, and more elaborate articles for the more affluent clients one would expect to order handmade furniture.

33. Writing cabinet of walnut and macassar ebony, 1929. Designed by Barnsley to rival work by Heal's of Tottenham Court Road, it was made by Charles Bray and Fred Eastlake in 1298 hours. The painted pottery is by Grace Barnsley.

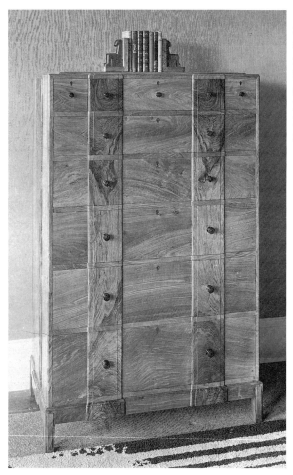

34. Chest of ten drawers in walnut, 1935. The design with its Art Deco flavour appears to have been based on a very similar piece by C. A. Richter for Bath Artcraft Ltd, shown at the Paris exhibition of 1925.

Barnsley also designed an increasing number of pieces for new applications, such as radio cabinets, phonograms, and cocktail cabinets, often with a faint Art Deco flavour borrowed from commercial work of the period. Sometimes this was more than faint, and designs exist for radio cabinets with lightning flashes zig-zagging across the loudspeakers.[25]

The plainest work was made for fellow craftworkers like Roger and Rita Powell, who had quite a number of pieces in the 1920s, including oak chests of drawers, oak beds, a walnut table, and a press for bookbinding, all good solid work with the minimum of decoration.

Most of Barnsley's relationships with individual clients were very amicable: if they did not begin as friends they rapidly became so. Charles Hawkins had known Sidney Barnsley[26] and presumably came to Edward on the basis of this past friendship. He and his wife had bought a house in the late twenties and rented furniture for it until they could afford their own. He then began to commission pieces for the house and his surgery as he could afford them, and like many of Edward's other clients he carried on ordering for many years. Barnsley became a big part of the Hawkins family's life and his periodic visits to stay in Cirencester were eagerly awaited, while Hawkins often visited the Froxfield workshop. The last piece made for him was delivered in 1965. Charles Hawkins particularly liked handcrafts and also bought metalwork from Alfred and Norman Bucknell, but in spite of living fairly near to Chalford, he did not commission anything from Waals.[27]

From Barnsley he ordered furniture for the entire house, where most of the rooms were painted in plain cream and had parquet floors. A dining suite, clocks, shelves, lamps, a radio cabinet, a writing bureau, mirrors, a fitted window seat, beds, dressing tables, wardrobes, and stools were all supplied, and he also bought the bread boards and trinket boxes which were made as 'potboilers' during the thirties and sold in the workshop or at Cotswold Craft exhibitions. Most were in 'Cotswold' style but several of the items made for him, apart from the furniture for the surgery, show tendencies towards Art Deco, which may reflect Hawkins's own taste; they include a sideboard which Barnsley later said was one of the pieces of his work he would like to destroy.

His list of items for the bonfire was not a long one and he was generally less concerned in later years by decorative features included for the sake of fashion than by peculiarities of construction. A bureau made for Sydney Wales in 1935 was another piece of which he later expressed disapproval.[28]

35. Bedroom furniture in walnut made for Charles Hawkins in 1928-9: an intriguing mixture of chamfered 'Cotswold' style and ziggurat-stepped Art Deco.

36. Writing cabinet in Japanese oak made for Sydney Wales in 1935 by Herbert Upton. The price was £38. Now in Cheltenham Art Gallery and Museums, it is one of the few pieces by Barnsley in public collections, since most are still in use in the homes of clients or their descendants.

presumably because, like a desk made for Hawkins in 1929, it has a feature which disobeys all Arts and Crafts rules about honesty of construction. The lower doors are not set into the framework of the front but are hinged onto it, and each door has a raised section down the outer edge, which looks as if it is part of the frame when the door is closed, but moves with the door.

Another client who became a friend, and whose daughters enjoyed Barnsley's friendship to the end of his life, was Mrs Ida Neale. She lived in Glamorgan and was involved in the organization of craftwork in the area. She was clearly conscious of the social ideas behind the craft movement, for at some time in the 1920s she bought furniture made at Brynmawr in Gwent, where ex-miners were trained in crafts. Having heard of Gimson and the Barnsleys, she went walking in the Cotswolds, looking in vain for workshops, but then recognized the name of Edward Barnsley when visiting her daughters at Bedales. Her first purchase was a tea tray in 1925, and from this small beginning she commissioned quite a number of items. Several desks were made for her in richly figured timber and two of these appear to have been favourites, for they feature in portraits of her by Conrad Felixmüller. She also bought from exhibitions, and at the 1931 Arts and Crafts show at the Royal Academy she purchased a distinctive burr oak desk which had been made some time earlier and appears in a publicity photograph of Barnsley's cottage interior (pl. 27). Like Hawkins, she also furnished entire rooms with Barnsley furniture and she ordered pieces over a long period, though the last cabinet made for her in 1950 was so expensive that she refused to show the bill to anyone in the family.[29] At her request, Bert Upton fitted this with secret drawers which were so well concealed that he eventually had to show her where they were, though she had hoped to discover them for herself (pl. 82).

37. Mrs Ida Neale, painted by Conrad Felixmüller in 1938, showing one of the several desks Barnsley designed for her.

Other clients who began to buy furniture in the 1920s and 1930s and who continued later or passed their interest on to members of their families were Mr and Mrs John Allan, C. H. St John Hornby, Mr and Mrs L. Hooper, Oliver Powell, John and Rotha Barnfield, and Drs Alec and Mary Capes. Often they furnished their homes gradually over many decades, fitting in new pieces as families expanded or they moved house.

Apart from domestic commissions, Barnsley also worked for architects on larger projects, and throughout his career these formed a significant part of the workshop's output, since they usually involved a larger amount of work time than ordinary furniture, though in terms of numbers of commissions, architectural work formed only a small percentage in the job books.[30]

At first these commissions were mainly through contacts from his father's generation and the earliest jobs, such as the ebony kneelers for St Andrew's Chapel at Westminster Cathedral, were to Sidney Barnsley's design. The doors for Khartoum Cathedral, however, another of Schultz Weir's schemes, were probably designed by Schultz Weir and Edward in collaboration,[31] and were made in 1929. The Barnsley workshop carried out several jobs for Schultz Weir up to 1938. An altar, reredos, and altar rails were made in 1928 and 1932 for St Mary's Church in Wotton-under-Edge, where Ernest Gimson's architect nephew, Humphrey Gimson, carried out

38. Oak screen for the Church of St Mary and St Edburga at Stratton Audley, Oxfordshire. Designed by T. Lawrence Dale and made in 1929 by the Barnsley workshop in collaboration with Eric Sharpe, a fine furniture maker who specialized in carved decoration.

alterations, and an oak screen for a church at Stratton Audley in Oxfordshire was made for the architect, Thomas Lawrence Dale, in 1929.

Francis Troup also commissioned work, though he was more interested in having his own designs made up in the workshop, as he had before at Gimson's. This was the ideal arrangement for someone who wanted things made properly but did not wish to run a workshop and who only required occasional pieces. Several architects used Gimson's workshop in this way and C. F. A. Voysey had pieces made at Waals's.[32] A walnut wardrobe now in the Victoria and Albert Museum was made at Froxfield for Troup in 1930. It is close in style to the work of Gimson and the Barnsleys but with subtle features like sliding handles which conceal the keyholes, probably of Troup's devising. Troup possessed it 'with pride and joy' until he died, according to his neice, Freda Levson.[33]

Gradually, Barnsley acquired new clients of his own from architectural firms. White Allom of Baker Street came his way in 1928 after approaching Waals for designs for furniture for the King of Siam. Waals declined the job, probably because he always lacked confidence in his own design skills, but Edward took it up with enthusiasm, producing drawings of solid 'Cotswold' furniture for this exotic destination. The surviving designs for beds have more written instructions on them than usual because they were to be made elsewhere and one is inscribed 'Made by White Allom & Co.'[34]

Other special and prestigious items were cases for War Memorial books for the Chapter House at Westminster through Charles Spooner in 1925, and for the House of Lords in 1927; the Ipswich Memorial Case for Graily Hewitt in 1930; and frames for various members of the Art Workers' Guild, such as Schultz Weir, George Clausen, and Emery Walker, for the portraits of Masters adorning the meeting room, which is furnished with Gimson trestle tables, the Master's seat designed by Lethaby, and turned chairs by Philip Clissett.

Barnsley's first work for a company seems to have been boardroom furniture for Arnold Levy at the I.T.S. Rubber Company in nearby Petersfield in 1930. This comprised a table, desk, ten oak chairs, and an inkstand, mantelpiece, and clock in ebony. This type of commission became very important after the war, but in the twenties and thirties little was done, and an order for thirty mahogany chairs for the Brewers' Society in 1940 was probably the largest so far. It was not completed until 1948 because of the war.

Fine furniture, then as now, was good for the corporate image and its value to companies in giving an impression of quality and solidity is obvious; it is less easy to see how Barnsley managed to get commissions for more utilitarian pieces for schools, especially against the increasing competition of firms like Russell's, which published well-illustrated and attractive catalogues devoted to school equipment.[35] From 1923 onwards he did much work for Bedales, including noticeboards, furniture for the library, and later repairs, but this was an unusual case. In the 1930s, however, Barnsley won two large contracts for school furniture at Charterhouse School at Godalming, Surrey, and at Dr Williams's School at Dolgellau.

First contact with Charterhouse had come in 1928 when a monitor's desk was ordered, but 1932 brought the larger, and for Barnsley rather unusual job, of six Chippendale chairs for the Common Room, followed in

39. An untypical example of Barnsley furniture: one of a set of six chairs in Chippendale style made for Charterhouse School in 1932 for £65/8/7d.

40. Dining room at Dr Williams's School at Dolgellau in Wales. The tables were
made at Froxfield in 1932 and the chairs in High Wycombe to Barnsley's
design. The photograph indicates the scale of such institutional commissions.

1935 by the furnishing of eight studies in oak, and a further eight in the
following year. The order for chairs and dining tables, a ceremonial chair,
bookcases, chests of drawers, beds, and art room tables for Dr Williams's
School provided a considerable amount of work between 1932 and 1937
and more chairs were ordered for Dolgellau in 1937 and 1939. These were
contracted out by Barnsley to the Hughenden Chair Works Limited in High
Wycombe and to Edward Gardiner, who had been taught by Gimson and
continued to make rush-seated ash chairs to his design. Thus Barnsley was
able to supply 275 small chairs at 30/6d each and thirty-six armchairs at
42/6d.[36] He also provided drawings for the college at Loughborough in
1938 but these were modified versions of designs by Waals and were for the
use of the students rather than for making at Froxfield.

Contact with questioning students and interested colleagues at Loughborough may have been one of the factors in a change of direction in
Barnsley's furniture design after the war, along with the influence of other
craftspeople and the watershed of the war itself. The wartime period was
very busy for Barnsley, but gave him, after nearly twenty years, a respite
from the pressures of running the business.

4. THE WAR YEARS AND AFTER

Wartime life at Froxfield – reduced pressure in the workshop – regulation of the furniture industry – debate within the craft organizations in the early 1940s – reassessment of the crafts and moves to secure their future – opening of the Crafts Centre of Great Britain, 1950

Although most of the craftsmen had left by 1940, guarantees from C. H. St John Hornby, a former client and friend of Sidney Barnsley, made it possible to carry on the business for a while,[1] and Edward spent more time in Loughborough in 1940, when his salary was nearly twice as much as in the previous year. When George Taylor left to join the R.A.F., however, Edward found an additional job further afield at the Mount School in York, teaching woodwork and English speech, capitalizing on the very clear enunciation he had developed as a child because of his mother's deafness. This kept him away from home for long periods in the autumn of 1941 but he gave it up in the following year.

The children, who normally attended Bedales daily, had become boarders in 1939 because of the practical difficulties of toiling up and down the steep hill every day and the feeling that they would be safer at school if a German invasion took place in what was felt to be a vulnerable locality. Since Bedales was one of the most expensive schools in the country[2] and the Barnsleys could not afford the usual boarding fees, the Head had agreed to Tania's suggestion that they should pay back after the war, and had also offered bursaries, so that the children boarded at the day rate. Even so, the repayments went on over a period of many years.

Jon loved the school, as his father had done, but Karin hated boarding and once absconded to Somerset with a friend who desperately wanted to be a ballet dancer in the face of parental opposition. Edward had great sympathy with children and went to retrieve them, returning the boy to his father without scolding, but with exclamations of pleasure at getting the 'delightful rascals' back, defusing a difficult situation and causing Mr Wright to approach his son with more understanding.

Edward was sympathetic about Karin's dislike of school and he and Tania allowed her to start a course in Theatre Design at the Central School in London when she was only 16. Some of their friends were a little shocked that the Barnsleys should allow such a young girl to live alone in a flat in Notting Hill, but their trust in her had its own sobering effect. When she overdrew at the bank, Edward sent such a disappointed letter explaining why they could not afford to give her more money and enclosing a purse of the softest leather, that she never repeated the mistake. Fortnightly on his way to Loughborough he would stop off in London to see her with a supply of fresh vegetables and fruit from the garden, and together they discovered a taste for French cinema at the former Studio One in Oxford Street.

From the beginning of the war, the garden was more intensively planted with food crops and income was derived from the sale, at 6d-8d each, of the figs which grew in abundance against the south and south-east walls of the workshop, arousing envy in friends. 'Yr. card with further news of figs just come', wrote Roger Powell in 1942, 'You lucky blighters! Have you any still to send away? I think price is quite justified. Miss Pilkington told me she sold all her surplus peaches @ 4s/6d ea.!'[3] Edward's skill with a shotgun added pigeons and rabbits to the rations during these years when there were a lot of extra people in the house, though he later decided that shooting was wrong and gave it up, partly because he felt his method of sneaking up on the sleepy rabbits early in the morning was unfair.[4]

In 1942 much of the workshop was fitted out with beds and became a first-aid post. In this and the following year, the only other craftsman in the Froxfield workshop was Oliver Morel, a Quaker and conscientious objector, who had come as a paying pupil in the mid 1930s. Morel was a product of another progressive school at Rendcomb, near Cirencester, which was financed by F. Noel Hamilton Wills of the tobacco family (incidentally a client of Sidney Barnsley) for the education of boys from local schools, who were chosen by scholarship. Its Head Teacher, James Simpson, was interested in craftwork and encouraged links with Gordon Russell's firm at Broadway.[5] After his period as a pupil at Froxfield, during which he had done some teaching at Bedales, Morel had returned to Rendcomb as a teacher but now came back at Edward's urgent appeal.

Morel's first task was to complete the work left unfinished when the men were called up, including furniture for the Jewish Scroll Room of the Cunard liner, *S. S. Elizabeth*, an interesting project because it had to be made to fit the contours of the ship. It was similar in appearance to Barnsley's 1924 cabinet (pl. 28), but with diamond-shaped fielded panels and latticed glazing bars intersecting to form a Star of David. This order came via H. H. Martyn of Cheltenham, a firm of furnishers and shopfitters which fitted out a number of the great liners.[6] Several more good new commissions were received and at least one client supplied his own timber. A walnut desk was made in 1942 for Janet Gimson, commissioned for her fiancé, then a prisoner of war, but mostly the work was small items such as tables and a trolley, stretchers and splints for the first-aid post, and repairs to local houses, gates, and cars. Morel and Barnsley did everything themselves until 1944, when they were joined by Glyn Philpot, who had just left Bedales and went on from the workshop after six months to a course at Brighton Technical College. In the same year, Edward told Eleanor Whittall at the Arts and Crafts Exhibition Society that he had volunteered his services as a joiner in Croydon, which had been badly hit by bombs, but nothing came of this.[7]

While the workshop was relatively empty, except when two people slept in the drawing office for a while, the Barnsleys' cottage now became somewhat overcrowded. A family of three conscientious objectors occupied one of the small bedrooms and the house became something of a meeting place for other C.O.s in the district, most of whom were doing forestry work. With their help in the evenings to work the land, and the loan of a field by a local landowner, Tania and Edward organized a scheme to grow vegetables which were sent up to Bishop Huddlestone for people sleeping out in London. Mrs Kellgren was living at the Bee House and friends came down from London now and again to sleep in the workshop and get away from the Blitz, so for the Barnsleys it was a period of conviviality mixed with great anxiety when, in 1942, Tania had a cycling accident while riding down Stoner Hill and required full-time nursing care for three months.

It was by no means clear that the workshop would be allowed to remain open. Perhaps because there were so few people to consider, the Board of Trade took a long time to decide what to do about small workshops, and even after an Order had been issued in 1942, the craftsmen themselves were not very sure about how it applied to them.[8] The furniture manufacturing industry had been subject to restrictions since the earliest months of the war, but much attention was being given to the development of the Utility scheme, the first samples of which appeared in October 1942, and the problems of craft workshops must have seemed of little moment to the politicians and civil servants in London.

The Board of Trade's Order stated that no-one would be allowed to make furniture after 1 July 1942, or in the case of small workshops after 30 September, without a licence, unless they were making scheduled pieces with limited timber and three-ply, for which supplies were released by the Furniture Manufacturers' Timber Supply Committee. Discussions on the position of craft workshops were still taking place between the Board and the Red Rose Guild of Manchester, which assumed a major part in the debate about practical aspects of the craftworkers' wartime role. The view of the Guild and other craft bodies involved, such as the Arts and Crafts Exhibition Society, was that it was essential to exempt some craftworkers from war service so that their skills were available to help in the rebuilding of society when peace came. The craftsmen agreed on this but needed to convince the recently formed Central Institute of Art and Design and the Ministry of Labour, and were divided as to the best methods of doing so. Harry Norris of the Red Rose Guild, for instance, favoured confrontation, and proposed to apply for a licence because he believed it necessary to get evidence of refusal, but in September 1942 he wrote to tell Edward of current discussions and advised him not to apply for a licence as yet, since a refusal would make his carrying on too obvious.[9] Norris was clearly worried by the prospect of being called up or forced to work in a factory.

Curiously, perhaps, Edward was not worried. He and Tania had registered at the Labour Exchange as unavailable for war work: Edward was fully occupied with teaching at Loughborough and running the workshop, and he was just too old to be called up. The responsibility of providing work for ten men had gone and it seems that he was able to relax for the first time in nearly twenty years. He felt that he should just carry on quietly until the final veto on new jobs was announced, especially as he had adequate stocks of timber and therefore had no need to apply for a licence. In the event, this proved a wise policy and at some point in 1943 Barnsley received his licence. In September he wrote to Norris that he liked the quiet life, had accepted what appeared to be considerate treatment for craftsmen and assumed the licence enabled him to go on as usual.[10]

This problem about the licensing of individuals was obviously of great personal importance to those involved, but it was also a question of principle, and discussion of this led on to the realization that the craftworkers needed to be more organized if their strongly-held beliefs about the importance of the crafts were going to be heard after the war. In common with many other sections of British society, the craft world found itself caught up in a mood of reassessment, which was described by Bernard Leach in his contribution to *Fifteen Craftsmen on their Crafts*, while in his autobiographical book, *Beyond East and West*, he mentioned the attempts of the craftsmen to prepare for post-war conditions in one bland passage which disguises the ferocious nature of the debate.[11] Edward, too, said little about this period in later years, except to state that he had helped John Farleigh to start the Crafts Centre in Hay Hill just after the war, but the Barnsley archive reveals many strands in a tangled web.

Why Barnsley got so caught up in this is not very clear. It may be that with fewer assistants in the workshop he now had more time for thought and that discussions with Oliver Morel encouraged him to act; or that he had been prompted to think by contact with students and staff at Loughborough; or perhaps that he had simply reached the age at which it seemed important to contribute to the wider world of his chosen work. He had been associated with the Arts and Crafts Exhibition Society as a Council member from 1932 and as a selector for exhibitions,[12] but now he had the opportunity for greater involvement.

Along with the practical skills of his trade, he had learnt most of his ideas about the crafts from his father, and to a lesser extent, from Gimson. He had grown up on talk of Morris and had read Ruskin and later Lethaby too.[13] From his earliest youth he had accepted the rightness of their beliefs, and had tried to practise them himself, but he had not often had to voice them. In his first talk at Loughborough College in 1938, he had spoken of the importance of keeping craftsmanship as a real part of life, not as a hobby or a sideline, and he stressed the point because by this date there was a considerable body of opinion that the crafts were useful as inspiration or as prototypes for industry, but had no real value in themselves. It was fundamental to Barnsley's belief that 'Man must create. Some form of creative expression is essential to a healthy balanced life and of all possible forms of creative work, that of the hands, under the direct conscious control of the brain, is the most satisfactory and the most healthy.'[14]

This is an argument based upon the effects on workers of particular kinds of work and it is one that Gimson had with Lethaby in 1916, when invited to design for the Design and Industries Association.[15] It was succinctly expressed in a Red Rose Guild magazine of 1948, probably by Margaret Pilkington — 'Craftsmanship is an activity, not a product';[16] and also by Eric Gill, who said 'The difference between art and industry lies in the fact that industry is interested in things made and art is interested in the making of things'.[17]

The Design and Industries Association's stand was about the effect of methods of work on objects, on the design of objects, and it did much to raise the standard of British design between the wars, but it also deflected discussion away from the principles championed by the Barnsleys and Gimson. One reason for this must have been that a life in the crafts involved a challenge to the traditional organization of society and accepted values, whereas the advocacy of better design within the parameters of industry fulfilled the accepted practical needs of society and also maintained the status quo. Gordon Russell, for instance, one of the strongest voices for design and industry, was conservative in outlook, with a traditional view of people's proper place in society.[18] Edward Barnsley was himself a member of the D.I.A., but he believed that this kind of attitude was the reason that Morris's views on the use of machinery had been so distorted and trivialized:

> It seems always to me, that Morris's political ideas were so unpalatable to his friends and his contemporaries of the same income group, or near it, that this part of him had to be dropped after he was no longer there to fight, and a sort of sentimental, one man one job, designer-maker ideology built up around him, exaggerated statements about his opinions on machines were invented, and the whole point about his warning about their dangers was missed, in asserting that he would have nothing to do with them. He never said, surely, that there was evil in the machines, only possible evils, probable evils, inevitable evils, from their misapplication. If they and not their users were of the first consideration.[19]

The views of Morris remained for Edward, as they had been for Sidney Barnsley, the foundation of his beliefs throughout his life, though like his father, he was not politically active. Tania, however, took part in local Labour Party politics from 1929, joined the Peace Pledge Union, and served as a District Councillor from 1950 to 1965; she was technically an Independent, as were all the Councillors, but everyone knew which side they were on. While Edward did not share her practical commitment, he believed in the socialism Morris preached, the vital contribution of the crafts,

> And the faith that man could again enjoy what Morris usually called labour, seems to me to be a basic of all his life and all his preaching. That true socialism (never yet attempted of course, let alone achieved), was a prerequisite to justice among men and a life that is worthy also seems a key-pin of his life, and to be irrefutably right ... The influence of Morris in the modern age seems to me to be small, it is too academic, too theoretical, talk rather than work. Or so it appears (on the whole) to me. But certainly it's there, and far from dead, and I hope rests waiting, like a seed lying dormant until

circumstances permit growth. And I fancy we must get our aprons on and take tools in our hands, whatever the craft, and MAKE THINGS, if we are to produce a soil in which the seeds of Morris can grow.[20]

By 1969 when this was written, Barnsley had virtually given up trying to prepare a seedbed by means other than craftwork. In the early 1940s, however, he still believed that talk would help, and his main talking shop was the Arts and Crafts Exhibition Society. This had been started in 1888 with the aim of exhibiting the best of modern design and craftsmanship and giving credit to the maker of goods as well as to the designer. From the beginning there were problems with this ideal, some manufacturers only grudgingly crediting their designers, let alone their workers, but the Society's earliest exhibitions were important showpieces for modern design and craftsmanship. By 1912, much of the enthusiasm had faded away and the exhibits of that year's show were left mainly unsold. Disillusion became the prevailing mood, as it became clear how little the Arts and Crafts Movement had influenced industrial production and how little the work had changed over twenty-four years. The Design and Industries Association was formed to remedy this failing, by a group inspired by the German Werkbund exhibition of 1914. Harold Stabler, Ambrose Heal, Cecil Brewer, Harry Peach, Hamilton Smith, Ernest Jackson, J. H. Mason, and William Lethaby were early participants, and although the Association was slow in its effects, by the late 1920s it had considerable influence.

As the D.I.A. succeeded in its aims, the designer-makers were left to struggle on their own against increasing unfashionability. Not only was the appearance of handwork outmoded because of interest in machine aesthetics, but Arts and Crafts style was no longer favoured by the artistic élite, who were quite different from the earnest, moralizing painters of the heyday of the Arts and Crafts. According to Aldous Huxley in 1923, real artists went for 'Louis whatever-it-was' or Empire, while 'Art and Craftiness' was irredeemably middle-class.[21] Others rejected the idea of long-practised skill and liked the notion of inspired experiment. Roger Fry and the Omega Workshops, for instance, relished the idiosyncracy of incompetent work and their experiments echo in some ways the early ideas of Morris and Company, but without the underlying respect for the skilled worker.[22]

Along with the artists, the Arts and Crafts had also lost its main group of supporters, the architects. Young architects no longer believed in the possibility of craftwork as an everyday remedy for the social ills of an industrialized society but were increasingly concerned to use intelligent planning and industrial methods to provide better conditions for ordinary people. The interests of the consumer now seemed to be associated with socialism and reform, leaving the interests of the worker out of the picture.

Many of the makers of craftwork were hangers-on of a once-serious movement and undoubtedly deserved the scepticism of their contemporaries. Responses to the crafts were also, however, conditioned by blinkered attitudes to the political views of the more committed makers, and, in some cases, wilful misunderstanding of what they were trying to do. For many of the educated middle classes concerned with issues of art and design, it was easier (and still is) to understand someone doing craftwork as a hobby than to see why they should want to do it as everyday work.

By the 1930s it had become usual to see the crafts as an adjunct to industry, even within the Arts and Crafts Exhibition Society, where debate took place in 1935 about the proposed mass-production section in the next exhibition. At the A.G.M. two years later, John Farleigh, the wood-engraver, declared that any member who refused to design for machine production was without social conscience, and at a further meeting it was agreed that Society members had a right and a duty to raise the standard in industrial products wherever they could.[23] Farleigh was not alone in seeing the question of collaboration with industry as a moral issue, for this was the period when nearly three million people, 23 per cent of the insured workforce, were unemployed,[24] and without its social-crusading element, the Arts and Crafts Movement had come to be seen even among its participants as retrogressive, and craftspeople as self-indulgent producers of luxury goods who were holding up the march of progress. Even the Director of the Victoria and Albert Museum could say in 1942: 'I do not, to be frank, much believe in what are known as "arts and crafts" in their present condition, as divorced from mass production. And I think a good many of the artists and craftsmen of this group are still living with their heads turned backwards, which is to be deplored'.[25]

Edward Barnsley had spoken at the 1937 meeting in favour of maintaining the Society 'within its own little sphere as a society for handicraftsmen',[26] and his experience early in the war confirmed his view, though he had sent a letter of resignation in 1940, presumably because of the difficulty of getting to meetings and a lack of income. He was given honorary membership for the duration and in 1942 was again on the Council of the Society, which was attempting to formulate a new policy in response to public interest aroused by an exhibition held at Hertford House the previous year. A leaflet about the Society's aims was to be produced, but it had become clear that these aims had not been properly defined and that there was still much disagreement within the group. In April, Barnsley received a letter from Roger Powell urging him to attend a meeting on the 18th:

> If the A. & C. Exbn. Soc. is to be any good to craftsmen in the future this is the last moment to guide its activities into the right lines, or it goes to stunt design, the commercial artists, & Gordon Russell & others. The Council is at present formed of people who for the most part are not craftsmen first & money grabbers second; the money grabbing comes first & they do not really give a damn for what they are making; they are ready to lick the boots of any king [sic] of middlemen who can hand out cash for a drawing. They would look at the suggestion that craftsmanship is a way of life with a blank look of understanding & dismiss it with a smile & "Oh yes of course, but ...".

He asked how Edward would feel about resigning if the voting went in favour of an officially regulated association of art and industry and craftsmanship within the Society, instead of the 'sort of living-in-sin association wh. Murphy, Capey, and Farleigh have tried to brazen out'.[27]

This is the beginning of a long and complex correspondence which, incidentally, is remarkable both for the letter-writing skills of the protagonists and for the efficiency of the Post Office, in spite of the war. Powell at this date was living at Letchworth in Hertfordshire, running the bindery established by Douglas Cockerell, who was now ill, and also working the land, and keeping goats and bees.

The three major issues for concern running as a thread through this correspondence were the immediate problem of ensuring that all the craftspeople were not called up so that some craft skills survived the war; the future of the Society, which was felt to be under threat of takeover by the industrial design faction; and lastly the creation of strong organizations of craftspeople ready to take their place in society after the war was over and able to influence future policy and convince the public of the value of craftwork. Both Barnsley and Powell were also members of the Red Rose Guild and the correspondence is often a three-way affair with Margaret Pilkington or Harry Norris of the Guild.

At the April Council meeting, Barnsley was delegated as one of a group of five to produce a report on the future of the Society's exhibitions. This group proposed that the Society should reaffirm the importance of crafts and craftsmen and that higher standards should be applied to the selection of objects for exhibitions. They suggested that a change of name to the 'British Society of Craftsmen' should be considered, and that Council should contact other like groups with a view to amalgamation into something like a Guild.

Barnsley was surprised when these proposals received overwhelming support from the members who replied, and impressed when John Farleigh, the Deputy President since January 1941, seemed eager to pursue these aims, even though his own views were somewhat different.[28] Farleigh (pl. 60) was an illustrator, probably best-known for his striking engravings for George Bernard Shaw's *The Adventures of the Black Girl in her Search for God*,[29] and he was also a teacher at the Central School. Reco Capey, an industrial designer, was President of the Society but had been in America for some time and was not involved in the discussions.

Farleigh proposed to hold a joint exhibition in 1943 with the Red Rose Guild, to show the public what the craftspeople could do.[30] Barnsley and Powell were not yet convinced that he was as committed to pure craftsmanship as themselves and Edward wrote to Farleigh in October to persuade him that he could achieve much for the crafts if only he could concentrate the efforts of the Society.[31] They were involved in producing another report which was presented to Council in November 1942 and this set out their aims in the clearest possible terms. The Society was to exclude factory production and industrial goods from its exhibitions and concern itself only with craftwork made in workshops. It was to encourage its members to undertake the preparation of their own raw materials if possible, rather than to acquire them from factories; and it was to attempt to clear up the confusion in the public mind about the production of such firms as Russell's and Heal's, which often looked like handwork but was made in industrial conditions. This report, too, was approved by Council and promoted to the members in a letter of December 1942 by Farleigh.[32]

The major task now was the planning of the joint exhibition, but an obstacle in the way of co-operation continued to be different approaches to the problems before them, in spite of the fact that several members of each group were members of the other, and in some cases influential members. Powell, Bernard Leach, and Harry Davies, another potter, were 'Master' members of the Red Rose Guild and in October 1942 had elected Barnsley and Norris to join them in this élite. Powell was now more confident of Farleigh, and he told Edward that he was prepared to work with Norris even though he had been horrified by an example of Norris's work: 'A huge wardrobe looks like (the worst) imitation-veneer paper on some mass produced article for a pretentious provincial hotel', he wrote.[33]

The two groups made the attempt to unite in common purpose but from early on it was apparent that there would be problems over the type of work to be included and over the personalities involved. The Guild proposed a three-part exhibition dealing with craftsmanship as a social necessity, craftsmanship in relation to industry, and craftsmanship as art. The second section was clearly in opposition to the new policy of the Arts and Crafts Exhibition Society and in February 1944, after a series of difficult meetings at which Norris antagonized everyone by his criticisms and dismissal of any alternative views,[34] Farleigh wrote to the Guild saying that the Society could not amalgamate or hold a joint exhibition at present, and closing negotiations somewhat abruptly. The Manchester group was understandably shocked, and Margaret Pilkington did her best to retrieve the situation, though she realized that the intransigent attitude of Harry Norris was an important factor in the decision.[35]

Throughout the whole affair, Barnsley favoured support of Farleigh, while Powell, in spite of difficulties with Norris and references to the need for Leach to 'lay off the Minor Prophet business',[36] thought that the Red Rose Guild was showing more useful concern with the essentials of the crafts-man's case, such as negotiating about Purchase Tax exemption and similar practical matters. He also felt it best for the societies to agree if at all possible so as to present a united front to the world, while Barnsley, who had insisted time after time that they should 'agree to agree', had by now given up. If all else failed, the work would just have to stand for itself.[37]

Powell was now thinking of resigning from the Arts and Crafts Exhibition Society Council in order to take a more active part in the Guild, with the aim of levering Norris out and persuading Margaret Pilkington back into the Chair, and thus being able to improve relations between the societies. Barnsley resigned as a Master of the Guild, writing to Norris to give his views on Norris's failings; Norris accepted his resignation but not his sermon.[38] Both Barnsley and Powell thought it still possible to get the two societies together if Norris were removed, but in the event, the Arts and Crafts Exhibition Society held an exhibition on its own in London at the National

Portrait Gallery in September 1944. Powell was very dubious about the wisdom of this, believing that the work available would not strengthen the craftsmen's case, but the exhibition was a great success, in spite of the threat of bombing, and for the first time in the memory of the Society's Treasurer, it actually made a profit.[39]

It proved to be a turning point for Edward's work because after it was over, John Farleigh, who was now President of the Society, called a meeting of members at which he made a plea for greater sensitivity to the spirit of the times. He could see, he said, that many of the makers were excellent at their crafts, but their use of unexciting colours, lack of interest in new materials, and over-concern with niceties of technique had led them to become severe and sad in their work. What they needed was to move forward, to be of the present, to get a sense of life as it is lived, and to use the light sides of their characters as well as the sombre.[40]

This exhortation struck home with Barnsley, who accepted Farleigh's criticism that the furniture in the exhibition had too much emphasis on clever joints and no elegance of line. He said that there had been discussion in his own shop because he felt they were missing an essential something, and he went away from the meeting with much to think about. The results were not evident in his work immediately, since his designs evolved at their own pace, but he often referred later to Farleigh's talk as the inspiration for a change of direction to a lighter style.

Farleigh also felt that the Society could not go on simply holding exhibitions every three years and letting the public forget the crafts in between. It had two alternatives, to have an exhibition every year or to establish a permanent home with showrooms, offices and a library in a central position, to provide a point of contact with the public and industry, and between craftspeople. He had already initiated discussions with the Board of Trade, and later he arranged meetings with Sir Thomas Barlow of the Council of Industrial Design and with Sir Stafford Cripps.[41]

The idea of a permanent showplace was not a new one but had been floated before in 1912 and in 1924. It became the most tangible result of all these wartime efforts and it seems from the correspondence that in this manifestation it was originally Barnsley's idea, proposed in a letter in January 1943, nurtured by Powell, and brought to fruition by Farleigh.[42] Barnsley had also been canvassing opinions about a new society to rise from the dead ashes of the Arts and Crafts (and presumably from the Red Rose Guild as well), which he proposed should be a selling organization with a half-time head, a full-time secretary, and money in the bank, probably intended to come from the government.[43]

Barnsley had been Deputy President of the Arts and Crafts since July 1944, and he was clearly active in the scheme and supported the President, but it was Farleigh who took the initiative and who managed to bridge the divide between the 'pure craftsmen' and the post-war public. In the same speech in 1944, he appealed for Society members to work together as a team or to break up the Society and work as individuals; unless they were prepared to think about changing to suit the times, Farleigh would have to resign as President since there was no point going to the Government seeking money and support if the Society did not have the right kind of work to show. In the next year he followed this by asking that the next exhibition be arranged as a town living room — it was definitely not to be cottagey.[44]

In 1945 Farleigh estimated that £3000 a year was needed to run a centre in London,[45] and he approached the government for grant aid. Barnsley had at one time proposed an appeal to interested individuals but then got cold feet at the prospect of losing private money, and in 1946 a leaflet was printed giving details of a scheme. The Crafts Centre of Great Britain was to be run by five societies, the Arts and Crafts Exhibition Society, the Red Rose Guild, the Senefelder Club, the Society of Scribes and Illuminators, and the Society of Wood-Engravers, with support from the Arts Council of Great Britain, the Rural Industries Bureau, and the Worshipful Company of Goldsmiths and the money coming through the Council of Industrial Design.[46] Its main objects were to be 'The preservation, promotion, and improvement of fine craftsmanship in Great Britain', through 'a permanent exhibition — constantly changed and refreshed — of the work of the best craftsmen in this country',[47] the development of closer contacts between makers and public, the encouragement of training, and the publication of a Yearbook. The Government had promised to match funds raised from private sources, apparently convinced by arguments that the crafts made an important contribution to design,[48] and once £2500 was guaranteed from supporters, work could go ahead on converting a building at 98 Portland Place.

Estimates of the necessary funding expanded and it was some time before the money was raised, though the Board of Trade agreed to increase the amount of its grant over a four-year period, and Barnsley's proposal at an Arts and Crafts Exhibition Society meeting that the Society should give rather than lend £1000 to the new centre was carried.[49] Difficulties occurred with Portland Place and new premises had to be found; Farleigh was involved in much complex negotiation over a long period, but in April 1950 the Crafts Centre of Great Britain opened its doors at 16-17 Hay Hill to show the world what the craftspeople could do.

Hay Hill runs parallel to Piccadilly near New Bond Street, so the site was central and in a good area for such a venture though not on a thoroughfare. The building had a large shop window, a display room with a mezzanine gallery reached by a spiral staircase, and an office at the back. Farleigh was still keen to dispel the homespun image of the crafts and the architect, Sergei Kadleigh, was clearly briefed to provide a simple and contemporary interior, 'a background of restrained elegance and taste that will prove the crafts capable of holding their own in an urban background'.[50] The walls and floor were plain and on one side of the room was a framework providing spaces of varying sizes for the display of textiles, pottery, glass, and other small objects. Furniture could be shown free-standing and objects were grouped as if in a house, with decorative flower arrangements.

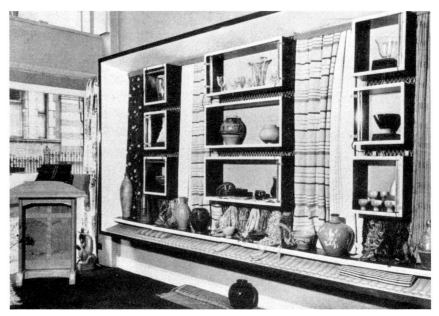

41. The Crafts Centre of Great Britain at 16-17 Hay Hill in London, as illustrated in *The Studio* in 1950. The stylish interior by Sergei Kadleigh was the result of John Farleigh's determination to do away with the homespun image of the crafts.

Initially the Centre was a non-trading body intended simply to provide a show-case for the crafts, but by 1953 at least, it also sold items for the makers, taking a percentage as a handling charge. Barnsley sold one or two pieces there most years from 1956 and over ten years his sales through the Centre averaged about £140 a year, but its worth to him was much more as a display area for his work, and he received a number of commissions as a result of people seeing pieces at Hay Hill.[51] These included a dining table and chairs and bedroom furniture made for the actor (later Sir) Alec Guinness, who purchased a chest of drawers from the Crafts Centre in 1955. For the craft world in general, the Crafts Centre was an important step in gaining government support for the promotion of the crafts and recognition of their importance for design and trade, and for those involved, it was the culmination of years of planning and hard work during the war.

5. NEW DIRECTIONS IN THE WORKSHOP

Return of the craftsmen at the end of the war – introduction of machine tools in the 1950s – handwork and standards of finish – changes in working practices and the increasing power of Upton – large commissions – designs for the Rural Industries Bureau in the 1950s – purchase of timber – extension to the workshop, 1961

In January 1945, Edward Barnsley was awarded the C.B.E. for his services to design. He had been proposed by John Farleigh for his work for the crafts, which included not only his role in the Arts and Crafts Exhibition Society but also his membership of the joint crafts committee of the Central Institute of Art and Design. The award gave a considerable boost to his own confidence and to the status of the workshop, but he debated with himself and with Oliver Morel over whether he should accept and he occasionally said later that he felt he should not have done so. 'Status matters cause me to shrink up a little', he later explained, but sometimes he felt it necessary to make use of the recognized marks of 'position' in society, and the C.B.E. represented a formal acknowledgement of 'the crafts' as well as of himself.[1] He refused to wear the decoration, though, saying that the colour of the ribbon didn't suit his hair.

42. One of the prestigious commissions which came to the workshop after the War: a cabinet presented to King George VI and Queen Elizabeth by the Government of Southern Rhodesia in 1947. On the left are Sandy Cockerell, Roger Powell, who bound the books, and Edward Barnsley.

Whether as a result of the honour itself, or the contacts Barnsley had made during the war, he gained a number of important commissions from government departments in the post-war years. He also became a member of the Advisory Council of the Victoria and Albert Museum in the 1950s, probably in recognition of his position as a pre-eminent craftsman.[2] Being known at the V&A also had benefits in terms of work: Dimitri Comino, for instance, became a regular client of the Barnsley workshop after approaching the Furniture and Woodwork Department at the Museum for advice on where to buy good-quality contemporary craftwork. He had bought from Heal's before the war but now he wanted something more lasting, which would be 'the antiques of the future'.[3]

On the death of his mother in 1944, the workshop had become Edward's and he no longer had to think about paying rent or the interest on his loan. For the first time ever, in 1943, he had started the year with a credit balance at the bank as a result of his work at Loughborough and the small scale of operations at Froxfield. From now on, the combination of a regular salary and rent-free premises made a big difference to the financial viability of the business. While the war was on, Barnsley and Bert Upton had met occasionally to discuss what they would do afterwards, and agreed that in future every job must be made to pay, though they do not seem to have worked out in any detail how to achieve this. It was generally accepted that Upton would come back, in spite of the fact that he was better paid in the aircraft industry than he would be at Froxfield and must have considered the alternatives.[4]

43. Barnsley, Tom Barnet and Glyn Philpot, 1945. While the workshop still operated with a small staff, Barnsley was able to spend time at the bench. This became increasingly difficult as the craftsmen returned after the war and the nature of the work gradually changed.

A letter from Barnsley to Margaret Pilkington of the Red Rose Guild in October 1945 set out the position in the workshop shortly after the end of the war, in the terms dictated by her request for information.[5] Edward himself was working full-time apart from his advisory visits to Loughborough. He still had large stocks of timber but no permit to purchase more, either for stock or for immediate use, though the salesman from the timber merchant thought that he should soon get a stocking licence. This was more likely to be granted if work was to be exported, but he did not mention his chances of selling abroad.[6] He saw no difficulties about sales but was faced with a liability for Purchase Tax. On the staff he now had one of his pre-war men, who had been invalided out, one apprentice, and one pupil.[7] His pre-war foreman, Upton, was to return from aircraft production the following week, and three positions for pupils were promised, one to an ex-serviceman.[8] He had orders booked for the next two years and felt that there was a considerable increase in enthusiasm for craftwork, and interest from schools in having well-made furniture, an optimism which he shared with Gordon Russell, who in his rather different firm also looked forward to a great expansion in the contract market.[9] Barnsley's view on this may have come from the fact that he was currently making furniture for Maplewell Hall at Loughborough College.

Upton returned as foreman and Taylor and Bray both came back in 1946, Taylor under the 'interrupted apprenticeship' scheme by which the employer paid the going rate for an apprentice and the government made it up to a working man's wages. Les Mundy and Bob Etherington decided to stay in the more remunerative work at the Bristol Aircraft Company, while Ron Bonner went to work for his father's joinery firm. Oliver Morel stayed until 1946, as did Martin Murray, who had been taken on in 1944, and the workshop gradually expanded with the arrival in 1946 of four pupils, Patrick Villiers, Peter Hensman, Robert Townshend, and David Powell, and another apprentice, Roy Cosham. Hugh Birkett had hoped to join the workshop as a pupil at this time but said that Upton refused to have yet another conscientious objector.[10]

The wages bill expanded rapidly from nearly £300 in 1945, to over £1000 in the following year, and Barnsley's overdraft reappeared in 1946, but fees from pupils also increased, from £31/10/- in 1945 to £185 in 1946. Barnsley's salary from Loughborough as shown in the accounts was very variable, probably only because he began to have it paid to his private account, though transfers were made back into the business accounts at various times.[11]

Unhappily there were increasing periods when Edward was subject to severe depression which left him unable to face the world. For two or three days he would keep to his room, communicating only with Tania, and then there would be days of long walks when he was unable to work, overwhelmed by worry about his ability to design, whether he could bring in enough commissions, and whether he would have enough money to pay the wages. These depressions had started before the war and were probably triggered by the financial problems of the thirties and the responsibility of fatherhood. During the war they had disappeared, but they now became more frequent, sometimes lasted a month, and caused considerable difficulties in the workshop when Edward was not available to make decisions, as well as great distress to himself and Tania.

In spite of this, the post-war period was one of optimism and enthusiasm for the prospects of the future. The order book was healthy and craftsmen and pupils worked well together on the whole.[12] The decade after the war saw a great expansion in the size of the workforce and there were often up to thirteen people in the shop until the mid fifties, when the number reduced again to six or seven, and then again from the mid sixties to four or five. Clearly, more room was needed and in 1948 an extension to the workshop was built by Edward and the staff on the site of the garage and sheds, using bricks from the chimney of Lupton's smithy, which was now demolished. A new timber shed in brick and wood was also put up next to the workshop.

Edward was still thinking through the ideas that John Farleigh had put forward at the meeting in London in 1944, and was beginning to develop a more personal style, moving away from the Cotswold idiom of his father and Gimson and looking at the more delicate lines and masses of eighteenth-century work. Bert Upton, too, was adapting his wartime experiences to suit post-war conditions and was eager to bring in the use of machine tools and to make changes in working practices. As a start, he began to cut down on the waste of materials by choosing the timber and making the cutting lists for each job, instead of allowing the craftsman do this as before the war.

Now began what appears in retrospect to have been a fierce battle of wills, though the craftsmen in the workshop at this time remember a happy working atmosphere, and changes took place over a long period. The struggle was between Barnsley, who wanted to retain the old methods of working, in which one man was responsible for one job, interpreting the design and working on the piece from beginning to end, using only hand tools; and Upton, who was keen to be more cost-efficient, who liked the idea of saving on hard labour by using machine tools, and who saw that the workshop could not survive unless it became more competitive. The relationship between the two had perhaps changed since Upton, who had joined Barnsley as an apprentice of 14, had now experienced working in a much larger organization in the outside world, and had acquired skills previously unknown in the workshop. As the 1946 Furniture Report suggested, the lessons learnt in aircraft production would have a major effect on post-war furniture making, and not just in the big firms.[13] Barnsley fought a strong rearguard action but in the end he had to capitulate. He, too, realized that he could not keep the workshops without using machine tools since it was only sensible to do some tasks by machine when economic factors were considered,[14] and he had to admit an admiration for the quality of work that was possible with them. In writing to friends he emphasized the positive advantages, 'The more we use machines the more I realise their possibilities and the more I realize the extent of nonsense or near nonsense that I and many others have spoken about them!'[15] but he also acknowledged the loss, as in another letter to Idris Cleaver of 1971:

> Alas, there are changes. I expect we have more powered tools than we had on your last visit, was the belt sander here, and the spindle moulder? Were you ever at a gathering when Edward Barnsley assertively remarked, 'the introduction of a spindle moulding machine into a craftsman's workshop is the beginning of the end?' I can see and hear myself, on at least two occasions. And, mind you Idris, I was right, except in so far that the 'end' precedes the end. Before we bought the machine we had already lost that something that only the 'hand' production can achieve. Things too accurate, too flat and too finished …
>
>   What we are all of us liable to do is to adjust to trends and to economic pressures, and then start to justify our adjustments.[16]

The spindle moulder was a tool Upton particularly wanted since it would do work on curves which was very slow by hand, and it is a measure of his persuasive skills that he was able to convince Barnsley to buy it in face of such deep-rooted objections. It may be that such compromise becomes inevitable in this type of workshop once the roles of the designer and the craftworker are separated, because each gives a different priority to particular aspects of the work. The designer, even when a practising maker, usually sees the aesthetic appeal of the object as the paramount feature, and the craftworker sees the quality of making as the measure of achievement, even though acknowledging the importance of the design. For example, some of the craftsmen made pieces for themselves after retirement in which the skill was still clearly evident but the materials were perhaps sub-standard, usually because of cost, thus slightly spoiling the appearance of the work. This was more acceptable to them than making something badly.[17]

An additional complication appeared in the work of the Cotswold group because they were also attempting to reconcile two different traditions. They admired the work of rural craftworkers whose products were functional and quickly made, with skill but without unnecessary finish, such as hay-rakes, hurdle fences, farm waggons, and the simple furniture found in farmhouse kitchens and country inns.[18] As architects they were also enthusiastic about the crafts of building, which involved a different scale of finish, and in later life Edward felt that something of his own attitude was conditioned by his enjoyment of the practical side of building.[19] But they also appreciated the appeal of fine cabinet furniture, made in city workshops in fashionable styles for richer customers by craftsmen who prided themselves on the quality of the finish as well as the basic workmanship. Such skilled makers were not impressed by the simple kind of work and some of Edward's employees dismissed Sidney Barnsley's furniture as having an 'agricultural finish', though Edward himself did not mind if a piece was not perfectly made if it was 'a thing that pleases'.[20]

Perhaps Sidney Barnsley's method, working on his own supported by private means and choosing to make 'good solid oak furniture with occasional pieces of a more delicate kind as a rest and change'[21] is the only way to resolve this dilemma, and Edward sometimes said that there was a special quality about such work, both as a finished product and for the maker. 'As far as I can judge, only those free of present-day monetary issues can possibly enjoy that something of personal hand controlled work which exists in no other form and in no other circumstances other than the truly individual maker, producing one at a time things, and enjoying the quiet tempo'.[22] Unfortunately this requires independence and considerable physical strength and ingenuity, and Sidney Barnsley experienced difficulties in spite of devising a pulley system for moving big boards. He was also restricted in the type of pieces that he tackled and did not do veneered work nor make chairs, the first difficult for someone working on his own and the second tedious. His position seems to have been very similar to that described by Michael Cardew in his autobiography, where he talks of the satisfaction in doing apparently arduous and boring tasks which demand a certain knack, acquire a rhythm, and allow time for contemplation,[23] and maybe the attractions of this depend on the temperament. Many hard-working people seem unable to see any value in such work; but the idea that someone who works on paper and asks someone else to execute the design thereby saves the tedium of the making, misses the point about the pleasures to be gained from craftwork.

In Gimson's workshop a certain compromise had been reached[24] because Waals's standard of finish was higher than Gimson would have liked, making the furniture more expensive than it would have been if less highly

44. Martin Murray planing a drawer, 1945: the use of hand tools was and remained the starting point of an apprentice's training. This simple oak cupboard indicates the continued production of Cotswold-style pieces into the 1940s.

worked, but allowing the craftsmen the pride in their labour which was one of the prime aims of running the workshop. Gimson was, however, uncompromising about the use of machine tools, on the grounds that they removed something from the maker's understanding of materials, that they took away from the variety in the working day which is an important part of handwork, and lessened the need for intelligent thought and personal responsibility on the part of the craftsman. His private income and fees from architectural work enabled him to continue on an uneconomic basis, but he did state in 1916 that he would rather have no workshop at all than have to use machinery.[25] His decision may have been different from Edward's in that machine tools were not so well developed in Gimson's day and could not be controlled in the same way by the maker.[26] It may also have been connected with the other major drawback of machinery that it is noisy and dirty, so that advantages of speed have to be balanced against nuisance value. It otherwise seems an odd decision for someone who was not physically strong and did not himself work at cabinet-making, though his stand was probably confirmed by the views of his friend Sidney Barnsley.

Edward's allegiance to the ideas of his father and Gimson was too deeply felt in the end for him to be entirely happy about the use of machine tools, but he really had very little choice, since he did not have the money to subsidize the workshop. His foreman was a craftsman without a background of Arts and Crafts ideas, and like Peter Waals he wanted to produce work of the highest possible quality, in the cabinet-makers' tradition. Furthermore, while appreciating the importance of contact with materials and the development of skills, he was an employee and therefore had different ideas about the value of physically tiring labour from someone who freely chose this kind of work. Among makers today there seems to be a consensus that it would be unreasonable to expect a woodworker to saw oak boards by hand when machine tools can do this with much less physical effort, even among those who believe that the worker gains knowledge from handwork which cannot be acquired when using machines.[27] It could take a week or more just to plane the parts of a chest of drawers by hand, and anybody without a deep-rooted antipathy to machinery could see the relation between wage costs, the price of the finished article, and the future of the workshop.

Upton also had a very different personality from Barnsley, who expressed some of the problems in a letter of 1965:

> It starts with me. I am to an alarming extent responsible, through my drawings which are often incomplete, not always accurate, showing insufficient detail of what I want, leaving too much to the intelligence of the maker, who does not have great practice in 'knowing what is the right thing'. The more reliance is placed upon drawings the less one's own thoughts and intelligence is developed during training, and the more one insists upon everything being put onto paper. And I tend, wrongly, to leave things undecided, materials not all on the spot ready (fittings etc) and all this causes delay and disappointment and consequent delay, and it's a viscious circle. Tonight my foreman meets Tania and myself, for a talk, and attempt to work

45 and 46. Bert Upton marking out timber with Clive Balcombe and interpreting a design with Oskar Dawson: two from a series of photographs taken by the Rural Industries Bureau photographer, in about 1954.

> out a revision policy. He is so excellent in most ways, but annoyingly 'always right' in manner, and unaware of the weaknesses of his own methods. Few people are willing to accept criticism, all too ready to criticise others, fail to see the motes and concentrate on the beams!![28]

While Upton was 'always right' and confident in his own skill, Barnsley was always unsure, questioning his own work, uneasy in relation to his employees and undoubtedly difficult to work for. Being more secure in his own estimation of himself, Upton was able to be firm, consistent, kind, and helpful to apprentices and pupils, who knew where they stood with him and were grateful for his clear instructions and patience, and impressed by his evident skill. Preoccupied by the need to secure orders, worried about the future, adjusting to alien machine tools and to changing social attitudes, Barnsley was only really happy with employees like George Taylor, 'my special craftsman',[29] who was not only easy-going and good humoured but also a very fast and accurate worker and, therefore, Barnsley's ideal of the fully responsible craftsman. Edward himself worked fast and was always impatient with anybody slower.

After the war, Barnsley's work became more involved with encouraging potential clients and advising at Loughborough, while the workshop was left very much in the care of Upton, who became 'the key pin of the place'.[30] Bert took over responsibility for production and quality control and gained considerable power. He enjoyed the challenge of the larger jobs and keeping a number of things going on all at once. He liked to find new ways to make things and new materials to cope with specific problems, and when contract work done outside proved unsatisfactory he taught himself new skills such as upholstery, favouring new materials and methods rather than traditional ones. From the early 1950s, he began to insist on full-size drawings, partly because of the increasing complexity of the work and the questions which inevitably arose when Barnsley was away and perhaps also because Barnsley was so fussy when he came back. This resulted in a change of relationship between the designer and the maker. Under the old system, whereby each craftsman was given a drawing to one-eighth scale, details of inlay and finish were decided by the maker from his own experience of working in the workshop over a period of time, and therefore each man was making decisions every day as part of the workshop team. Under the new method, most of the decisions were made by the designer and the foreman and there was less scope for the contribution of the maker.

Gradually from 1956 into the 1960s, machine tools appeared in the workshop and new working practices evolved. Apart from the problem of standards of finish, there was another loss for Barnsley in these changes, and it is difficult to see if this was deliberate on his part or indeed if he recognized that it was happening. After the war he became much less involved in the actual making of furniture. He had never had quite the same delight in dovetails and through tenons as his father, but his construction techniques were usually traditional, following the example of Cotswold work. Now, as his style became more elegant in the eighteenth-century manner, the methods of making changed and became more complex. Barnsley was firm that he would not change his design to suit the way the machine tools worked, this being his major objection to the use of machinery, but one might question whether he was able to control this natural tendency entirely, for he was occasionally confronted with a dilemma. Upton, for instance, devised a special tool for making decoration on chairs in a cost-effective way and Barnsley had to decide whether to make more designs to suit this tool.[31]

Bert Upton prided himself on being able to adjust a machine to do anything that was required, but as time went on, Edward became more divorced from the making of the work to the point where Upton believed that Barnsley no longer knew exactly how it was done.[32] Upton said, for instance, that Barnsley's design for an octagonal mirror, which became a standard product of the workshop, had no indications on it of how the thing was to be made and the foreman had to work this out in the most economical way possible, finally achieving a method which took sixteen hours.[33] If this was so, it brings into question the nature of the designer's role, which had changed from being that of a craftsman designing with full knowledge of all the techniques and possibilities, to that of a designer working with line and proportion on paper and making the craft suit the design rather than vice versa. Barnsley's own frequent references to his lack of ability in comparison with his employees, and to being a fraud because he spent all his time at the drawing board, suggest that he was conscious of a change, and perhaps his gradual withdrawal from practical work reflects his lack of interest in this level of skill.[34] He appreciated the results and he knew this work was essential for the workshop, but he did not really want to do it himself.

Such changes came about slowly because, for all his enthusiasm for new methods, Upton was unable to do anything about the lack of electricity in Froxfield until the Electricity Board extended the service in 1955. In spite of the complaints of the workshop's insurers, the paraffin lamps and stove were fixtures until the mid fifties. When electric power did arrive, the lamps were replaced by 'anglepoise' lights on each bench with twenty-watt bulbs, and Barnsley began to acquire electric machine tools.

The need for these was already clear since Barnsley had been having wood planed at Bullock Brothers in Grayshott, Haslemere, from about 1947 onwards,[35] and in 1951 or 1952 a petrol-driven circular saw had been purchased. Upton was particularly pleased with this machine as he could fit different types of jig to it, and he was much admired by Barnsley and by the other craftsmen for his ability to adapt and customize it. A petrol-driven bandsaw was not such a success, however, and prompted much correspondence between Barnsley and its makers because the band kept breaking, until it was replaced by an electric version from Wadkin's in 1955.

A veneer press purchased in 1954 also proved a disappointment, but this was at least partly to do with faulty lamin board and the solution lay in buying German material as before the war.[36] In 1955 the circular saw was converted to electricity and Barnsley ordered a mortise machine with drilling attachment. He also considered buying a planer, but once again the remote position of the workshop proved a disadvantage when it was found that planers required three-phase electricity and Froxfield could only run to single-phase, though this difficulty was soon overcome.

The installation of machinery was an expensive business, so in spring 1956 Barnsley circulated a leaflet to clients and had a sale of stock in the workshop, at which a large proportion of the items was sold.[37]

It was probably also because of the introduction of machine tools and a new emphasis on cost-effectiveness that from 1955 Barnsley stopped taking pupils for some years. In 1950 there were five pupils, Peter Hensman, Kenneth Marshall, David Corbett, John Houghton, and John Lucas, all paying a premium, though when their work was good enough to be sold they were paid for their time, and some were able to recoup the whole of their fee. Others, such as Idris Cleaver, came for shorter periods as a refresher course from teaching, but the number of pupils gradually dwindled and Sandy Mackilligin in 1955 was the last until 1970. In the early 1950s the core staff was Upton, Taylor, Bray, and Oskar Dawson, a fully-trained craftsman taken on in 1947, and three apprentices, Leal Wyatt, who started in 1948, Alan Peters in 1949, and Clive Balcombe in 1952.

The introduction of machinery inevitably led to changes in the day-to-day working practices of the workshop, though the apprentices and pupils were not allowed to use machine tools until Upton felt they had enough experience of handwork. Most of them appreciated the value of this later on,[38] but at the time some were a little dismissive of what they considered to be slow, old-fashioned methods. Alan Peters joined the workshop before the machines were bought and has written a graphic account of the hard work involved in using the hand- and foot-powered circular saw, of planing a table top by hand and of his return from National Service to find that electricity had arrived and with it a roaring, belching planing machine which had been installed next to his bench.[39]

Peters was taken on when he was 16 years old, after learning woodwork at school with the teacher who had also influenced George Taylor and Leal Wyatt. He was very pleased to be doing what he had always wanted, but a letter from Edward Barnsley to Peters' father indicates that Alan was somewhat impatient of the more menial tasks expected of apprentices and would have to learn that these jobs were important.[40] Peters senior was an engineer and had probably had a similar training himself, so he was more sympathetic to this argument than his son was at the time, though Alan Peters' energy, speed and skill of work, and efficiency in running his own business give evidence of a different type of temperament. He later wrote that his experience of building at Froxfield came in useful when he had his own workshop and house to renovate.[41]

As before the war, the apprentices were taught practical skills only. They started by making very simple things, like bread boards and stools, and moved on to plain tables and then tables with drawers and suchlike. Bert Upton thought that his own training under Charlie Bray had been chaotic, so he ensured that there were changes when he was in charge and all who trained under him valued his care. He was concerned about their welfare and their future, and it was his idea that money from the apprentices' wages should be set aside so that they would be able to buy tools at the end of their five years. There was no formal training in design for apprentices because Lupton had never given any advice on design and Barnsley followed his example.[42]

While the apprentice's life changed little, the work of the trained crafts-man did alter. Each man often had up to six pieces on the go at once and some degree of division of labour was introduced, mainly for the production of chairs in batches. Bert Upton realized that the price of chairs, which is generally high because of the complexity of their construction, could be reduced if the component parts were produced in larger numbers when machine tools had been set up to do similar jobs. If a set of six chairs was ordered he would suggest that a similar set be made at the same time to save on setting-up costs, and since he enjoyed the challenge of the task, he was usually the one to do the cutting out. Similarly with dining tables, much time could be saved by making several at once, using the same mould for the laminated stretchers and having two men working co-operatively on lami-nates, veneering, and other tasks; in 1974 Barnsley wrote of the production of seven tables at once, all in different woods and with varied details.[43]

As the workshop became able to deal with large orders and to compete in price, more commissions came in from companies and colleges. A large dining suite was made for the boardroom at Appleby Frodingham Steel-works in 1956 and dining furniture for Nuffield College, Oxford in the following year. Such work was not without its problems and involved a considerable commitment of money for materials, with great risk of miscal-culation over prices. The architects, Harrison, Barnes and Hubbard commis-sioned the Nuffield College job, which was originally to include tables, benches and sideboards, but the sideboards were left out because of lack of

47. Dining furniture at Nuffield College, Oxford, designed by Barnsley in 1957.

funds. The college Warden wrote to Barnsley expressing pleasure that he was to have the commission and regret that the budget was too small to allow the kind of fine work he had recently seen at the Crafts Centre.[44] Costs became critical because the timber had to be kiln dried to cope with underfloor heating and was thus more expensive than expected, leaving Barnsley in a particularly difficult position because he had sub-contracted part of the work, as previously arranged. Richard Fyson, a furniture maker at Kencot near Lechlade, whom Barnsley seems to have met through the Rural Industries Bureau, had agreed to make the benches but found his profit rapidly disappearing in the cost of timber, and on completion Barnsley appealed to the college authorities to increase the payment to Fyson to make up for this. He also expressed concern that payment was tardy and sent Fyson £200 of his own to tide him over until the college paid up.[45]

In spite of the size of such commissions, the greater use of machine tools led eventually to a reduction in the number of staff required and at its period

48. Display fittings for Saccone and Speed, wine merchants of Sackville St, London, 1953. Such work for businesses was a growing element in the workshop output in the fifties and sixties.

of greatest production in the late sixties the Barnsley workshop employed only four men, all fully trained. This was partly because Bert was fed up with having to spend so much time on pupils, partly because the size of commissions required more space in the workshop, and partly because of continuing uncertainty about orders.[46]

The commercial necessity of serving the contract market seemed to be self-evident and was perhaps connected with a feeling of pessimism about the prospect of orders from individual clients. Stanley Davies, one of the very small band of furniture makers running a similar workshop at this time, in a letter of 1955 analysed why post-war customers no longer wanted craft furniture. There were fewer wealthy people than before the war, he said, few large houses and a general preference for small ones, and a lack of domestic help, necessitating light-weight flimsy furniture; the number of 'masters of business' had declined, with more people in jobs within large concerns having to move often, with the result that few married couples decided to build up an ample and enduring family home to pass on to their children; and customers lost their eye for quality as the attraction of fashion became more prevalent through advertising in magazines.[47] Ten years later, Barnsley's view was that people who would have been his clients were in the group which lost income after the war when others became better-off, and that there was now a wider range of attractive goods available to them, such as Scandinavian furniture.[48] Another explanation may lie in the semblance of egalitarianism in the sixties, when pop culture disapproved of élitist images and Habitat provided simple and cheap furniture which catered to both purse and fashion. This would also explain the present-day resurgence of the crafts along with the decline of socialism and the rise of the right. Art in the sixties was for everyone, in principle at least.

Barnsley's designs did reach a wider, though still limited, market through his work for the Rural Industries Bureau. He seems to have come into close contact with this body through G. E. Marston, who had been an official artist on Shackleton's Antarctic expedition of 1914-17,[49] now lived in Hawkley, near to Froxfield, and was Head of the R.I.B. from the early 1930s to 1942.

The Bureau had begun its existence in 1921 as the Rural Industries Intelligence Bureau, under the auspices of the Development Commission, and represented a government attempt to assist skilled workers to stay in business in the crafts allied to agriculture. Throughout the 1920s and 1930s these crafts were hard pressed by competition from mass-produced factory wares delivered to all parts of the country by modern transport, and by the slump in farm prices, which affected the farmers' ability to pay for goods and services. It was the R.I.I.B.'s job, along with the Rural Community Councils which were created at the same time, to help the craftworkers by suggesting profitable sidelines, such as the construction of poultry houses by agricultural carpenters, and by providing designs for these and, occasionally, for simple furniture.[50] The Bureau's County Organizers also advised on modernizing equipment and workshops, and on financial matters.

The Second World War brought some respite from the pressures on rural craftsmen because the need for food resulted in renewed prosperity for farmers and the 'make do and mend' spirit brought forth many old tools and machines to be repaired. A loan fund was introduced at the R.I.B. to help craftspeople to buy new equipment, and between 1939 and 1948 the Bureau doubled its staff.

In 1942 a new Director was appointed, Cosmo Clark R.A., a charismatic man who 'collected craftsmen around him'.[51] In 1948 he asked Edward Barnsley to become Furniture Consultant to the R.I.B. for a new scheme aimed at helping rural woodworkers to make better-designed pieces. Barnsley was to provide designs which would be made up by the Bureau's cabinet-maker in a workshop at the Wimbledon headquarters to test the difficulties of construction. Once approved, the pieces would be displayed at the head office and photographed and included in a catalogue produced by the Bureau, and full-size and scale working drawings could be ordered from the R.I.B. or its County Organizers, 'by rural craftsmen only'.[52] In an undated folder of designs of about 1959, these drawings ranged in price from two to nine shillings and were chosen to suit craftsmen of different standards of skill, simple stools and table lamps being included along with a boardroom table and chairs and a writing bureau (pls 50 and 51).

In May 1948 it was agreed that Barnsley would be paid three guineas a day plus expenses, and at first he worked on some of his existing designs, amending them for their new purpose. As he began to develop new designs specially, and realized the implications for his own business of making his ideas widely available, negotiations took place over a fee per design and the

R.I.B., unsure what to offer in a new situation, hazarded £10, £15, £20? Characteristically, Barnsley agreed on £10 but then had second thoughts and arranged a compromise by which he would charge a higher fee for designs he felt were more original or more useful than most.[53]

His work on the scheme took up much time in 1949 and 1951 and provided a variable income until 1957.[54] As well as making the designs and discussing their production with Alan Smith, the cabinet-maker, Barnsley was also available to visit craftsmen in their workshops to deal with technical and design problems[55] and he was issued with an official R.I.B. Austin which he could pick up in London when necessary.

Other concrete advantages of the project for Barnsley were that the R.I.B. began to collect fine woodwork and then thought of exhibiting it. Initially the collection consisted of the samples made up by Smith, but it was later increased with pieces bought from Barnsley and other makers, such as Hugh Birkett and Stevens and Scrubey, who also provided designs for use in the scheme. A competition was organized in 1949 for rural craftsmen to submit pieces made to designs approved by the Bureau, which were judged by a

49. The Rural Industries Bureau exhibition at the V&A in 1950, showing pieces from the Barnsley workshop alongside furniture made under the auspices of the scheme. The competition clearly elicited a good response and was fittingly displayed with quotations reflecting the ideals of the organizers.

panel of furniture designers and makers. The winning entries were shown in 1950, along with other examples of fine handmade work by Barnsley and others, at the Victoria and Albert Museum, where Ralph Edwards took a personal interest. Edward had been much involved in this from the beginning, visiting makers in their workshops to see who was in business and whether they would be interested in taking part.[56] James Noel White, the R.I.B.'s Information Officer, got together a small exhibition which was sent out by the V&A to museums all over the country and other events were also organized to add to the educational value of the display, such as the discussion between Barnsley and Gordon Russell, which Noel White set up at the Geffrye Museum.

A second competition in 1952 for furniture makers to produce their own designs resulted in more items being made, after discussion of the designs with the competition judges, and these were added to the exhibition. A photograph of the display in the R.I.B.'s 1950-52 Report shows an attractive mix of furniture, pottery, and woven textiles, which in 1952-4 was seen in Bilston, Warwick, Letchworth, Norwich, Halifax, Bristol, Colchester, the Crafts Centre in Edinburgh, and the Geffrye Museum in London. Many items from the collection are still in the possession of the R.I.B.'s successor body, the Rural Development Commission, at its offices in Salisbury, though some were sold after Cosmo Clark left the Bureau.

Smaller-scale displays were also organized by the R.I.B. and Arnold Pentelow, the Wiltshire Organizer, was surprised at Barnsley's interest when he put on an exhibition at an Agricultural Show in Salisbury in the early fifties and Edward brought along a selection of pieces from his workshop, set them out in the open air, and sat with them all day as steward.

In 1955 the R.I.B. was involved in trying to set up a Furniture Makers' Association to provide publicity, collective insurance, an apprenticeship scheme, a library of designs, and other services, and though Barnsley believed that he might have prompted this plan through expressing opinions at the Bureau, he was dubious about its merits. Stanley Davies agreed and thought it might be detrimental to designers like Barnsley, who could find his 'style travestied by cheaper & inferior substitutes'.[57] Something like this did occur some years later when Richard Fyson, who had collaborated on the Nuffield College dining furniture, reported that he had recently visited Oxford and found that a couple of extra benches had been made up to Barnsley's design by someone else, presumably more cheaply. These had warped and looked worn, doing Barnsley's reputation no good.[58]

In the 1955-6 R.I.B. Report, reference was made to experiments with new materials and techniques and the development of new designs for inclusion in the Furniture Catalogue, but though Barnsley's name appeared in the list of consultants into the 1960s, his real involvement with the Bureau stopped around 1957, perhaps because there was by now a considerable body of available designs, or because of a shift of interest within the organization towards the agricultural support crafts.

RURAL INDUSTRIES BUREAU

Bureau

Designed by Edward Barnsley, C.B.E.
This Bureau is shown in walnut but
may be made in any fine grained
English or imported hardwood.

> DESIGN No W 55
>
> HEIGHT 3 ft. 6 in.
> WIDTH 2 ft. 9 in.
> DEPTH 1 ft. 4 in.

Dining chair
with arms

Designed by Edward Barnsley, C.B.E.

This loose-seated dining chair is shown
in oak; English or imported hardwoods
of fine grain may also be used.
A dining chair without arms is also
available. Both designs match the
the large Refectory Table (Design
No. W 54).

> DESIGN No W 22
>
> HEIGHT OF BACK 2 ft. 11 in.
> HEIGHT OF SEAT 1 ft. 5 in.
> WIDTH OF SEAT 1 ft. 8 in.

RURAL INDUSTRIES BUREAU

50 and 51. Two sheets from a catalogue of designs available from the Rural Industries
Bureau, about 1959-60. Rural makers could buy detailed drawings for these pieces
from the R.I.B.

The R.I.B.'s policy of helping 'producer-craftsmen' came in for criticism from M. W. Williams in his report of 1958, *The Country Craftsman*, which accused the Bureau of a romanticized view of the rural maker and a muddled policy in relation to craftspeople who worked in the countryside for preference rather than because their work was intimately connected with country life. Throughout its existence as the Rural Industries Bureau and subsequently from 1968 as Co.S.I.R.A., the Council for Small Industries in Rural Areas, it continued actively to promote fine craft in the countryside and this scheme of providing good designs in the 1950s played a part in this policy. Barnsley later concluded that it had not been a success and that, understandably, few craftsmen wanted to use designs that were not their own.[59] But it was certainly taken up with enthusiasm by some of those for whom it was intended, both amateur and professional,[60] and some cabinet-makers, such as Trevor Pate in Plymouth, still use these designs today, with due acknowledgement to their originator. Some of the woodworking magazines now fill the gap by publishing designs and instructions by leading makers.

At the Rural Industries Bureau it was accepted as inevitable and beneficial that craftspeople should work with modern machine tools and new methods, and the attitude of Cosmo Clark and his County Organizers may have had some effect on altering Barnsley's position. In the workshop, the changes brought by machine tools included the use of techniques which would formerly have been too time-consuming, and which formed part of the development of Barnsley's style in the fifties and sixties, such as laminating lengths of wood to make curved sections for drawer-fronts and stretchers. This type of experiment was specifically mentioned in the R.I.B. Report of 1955-6 and the Bureau's trials must have been of help to the Barnsley workshop in such developments. Certainly in 1957 when asked to send his account for consultancy work, Edward wrote that he felt the obligation was all the other way, since the Bureau had done experiments for him on materials for chair seats and suchlike and he had done nothing for them.[61]

Another recurring feature in the reports was the increasing scarcity after the war of timbers which had formerly been widely used. While the supply of timber was controlled, the R.I.B. acted as the approving body for applications to the Board of Trade for the artist-craftsman licence which was needed to purchase hardwoods, and after the controls were lifted in 1950, a licence was still required to buy some plywoods and veneered boards. The R.I.B. saw it as part of its service to advise on the use of new imports such as Australian walnut, black bean, opepe, ramin, and makore[62] and here it is difficult to see whether Barnsley's own interest influenced the Bureau or vice versa.

The purchase of timber continued to be one of Edward's greatest pleasures and he enjoyed a particularly friendly relationship with William Inman of Turner's of Lewes, whom he had first met in 1926 when Inman visited the workshop with his parents as a customer. Their first professional encounter occurred some years later when Inman was training in the timber business with a firm in Hook and suggested that Barnsley might be interested in a particular walnut butt, which on sawing proved to be defective. Disappointing as this was, it was the beginning of a long association because Inman was interested in craftwork, and was able to foster that interest when he became a director in his family's firm after the war.

Barnsley became his client after the death of Inman's brother in 1949. At first he was regarded as the firm's fussiest customer, and he did not endear himself by arriving at the sawmill well before the appointed time in order to have a good look round for anything special which might have been hidden away. Inman probably told him at some time that it was essential to serve every customer with a quality just suitable for their purpose, not too good and, of course, not too bad. It quickly became obvious that only the very best was suitable for Edward and so anything hidden away was hidden for him, ready for his next visit. This became eagerly awaited, for Inman found him a delightful person and also the source of much useful knowledge about sawing, stacking, selection, and the behaviour of various woods. If a log was sawn for him, he was always present, deciding the thickness of each board according to its grain, figure, quality, or size. On one special occasion three logs were sawn simultaneously for him on three separate saws and Edward darted enthusiastically between each sawbench until all were cut. Inman later told Barnsley of some of his shortcomings as a customer and Edward replied contritely that 'until I experienced your own sensitive ways of doing business, I had the impression that timber merchants were charging me

52. The timber store at Froxfield in 1977. Barnsley's stocks of carefully selected wood were his pride and joy.

quite suitable prices from their point of view, and I became fussy and awkward with their valuable time, took a lot of their time for nothing, was a bad payer and the lot. However, I hope I was a buyer, sometimes, who added to the profits of the seller'.[63]

His purchases were not large and he was very particular about when the tree should be felled, in midwinter when the sap was at its lowest, and how it should be sawn and dried, though he had to accept kiln-drying in the late sixties. But the relationship was mutually educational and Barnsley's recommendation counted for a good deal with the other craftspeople Inman was keen to have as customers. These included Eric Sharpe, Barbara Hepworth (who didn't mind if logs supplied to her had holes in them), and John Makepeace. Oak became rather unfashionable after the war but Turner's continued to supply walnut and other English woods and some of the new imported timbers, though not the black bean which Barnsley used a great deal in the fifties and sixties and which he purchased from Mallinson's in London. He also seems to have had a friendly relationship with Mallinson, who expressed pleasure in being able to assist with work of such high quality as Barnsley's, though he was clearly as fussy with them as with Inman.[64] To the end of his life Edward retained this interest and letters of the late seventies and early eighties document his pursuit of timber and his pride in his stocks.[65]

Once the timber was in the store it was Bert Upton's responsibility, and it was he who selected it for everyday work, except when Barnsley knew of a

53. Barnsley and Bert Upton moving planks of bubinga from the stock for inspection, 1970.

special log which he wanted for a particular piece. It would then be moved from the timber shed to the workshop to acclimatize for some months before it was worked, and Upton would cut out the basic shapes with the different saws he kept sharpened differently for the various woods. He would then explain the design to the craftsman if necessary and supervise the making, and when the piece was finished he would talk to the maker about how he felt about his work.[66]

Barnsley was away from Froxfield for long periods, at Loughborough and elsewhere, and also trying to drum up custom by dropping in on old clients and casually suggesting that they might like to order something new. This was his main way of finding new business apart from contributing to exhibitions. In his early years he seems to have paid for advertising in magazines such as *The Cabinet Maker* and *The Architectural Press* but though he occasionally thought about advertising in the sixties, he never did.[67]

Tania Barnsley was still in charge of the finances, which became considerably more complex after the war because of Purchase Tax and then Value Added Tax, and she and Upton were very much responsible for the day-to-day running of the workshop, where Edward's absence frequently caused problems. Of particular annoyance was his habit of assessing the aesthetic qualities of a piece when it was finished or nearing completion after he had been away, and changing the design if it did not come up to scratch. Several of the craftsmen have said that although they later appreciated the importance of this maintenance of standards, it was not considered helpful at the time, and Barnsley himself was quite aware of this.[68] He probably justified it partly by memories of Ernest Gimson; he remembered at Daneway seeing the men removing the back from a veneered cabinet because 'Big Uncle' didn't like the pattern and was very particular to have things altered if he felt it necessary. Gimson's cabinet-makers also found this annoying.[69]

The official workshop accounts are difficult to understand at this period because some features, such as payments from Loughborough and income tax, appear only at irregular intervals, while transfers were often made into the workshop account from Barnsley's private account. They seem to show a net profit in the fifties which see-sawed from £448 to £1138 and averaged out at about £740. As before the war, the accounts tell only part of the story, and the cashbook shows that although Barnsley started every year in the 1950s in credit, the amount varied enormously. In the period 1949 to 1954 the credit balance was always under £200, then in 1955 it went up to over £800 and stayed regularly above £300 until 1961 when it was down again to £115. Apart from his work for the Rural Industries Bureau, Edward gained further income from lecturing to groups of craftworkers and trainee teachers, and advising at Loughborough provided a welcome regular salary, which allowed him to think of spending capital on the buildings.

The addition of machinery resulted in increased noise and dust in the workshop and by 1958 he was planning alterations to ameliorate working conditions.[70] His son, Jon, was now an architect, working for himself in London, and he designed the extensions, which were carried out over the

54. Barnsley digging foundations for the new machine shop and spray-bay in 1961. This was a fairly minor hole by comparison with some of his excavations.
55. The workshop photographed in 1981. The machine shop is in the centre, the original workshop just behind, and the 'top shop' obscured by the car.

next few years. Edward had decided that he should do the job properly this time 'having muddled along more or less in the past with make shift appliances'. [71] An oil-fired boiler was bought and installed in the new part of the workshop, but it blew out heat from above and the staff hated it, so it was quickly removed. The Trust much later found an efficient one, but up to then the workshop continued to be heated by an old coke stove, which, until he was well over 80, Edward stoked in the very early hours of the morning to keep it alight. The major change in 1961 was the addition of a machine shop to the right of the front elevation with a spray-bay behind and a timber store below this. As usual, Edward revelled in the hard physical work of digging out the foundations for the store, which gave him the two-fold pleasure of saving money and enjoying the labour. This he got from his father, whose attitude is summed up in a letter to Philip Webb quoting the American philosopher, Thoreau, on preparing firewood, 'that one gets warmed twice — once in sawing it and then in burning it', and 'the pleasure of splitting a big log and thinking of future pleasure in watching it burn is worth a good deal'.[72] Edward also liked the idea that he was adding to the value of the property by building a structure which could be converted for use as a garden room if the business ever finished.[73]

He and Upton decided how best to accommodate the extract plant and machine tools, by now a circular saw, planer, and band-saw, and Jon put their requirements into design form in 1961.[74] The extension continues the roof line of the original workshop and is an unassuming and fitting addition of simple practicality. It provides concrete evidence of the new underlying stability of the business, and heralded in the 1960s, which proved a decade of change, both for the workshop and for Barnsley himself.

6. THE WIDER WORLD OF THE CRAFTS

Restructuring at Loughborough in the 1960s and Barnsley's retirement – changes in craft and design teaching – financial viability of the workshop and relations with employees – debate on a new image for the Crafts Centre – formation of the Crafts Council, 1964, and the Crafts Advisory Committee, 1971

Edward Barnsley's three major preoccupations in the 1960s were the continued running of the business; the future of the crafts as a vital part of modern life; and a renewed interest in the background of the Arts and Crafts Movement. Some things remained much as before, especially Edward's alternating confidence and pessimism about the viability of the business. The expansion of the workshop space in 1961 and the addition of a bathroom, cloakroom, and two inside W.C.s to the cottage in 1964 at a cost of £977, were rapidly followed by a net loss to the business in 1964 of £466. A prestigious order from Courtauld's for two large tables and thirty-four chairs, which had prompted him in 1963 to gamble on the future and for a short time acquire a second car, had not yet worked its way into the accounts, though the following year saw a profit of over £1000.[1] The

56. Barnsley in the late 1970s with a model of the boardroom table made in 1964 for Courtauld Engineering Ltd. The table was in rosewood, and twenty-four feet long. Models and mock-ups were made very rarely in the workshop.

Courtauld commission soon caused major headaches, though, when the lacquer crazed and veneers blistered in the dry heat of the building, necessitating remedial work.[2] Another large corporate commission of the sixties caused a different kind of problem: after protracted negotiations with Magdalen College, Oxford, over an order for fifty rosewood chairs which were quoted at as slim a price as he could manage, Edward found that the college wanted to spread the cost over two financial years, starting in nine months' time, when wages would already be considerably higher.[3]

In the mid sixties, he also had to face the prospect of retirement from his job in Loughborough, an event he viewed with some trepidation, partly because of the financial consequences and partly because of the work itself.

Barnsley enjoyed advising, which appealed to his self-confessed tendency to pontificate. He liked the earnest young men who took teacher-training courses, many of them paying for themselves in an effort to improve their job prospects, and they respected him for his enthusiasm and his straightforward, unpatronizing, 'man-to-man' attitude to them. If time allowed, he would join them at their tea-break in the canteen and the relationship was much easier than the complexities of workshop life, with everyone benefiting from the lack of tension. Many of Barnsley's students have said that he was an excellent teacher who taught them to appreciate the difference between good and bad design, who showed them how the removal of a mere sixteenth of an inch could improve the appearance of a piece of furniture, and who encouraged them to make fine pieces which they can still enjoy.[4]

For over twenty years, he had made his regular trip to Loughborough, enjoying the break from the workshop, the discussions with colleagues, and the contact with students, and in 1949 he was awarded an honorary Diploma. The college expanded steadily, extended the length of its courses, changed its name to Loughborough Training College, and began to reorganize its course components. John Bridgeman retired in 1963 and as Barnsley approached the standard age for retirement, ideas about the teaching of Handicraft in schools were changing. Though he hoped to be kept on, it became clear that he would have to go.

Don Porter, a retired H.M.I. who had much contact with the college, has described the situation clearly :

> Critics of what happened at Loughborough during the late 1960s often failed to appreciate that it was to a large extent due to changes in the College itself, and to developments in schools. Herbert Schofield's brilliant plan for a mini-university on the new campus was, for a time at least, set aside when four new colleges were established. Two served mainly local needs, while the College of Education and the College of Advanced Technology recruited nationally. By 1965, plans were in hand for a further expansion of the College of Education, this time to include a broader intake. It was no longer to be almost wholly devoted to training male teachers of Handicraft and Physical Education for Secondary schools: there would also be men and women who would teach in primary and middle schools. More residences were built, and the Bridgeman workshops were extended to include facilities

for art and pottery, and laboratory provision for the study of materials and structures, and for studying the impact of electronics and plastics upon handicraft.

At this period ideas about secondary education were under review and the Crowther report, plainly influenced by the pioneering work of some secondary technical schools, emphasized the value for all pupils of continuing beyond the age of 13 or 14 with practical/aesthetic subjects. It also suggested that many boys and girls would do better following a more practical approach, which it called 'The Alternative Road'.[5]

> By the mid 1960s there was also the second raising of the school-leaving age (to 16), and a drive towards a more comprehensive system, involving in some cases the establishment of middle schools bridging the hitherto universal 11-plus transfer age. All these changes inevitably affected specialist colleges like Loughborough. Whereas formerly students had left to enter schools of modest size, often with two workshops and maybe a technical drawing room, now schools would be much larger, often with a suite of workshops flexibly planned with space for a project area. Handicraft, which despite its successes had been regarded as a fringe subject, could now claim a more central place in the curriculum.
>
> The combined effect of all these changes was to emphasize that continuing with a relatively limited range of woodwork and metalwork, however excellent, was no longer an option open to the college authorities.[6]

As Porter says, all this must have been known to those who were in touch with Local Education Authorities and schools in the teaching practice area where pioneer work was going on, yet there seems to have been a failure of communication when Bridgeman retired in 1963, to be replaced by J. W. S. Hardie, who saw the restructuring of the college as his first major task. Unfortunately he did not fully appreciate the existing strengths on the Handicraft side, or the critical parts played by Barnsley and Waals before him. It should have been possible to broaden the college course while retaining cabinet-making as one of the important options open to the students, but Hardie went too far, too fast, alienating some of the staff. As a result, controversy reigned within the department and among former students as to the relative merits of the old and new style courses.

The debate was about the type of training which should be offered to children in schools. Some felt that there should be more recognition of new technology and materials, and that teaching traditional woodworking techniques was of little relevance to twentieth-century children, especially to those without natural ability. Design was seen as a problem-solving process which could be applied to the making of almost anything, in all kinds of materials. It was felt that greater emphasis should be given to the teaching of metalwork, which had become very limited in relation to the techniques and equipment available. Good-quality timber had become prohibitively expensive since the war, so the idea of being able to use cheaper plastics and ply had an appeal for hard-pressed schools, but the main aim of the new thinking was to involve the student or pupil in the activity of designing and making as a whole, and to encourage them to further effort by ensuring good early results. It was also intended to raise the status of craft teachers by emphasizing the intellectual side of the design and making process.

Younger teachers, and a few older ones,[7] embraced these ideas, and at Loughborough, 'Design Technology', including mechanical and electrical engineering studies, was introduced in 1966, and the department's title was changed from 'Handicraft' to 'Creative Design'. Geoffrey Harrison, the Head of Department after Ockenden's retirement, was an engineer with ideas on how students could put theory into practice through workshop experience. Few objected to the introduction of technology, but among the staff feelings were divided about so complete a change of emphasis and for Barnsley and many of his ex-students, now teaching in schools, it seemed a betrayal of all they stood for.[8]

Barnsley had always believed that design was a product of experience, intelligence, and intuition, not a cerebral process which could be applied to any set of materials, and he thought that the new attitude denigrated the work of the experienced maker by implying that hand skills were not important. Even under the existing conditions he felt that practical teachers like Cecil Gough were discriminated against in terms of salary and promotion prospects in comparison with their more academic colleagues, and the new ideas would increase the split between 'designers' and makers. The status of the craft teacher in relation to colleagues teaching other subjects might be enhanced, but only at the expense of continuing prejudices that academic abilities were superior to practical skills.

Patrick Nuttgens has put forward a similar argument, quoting a story told by Sir Alex Smith, former Director of Manchester Polytechnic, who when visiting a school 'came across a most superb model of a boat. He stopped to admire it, and the Headmaster said what a pity it was that the boy who made it was one of their least able children. The story speaks for itself'.[9]

Aesthetics, Barnsley felt, were an adult interest and would bore children, who learn best from doing,[10] and in giving freedom to the students' own imaginations the new methods would pander to the easy option. What ideas could they express if they had no real understanding of materials and techniques and why should they be encouraged to develop impractical 'original' ideas when they could be learning from others? 'Few young people have anything worth expressing, and they are NOT necessarily made verbally constipated for life by experiencing the diciplines of an art or a craft. After experience it's sometimes found that a small number per cent have ability that's worth expression, and by then they can express it.'[11]

In the hands of skilled and imaginative teachers the changes could be made to work, but the wholesale swing to the fashionable ideology in the sixties and seventies resulted in a generation of art and craft students leaving college only to realize that they did not have command of the basic techniques of their subject.

Critics of Barnsley's method say that the standard of craftsmanship was

57. Students' work at an exhibition at Loughborough College in the mid 1950s. The influence of Barnsley and the Cotswold style is very clear.

too high and produced expectations beyond what could be required of school work. They point out that pieces made by students under his supervision were predominantly in Barnsley style because he did not recognize any merit in their own ideas and unconsciously took over their designs in making corrections to their drawings, and that many of his students developed their work no further after they left. On the other hand, Bill Elloway, who worked with Barnsley and continued at the college until 1983, felt that one of the strengths of the system was that the students were not producing designs of a random nature, responsible only to themselves, but were extending a fine tradition, adding to the accumulated experience of many years.[12] His understanding of this echoes Sir George Trevelyan's description of the benefits of his training at Waals's workshop as 'submitting to the discipline of a great craft tradition'.[13]

The issue still raises strong feelings among craft teachers today, and is further complicated by the effects on established Craft, Design and Technology courses in recent years of the demands of the National Curriculum.[14]

'Poor old Edward retired from his lucrative lectureship at Loughborough when the 65 years was reached', Barnsley wrote in 1968, 'and overnight loss of about twenty five pounds a week. It took me a long time to get over that, but, so far we have done something which no other "craftsman" has done since the start of the Arts & Crafts movement as it's called, that is made an adequate income directly from the work. Long may it go on. Some people would not consider income adequate!'[15] Stanley Davies had told him in 1955 that he had not made a financial success of his business,[16] but Alan

Peters suggests that by 1968 Edward was mistaken in thinking he was the only one who had a self-supporting workshop, since he himself was still teaching one day per week only to satisfy his bank and could have lived from his work. He believes that Sandy Mackilligin was one of the first and that John Makepeace was also self-sufficient by this time.

In 1965, Edward had told Vera Simpson that he had calculated his average net income for 1954-63 as £700 per annum, including the £200 paid to Tania.[17] Later in the letter of 1968 quoted above, he amplified his comment about income. 'For many years it must remain something of an uncertain job, with years when the net total profits are little, alternating with other years when I could count on an income approximating to a junior director in some firm! With a sixty hour week, practically no holidays, enjoying the benifits of having to "do it all ourselves" and no complaints whatever.'[18]

This last was of course not strictly true; he took great pride in the fact that the workshop was able to survive without his teaching salary and mentioned this to several correspondents, but he was also conscious that his income was not what he might have expected at his age. Perhaps his visits to clients brought home to him the reality of his simple standard of living; certainly for a while he became rather status-conscious and mentioned in a joking fashion in letters the idea that 'there may come a time when it will be a custom, when friends drop in at homes around the country, for the host or hostess to say, in effect, "Oh, just before we have our drinks do come and look at my latest Barnsley", not the Bently or the Rolls or the Jag or the mink.'[19] He had always had a certain element of guilty delight in status and rather liked his daughter's new title of Contessa when she married (though she sometimes found the title embarrassing), but his whole philosophy worked against his achieving the widespread recognition which would be needed to make his furniture a status symbol — though among his clients no doubt some did show off their new acquisitions in just such a way to their friends. It was left to John Makepeace to bring about a major change in attitudes to handmade furniture and since he did this by allying his work with that of artists and by stressing new qualities in the design, saying that he wished to owe nothing to the work of the past, Edward disapproved.[20] Makepeace also believed in the efficacy of publicity and employed a publicity agent; this Edward saw as immodest self-seeking, though his own business would probably have benefited from similar treatment.

He was indignant at the lack of understanding of his view of the crafts and the craftworker's life, and his interest in recording the history of the Arts and Crafts, and his reading and re-reading of Ruskin and Morris, balanced out his hankerings for worldly glory and made him appreciative of his situation: 'Fortunately I think we shall carry on. Wages and all other costs continue to mount. We work under conditions which are right for our things, but bear little relation to and are in conflict with the industrial set-up, to our disadvantages. We remain unique however, and reputation does not decline I trust.'[21]

Since the 1950s, Barnsley had been charging more standard amounts for his percentage and 'shop', his design work being costed at about 25 per cent of labour plus materials and overheads, while 'shop' was calculated at approximately 33–50 per cent of wages. Purchase Tax was accounted for within the figure for overheads. The loss of his teaching salary seems to have made Edward Barnsley think harder about the economics of the workshop and to analyse what was needed in terms of productivity. In 1967 he estimated that each bench had to produce a profit of £5 per week to provide his income and that it was essential to estimate how much work each assistant could produce in a week, month, or year. It was also vital in his view that the cost of the finished article was made up mainly of wages and materials and not high overheads, and he recognized the privileged circumstances of his rural workshop in this regard. The hidden profit on seasoning materials was another factor (though there was also the risk of a timber becoming unfashionable and redundant), along with other items which could be claimed against tax, but the whole business relied on a steady flow of work, and problems arose when there was any slump in orders.[22]

In spite of good intentions for greater efficiency and self-reform, however, Barnsley continued to muddle along. He took on uneconomic jobs, both fine work like inlaid boxes for friends, and simple machining tasks such as parts for 'stink cabinets', which were highly paid but mechanical, and he occasionally did them himself because the price would be too high if he charged the proper rate for a craftsman's labour.[23] He did not consult his employees about how long it would take to make up his designs and he never told them

58. A table of the late 1950s with characteristic inlaid decoration. The pottery figure by Margaret Hine belonged to Barnsley, who bought a number of ceramic pieces from the Crafts Centre in the fifties and sixties.

how much time he had estimated and quoted for. George Taylor suggested to him that he should do this so that the maker had something to aim for, and on one occasion they tried it. George got on so fast that he congratulated himself on being well within the period allowed, until Barnsley suggested adding some decoration since there was time available. At this point George despaired of Barnsley ever being able to accept making a real profit.[24] It was the long-standing problem that Barnsley wanted to make things to the highest possible standards at prices which would not deter clients from coming back for more, but for craftsmen on low wages it must sometimes have seemed that rich customers were being subsidized by the poorly-paid workers.

Although he often said that the maker of things was more important than the thing made, his own difficulties with staff and money usually got in the way of his ideals. He was disappointed in makers who did not come up to his idea of the 'thinking craftsman', but he did little to encourage initiative or involvement within the workshop, and although it was suggested to him that work would get on faster if everything needed for a piece were ordered when it was started, he would neither do this himself nor delegate to others. The craftsmen came to recognize that the business was doing well when the Guvnor spent his time working solidly in his drawing office and they knew that if he was in the workshop chivvying them along, the order book was not so healthy. He seems to have had little understanding of the duties of an employer towards his staff in terms of wages and conditions of employment, no personal interest in their lives or welfare, and no knowledge of working life in the outside world, though he did have some understanding of his ignorance in relation to 'what the younger craftsmen have to face up to' without his privileges.[25] In spite of all his attention to calculating overheads, he never realized how much it cost the workshop to train staff and then to lose them because of low wages even though many of them were eager to stay on.

He was aware of some of these problems but wrote in 1965:

> It's a little late in life for me to bring out a fresh spurt, to change from a rather haphazard chap, not much practical neat efficiency, no interest in the ambition of success, untidy, imprecise, often to a degree of vagueness and uncertainty, a marked dislike of being definite, hopeless with assistants in many ways (family shyness the main reason for this) easily annoyed and irritated by others' foolishness assumed or real. And now it seems that one of THE main causes of our troubles is me, the drawings etc etc, and so, I repeat, it's a little hard to look forward to trying to alter the whole approach, the whole method of work, when I want more than anything else to ease off, spend time walking the fells and staying with friends and chatting and putting up seats and gates and odd jobs free of responsibility, & digging holes in the ground & felling trees!!
>
> I guess the future is preparing to test me hardly.[26]

And yet, he had already said earlier in the same letter, 'it would be a wrong thing indeed, wouldn't it, if we fail to go on producing.'

By the late fifties and early sixties the staff was down to six or seven and by the mid 1960s Barnsley felt reluctant to take on apprentices because he needed all his workers to be economically viable and this only happened when they had gained some years of experience after the apprenticeship was over. His excellent team of craftsmen comprised Upton, Taylor, Dawson, Clive Balcombe, Leal Wyatt, Malcolm Clubley, and Paul Way, and Charlie Bray also did occasional part-time work. Way, who started in 1960, was the last apprentice to be taken on for some fourteen years, and Edward began to feel that although such training was essential for young makers, it was no longer economically feasible for a small workshop, and should become part of the function of the Crafts Centre and Crafts Council.[27]

His involvement with the Crafts Centre remained strong in this period, and he wrote frequently to Sheila Pocock, the Secretary, asking that they be more careful about the standard of furniture shown at Hay Hill, commenting on proposals to change the Purchase Tax scheme, and suggesting ways in which the Centre could improve its income, such as by charging a percentage on all commissions received by a maker from clients who had first seen work at Hay Hill. Sometimes he simply thanked Miss Pocock and the Centre staff for all they had done for him over the previous year. He said he was surprised at how few commissions came to him through the Centre but he felt that there were always benefits. He certainly received his share of space and was even offered a one-man show for 1962 but had to turn it down because the workshop was being extended.[28]

Along with others, however, he questioned whether the Crafts Centre was as good as it could be and whether it was fulfilling all the aims for which it was originally founded. Unfortunately the correspondence is not as illuminating as during the war, because Roger Powell had moved back to Hampshire in 1947 and there was no-one else involved with whom Barnsley was quite so frank in writing. Papers in the Barnsley archive from the various groups of which he was a member and in the Arts and Crafts Exhibition Society collection at the V&A Archive of Art and Design, show that there was much discussion about the future of Hay Hill.

In 1960, David Kindersley, the letter-cutter, expressed concern that the Council of Industrial Design (also known as the Design Council) was building up a crafts section, and he urged the Council of the Crafts Centre to ask for discussions and liaison as soon as possible. Some months later, Kindersley was elected to the Council of the Crafts Centre and told Sheila Pocock that he hoped to be able to help the Centre more than in the past, since it had not achieved the success he felt it deserved.[29] In November he circulated a paper entitled 'Image of a Craft Centre'. This argued that the Centre was at a crossroads and that a new image was required. Its first loyalty should be to the designer-craftsman, not to the traditional maker or the pure designer, though their work should be displayed to help in the cross-fertilization of ideas and assist in defining the differences between them. The main purpose of the Crafts Centre was to prevent the death of craft skills and to encourage the development of new ones, but its work was

59. David Kindersley, the letter-cutter, a key figure in the moves to reform the image of the Crafts Centre in the early 1960s which culminated in the foundation of the Crafts Council of Great Britain. He succeeded John Farleigh as Chairman of the Crafts Centre in 1964.

hampered by a lack of support. The arts were well covered by the Arts Council, the rural craftsmen had been saved from extinction by the Rural Industries Bureau, and the designers had the Council of Industrial Design, but the Crafts Centre's standards had not been high enough and its image had been compromised. What was needed was a body with similar status to the C.O.I.D. All the best craftsmen should exhibit in it, regardless of their own school of thought, and it must be seen as a repository of readily available information about makers and their products. The Design Council's index of potters should be transferred and discussions should take place between the Crafts Centre, Arts Council, C.O.I.D., and R.I.B. to ensure no duplication of activities. Consideration must also be given to who ran the Crafts Centre since it was clear the craftsmen should not do this, though their support was needed.

Kindersley's paper continued that the idea behind the Crafts Centre had been right but the country's economy had been unfavourable, and more emphasis should be given to the export value of craftwork. The position of the Centre at Hay Hill was out of the way and a new position in Piccadilly had been suggested by James Noel White. There should be a monthly magazine with illustrations of both traditional and experimental work so that the word craft would cease to have a derogatory meaning, and this should be run on a sound commercial basis. It would be impossible to remedy the inherent inconsistency between sales and exhibitions because unlike items shown at the Design Council, craftwork was not widely available in the shops.

It was proposed that a trust comprising men and women in business, industry, and the crafts should be formed and an inspired impresario, who should be a maker, be appointed to run the centre without interference after an initial briefing. Selection meetings of members of the five constituent societies and two representatives from each craft if possible, should be held to choose work to be shown, so as not to break faith with the societies, but they should relinquish direct control.

In summary, the paper proposed a change of name to the Crafts Council and suggested that the day-to-day running should be independent of the craftspeople and in the hands of staff chosen for their ability to organize, select, display, and sell. Membership would be sought after by designer-makers, whose work would be brought to a wider public. A permanent but changing display of craftwork would be needed with the support of a comprehensive record, and a well-produced monthly magazine. Staff should be properly paid.[30]

This seems to reflect discussions which had taken place at the Art Workers' Guild as well as the Crafts Centre, and at the Arts and Crafts Exhibition Society, which in 1960 had changed its name to the Society of Designer-Craftsmen.[31] James Noel White, the Deputy Director at the Design Council, who was interested in the crafts and their relation to industrial design, was also much involved and in the following year he and Kindersley, with David Thomas and Victor Margrie, prepared a report on the future of the Centre for the Society of Designer-Craftsmen. This was partly prompted by the warning from the Board of Trade that it planned to withdraw its grant from the Centre in 1962.[32]

Barnsley was also on the Council of the Designer-Craftsmen and clearly felt some responsibility for 'stirring up trouble' within the group because he had written in March 1961 to John Farleigh requesting an informal meeting to explain that the aim was to make the Centre more as originally intended, but he does not seem to have been involved at this later date. Unfortunately, there is surprisingly little correspondence in the archive between him and Farleigh.[33]

The Board of Trade was still adamant about the removal of its grant but Kindersley proposed that the craftworkers should guarantee an increased subscription to maintain the Crafts Centre, with some success, and in September 1962 the Council of the Designer-Craftsmen heard that the Pilgrim Trust was to provide a grant which would enable the Centre to stay open for another two years, giving time for more work on the new plans.[34] The Council of Industrial Design was still involved at this point and Kindersley felt this was an advantage: he saw the craftsman's role as close to the designer's, while Barnsley was always suspicious of 'design'.

For many years since the wrangling of the wartime period, Barnsley had felt that it was impossible for craftsmen to agree and to work together, a view incidentally shared by Kindersley, and that a national crafts organization should be formed with a professional salaried Director, who should be given authority to act, supported by a council composed of lay members as well as makers. In this respect his position was close to that of the 'Image of a Craft Centre' document, but somehow over the next few years his ideas on how this should be put into practice diverged from those of the writers of the paper and he found himself isolated.[35]

As discussion built up on these questions, a new character entered the picture, who seemed to Edward to provide many of the answers to long-standing problems. Cyril Wood had recently retired after a distinguished career in the arts as a theatre producer and director, a broadcaster, administrator with the Arts Council, and first Director of the South West Arts Association. In 1962 he compiled a report on the crafts for the Gane Trust and he wrote to Barnsley about this in March 1963, wanting to visit Froxfield.[36]

Thus began a new and extensive correspondence which grew so rapidly that by June, Edward was joking that if it 'keeps going like this I shall have to consider switching my building operations from a bathroom to an annexe for our files'.[37] It started on a friendly basis, at least partly because both men were the type to respond to letters immediately and both appreciated a reply by return. It grew so rapidly because Wood had become interested, wanted to do more for the crafts, and decided to organize an exhibition of craftwork at his home in Gloucestershire, a farmhouse called Swyre at Aldsworth. He solicited Barnsley's advice about work to be included, a responsibility Edward tried to shrug off by suggesting that Wood should get recommendations from others apart from himself. The real problem, he thought, was to find furniture makers able to cope with both aspects of the designer-craftsman's role, the design and the making; Robert Townshend and Alan Peters he considered to be above the line of doubt, but the list of those he put below it was a long one and included Eves, Makepeace, Mackilligin, Baly, and McCurdy. This was not a consistently held view, for in June he was glad to hear that Makepeace was on Wood's list since 'he strikes me as one of the coming young furniture makers'.[38] In spite of protests of unfitness for the job, he soon became absorbed in the task of proposing suitable exhibitors and suggesting ways of breaking down the formality of the exhibition by, for instance, allowing visitors to sit at the table and eat, by including humorous items, and by inviting people to come and talk.[39] He also offered pieces from his own house, such as an ebony sea lion by Ferelyth Wills, and he put forward the name of Lucie Rie, whose work Wood did not know.

As plans developed for the exhibition to be held in September 1963, Barnsley became embarrassed at the privilege of having a whole room of the display to himself, financed by the Gane Trust. However, since this was intended to be the first of many such shows, he reconciled himself to it and bent his mind to problems of whether commission should be paid to the Trust on items ordered as a result of the exhibition, and the organization of an opening and a meeting suggested by David Peace, the glass engraver, to discuss the future of the crafts and the continuation of the Swyre project.

The exhibition, called 'The Mark of the Maker', took place in the farmhouse and a barn, which was turned into an exhibition hall with help from apprentices from a local college on the suggestion of Arnold Pentelow of the Rural Industries Bureau. Barnsley expressed his appreciation to Wood and his wife, Rosalind, for the attractive arrangement of the display, and Wood began to formulate more ambitious plans for the future. Barnsley's letters throughout had been concerned with the place in society of the craftworker and the usual problems about machinery and the association of the crafts with industry, and he clearly felt that in Wood he had a sympathetic ally. In preparation for a meeting at Swyre he sent a letter outlining his views; the main object was to 'Maintain, develop, stimulate, and in every possible way increase the total production of works of those people called designer makers. Follows that this implies approach to those other than craftsmen, so that they become increasingly aware of this particular work, and become convinced of its values'. This was to be achieved, he suggested, by building up conviction that 'ART (not so much individual artists!!? but art, which includes craft, is a LIGHT OF THE WORLD, nothing less'. A revolutionary, no-compromise approach would start with a Swyre board of Wood as Chairman and Lord Eccles as first director; these two to appoint more directors, including 'at least one woman member of top rank', who would bring a feminine sensitivity to bear on the choice of future exhibits. 'No craftsmen to be members of the Board, or of any committees which the Board might appoint. As far as possible no direct advice sought from craftsmen at any time.' The craftspeople were to concentrate on the work to which they were suited, making things to the best of their ability, and should be kept out of contact with their potential customers since 'collectively they don't make too good an impression, their individuality is their strength, but results in their being better advocates when in their own habitats, with their products, not at the council tables, not in committee.' Swyre could become the home of an annual exhibition at which it would be an honour to show, and which would particularly encourage younger makers.[40]

He knew that the craftsmen would not like it: 'They are unable to agree about any one single thing, as a specie they grouse, find fault with anything that is not of their own creation, belittle and denigrate, and are temperamentally unsuited to evolve policies or carry through actions for their own good'.[41] He believed that his views did not carry much weight because he disagreed with modern trends and lacked the tact to express himself persuasively, and the only reason he continued to contribute to the debate, he said, was that he wanted to see a future for craftwork and that future was in the hands of the younger makers.[42] Unfortunately he also felt some doubt about who these younger makers actually were, since 'Roger Powell made the point that the young craftsmen are not as the older ones are, and that Haymarket under more or less any terms, is their pitch, not Swyre.' In other words, they wanted their work represented in the Design Centre, not surprisingly perhaps, in view of its lively display policy, publicity value, and popularity.[43]

Barnsley urged Wood to talk to Mrs Pocock at the Crafts Centre to make sure that there was no misunderstanding about encroachment, but already Wood's proposals for Swyre were coming into potential conflict with plans for Hay Hill. Barnsley felt that the essential was to have a thoroughly convincing Crafts Centre of Great Britain and he was anxious lest money be drawn away from this ideal towards the Swyre project.[44] As Wood began to think in bigger terms, Edward drew back a little, suggesting that views should be sought from others, insisting that consideration be given to the position of staff at the Crafts Centre, and urging patience while Wood established himself.

By now, Wood's ideas had moved a stage further and instead of providing a small exhibition gallery in Gloucestershire, his aim was to reform the Crafts Centre. Barnsley was quick to tell him to consult with John Farleigh or members of the relevant societies. 'Perhaps Francis Cooper's plan is a sensible first move', he suggested, and 'Sandy Cockerell is clear headed in ways which I am not, and combines the right ideas with practical outlook & sensible knowledge of "people", or that is how I see him. A better man for talk than Barnsley I fancy.'[45]

David Kindersley reported to the Council of the Society of Designer-Craftsmen in December 1963[46] that Wood had proposals to put forward, and at a meeting of the Council of the Crafts Centre, Wood's plans were supported by Barnsley, Kindersley, Cooper, and Margrie, and he was asked by Farleigh to prepare a memorandum detailing his proposals. At a meeting on January 18th, Farleigh resigned as Chairman of the Crafts Centre Council and Wood saw prospects of himself becoming Director.[47] Barnsley, however, was still urging caution. To ensure success he thought it necessary to get a commitment from about 85 per cent of the craftsmen rather than a simple majority which might break down later, and he was adamant that makers should be excluded from the organization, though 'this point is a dangerous one, and probably best left out or played very gently. Norris and his lot, if he carries them with him, are absolutely dead against admitting that they are not best qualified to do all this sort of thing. (Against the evidence I should assume, wouldn't you?!!)' He also wanted to be sure that any challenges were properly met and, if justified, incorporated into the plan, which would be strengthened by the 'honest facing of opposing views'. 'Even a Norris has his contribution to make! How I like to pontificate. John Farleigh should not be left out, it may take time. He's done a great deal for "the crafts", and the way in which he has gone is a sorry one, it seems to me, not altogether worthy, and certainly hardly just'.[48]

Taking time was not part of Wood's plan to establish the Crafts Council of Great Britain; he saw a need for it now, and at this critical moment, the less said about Farleigh the better.[49] The aim was to set standards, make the crafts more accessible and more widely understood, to promote research, to establish relations between the crafts and industry and to provide a variety of services such as publicity, a newsletter, an index of makers, touring exhibitions, and training. His plan was very similar to that set out in Kindersley's earlier document, but unlike Kindersley and others, he was against a close association with the Design Council and wanted an organization for the crafts on the same basis as the Arts Council, with money from the government provided without strings. The Board of Trade had anyway made it clear that it was against a Crafts Centre within the Design Centre.[50]

At the Extraordinary A.G.M. called in January, Farleigh resigned from the Crafts Centre as Chairman, Council member and ordinary member, in

60. John Farleigh, the wood-engraver, whose tireless campaigning for the crafts had brought about the foundation of the Crafts Centre of Great Britain. He was Chairman from its inception in 1947 until 1964.

spite of efforts by Kindersley to persuade him that the proposed changes owed much to his own ideas. Wood's scheme was explained and questions were asked about the representation of craftsmen on the new proposed Council, with Barnsley promoting his usual view that makers were not competent to run such things and Bernard and Michael Leach holding out for a 50 per cent representation. It was proposed that the Crafts Centre should change into the Crafts Council of Great Britain, but solicitors advised that there should be two bodies, with the Crafts Council responsible for raising money for the Centre. Wood was invited to become Director, but wanted to know the views of the members before he accepted.[51]

The members were persuaded by his arguments, he did accept and the Crafts Council of Great Britain was formed in 1964, housed at first within the premises of the Crafts Centre and later at 47 Victoria Street, London SW1. In early February, Edward sent a long list of suggestions for potential council members, including craftspeople, since he recognized that his view on their exclusion was a minority opinion, but a leaflet produced not long after shows how effective his earlier arguments had been. Members of the general Council were Barnsley himself, Sir Cyril Black, Sydney Cockerell, Peter Collingwood, John Cordle, John Dunkerley, Viscount Eccles, David Hardman, Laurence Irving, Lady Jamieson, A. Everett Jones, Lieut-Col. Alister Maynard, J. D. B. Mountrose, Nicholas Ridley, Gordon Russell, Lady Sempill, and Lord Wilmot of Selmeston. The Duke of Edinburgh, who had been President of the Crafts Centre, agreed to be President of the new Crafts Council.[52] The aims of this body were similar to those put forward by Farleigh in 1948, the major difference being one of ultimate control: the five societies which ran the Crafts Centre would no longer control the Crafts Council, which was to have policy formulated by trustees and administered by the Director.

Wood as Director had the advantage of years of working in arts administration and a sharp political sense of whom to approach for money and help. A dapper man in black suit and bow tie, he appeared very much an establishment figure, and this probably assisted his negotiations with civil servants and government bodies. He enlisted support from a wide range of influential people and raised a lot of money, but many of the craftspeople resisted his charm. Like Farleigh before him, he wanted to change the image of the crafts, but he could be undiplomatic and he alienated some of the craftspeople by expressing a desire to do away with the 'beard and sandals' image at a meeting chaired by Kindersley, a bearded craftsman of the Eric Gill school. Some who supported him and helped with exhibitions or events also felt that while he was friendly when they were needed, he would often cut them when the work was done and there were more important people to talk to. Perhaps also because he was not a maker, he never received the whole-hearted support necessary to make a truly representative body of his Crafts Council, and he tried to make changes too fast. He wanted to decentralize from London, for instance, which caused disagreements with Kindersley and Margrie.[53]

The Crafts Centre carried on under the chairmanship of David Kindersley, until the problem of funding recurred in late 1964 and the newly formed Crafts Council proposed to close down Hay Hill. Kindersley appealed to the Council to think again, for the Centre had been operating for sixteen years and decisions were now being made with scant regard for dedicated staff, who had built up contacts and knowledge over this period. Moreover, although it had been in existence for six months, the Council had not yet stated what plans it had for a London showroom, nor its arrangements for choosing objects. Kindersley was clearly worried that the Council's ideas were too commercial, that too much emphasis would be given to saleable work at the expense of the Centre's role as a showplace, and that expertise would be lost as a result of too-rapid change, concerns which sound remarkably familiar from events in the 1980s. In addition, the Crafts Centre was hampered in its appeal for money by the fact that the Duke of Edinburgh was now President of the Crafts Council and no longer of the Crafts Centre, a change Kindersley had warned against for this very reason.[54]

Barnsley took exception to Kindersley's paper and drafted a letter disagreeing with his direct approach to members of the Crafts Council. He also wrote to the Editor of *The Times*, suggesting that the crafts needed a clean break, and that full support should be given to Wood. In December another letter to the Secretary of the Crafts Centre gave his opinion that the recent A.G.M. had been the most deplorable and despicable event in the history of the Arts and Crafts Movement.[55]

Eventually it was decided that the Crafts Centre and Crafts Council would have to be divorced and the available government grant split between them. The Centre was to remain as a showcase in London with a modified constitution and from 1965 a new Chairman, Graham Hughes, formerly Art Director of the Goldsmiths' Company.[56] By 1969 the Crafts Centre was ensconced in new premises at 43 Earlham Street in Covent Garden with an annual grant of £4000 a year and further income from sales and recommendations, while the Crafts Council received a grant of £5000.[57] The Crafts Council had Gordon Russell as its Chairman for four years until he resigned because of pressure of work. It continued working on exhibitions, and over the following years toured a number of successful shows to all parts of Britain, making links between craft and industrial skills by putting displays in venues such as the Bristol Aeroplane Company and Rolls Royce factories in Coventry and Shrewsbury. Such exhibitions included work by makers across the whole spectrum of the crafts and design. It also continued to campaign for more funds 'to provide a service to the crafts comparable to that given to the arts by the Arts Council', and some consider that Wood's work sowed seeds which were reaped later.[58]

In addition to the exhibition service, the Crafts Council established an index of craftspeople and in 1971 it moved to premises at 12 Waterloo Place. Barnsley hoped that people would support this, but he had realized some years before that others did not approve of Wood and he thought that he himself had lost the confidence of other makers because of his role in the formation of the Council. He also believed they felt he had used the Swyre exhibition for his own ends. His justification was that he had tried to set a standard and had also sent other people's work, but he was aware of his 'incorrigible habit of criticism and preachifying' and now felt he had made a mistake over the directorship.[59] He had discovered the drawbacks to the policy he had urged upon his contemporaries, of non-interference with the executive powers of the Director, when Wood appointed two designers of whom Barnsley disapproved to choose and display objects in a 1965 exhibition: 'And the Director certainly directs! He and chairman selected these two men, and no consultation as far as I know with Council members. I suppose it's got to be like this, but it does make me anxious about CW, as so many have been.'[60]

When asked to be on committees and to take on such roles as the Mastership of the Art Workers' Guild, Barnsley usually suggested alternative names and claimed that he was unsuitable for various reasons.[61] He did, however, serve on the Crafts Council and in 1967 he was back on the committee of the Designer-Craftsmen, where he suggested an exhibition limited to makers under thirty, an idea which 'didn't go down well'.[62] By the following year he had given up, though he regretted that he was no longer actively contributing something to the future of crafts, because he was worried that the 'gentler people are pushed out by the less gentle and that on the whole the less gentle are pushing for the wrong reasons and they destroy'.[63] He himself was not involved in the formal world of the crafts in 1971 when the Crafts Advisory Committee was established, but the policies of the C.A.C. and its published aims were clearly based on those of both the Crafts Centre and the Crafts Council, and its grant of £45,000 a year, increasing very rapidly every year (to £178,000 in 1972/3 and £304,700 in 1973/4), made the success of these aims more likely than ever before.[64]

The Crafts Advisory Committee's grant was obtained by the persuasive powers of David Eccles, Minister for the Arts, and came from the Arts branch of the Department of Education and Science. It started with administrative services provided by the Design Council and with Paul Reilly from the Design Council as its Chief Executive, but was emphatically not under the control of the Council of Industrial Design.[65] Sir Paul Sinker of the Rural Industries Bureau was Chairman and Victor Margrie, Secretary. Its predecessor bodies were persuaded (or forced?) in 1972 to merge as the British Crafts Centre and in the following year the Crafts Advisory Committee took over the Waterloo Place building, while the British Crafts Centre retained the gallery at Earlham Street (where it is still based, though now known as Contemporary Applied Arts). It was for this gallery, at the request of Lord Eccles, that Barnsley designed one of his major pieces of the next few years.

7. RENEWED INTEREST IN THE ARTS AND CRAFTS

Barnsley's plans for a book – lectures on the place of the crafts in society – Gimson exhibition, 1969 – 'the grand old man of Designer Craftsmen' – Barnsley's reliance on his craftsmen – batch production in the workshop – more exhibitions – the last piece made by Barnsley, 1976

In the post-war period, the demands of the workshop and garden, teaching, and craft committees left little time for leisure. The few holidays the Barnsleys took were usually spent in the Lake District, where Tania's brother had a weekend cottage on which Edward would work in gratitude for the use of the place, and where he also enjoyed long walks. Much of Barnsley's social life, such as his pleasurable visits to clients, was bound up with his work and even his commitment to the Campaign for Nuclear Disarmament and regular attendance at the Aldermaston marches in the fifties and sixties resulted in a commission, for a wooden cross carried by Christian pacifists. He continued to enjoy singing Gilbert and Sullivan and maintained his contacts at Bedales, and also attended meetings in London of the Art Workers' Guild and, later, the William Morris Society, where he

61. A demonstrator carrying the cross made for the Anglican Pacifist Fellowship in 1961. Barnsley later recalled that he and Tania were the only people from Petersfield to attend the first Aldermaston march.

found interesting company and pleasant conversation with people concerned with the same issues as himself.[1]

In 1959 and the early 1960s, Barnsley had devoted much of his early-
morning writing time to making notes for a book, which give a clear
indication of his preoccupations at this date.[2] He wanted firstly to set the
record straight about the work of Gimson and the Barnsleys, and to rescue
the reputation of his father, whose contribution to the Cotswold style had
not been widely recognized. The work was known to a small band of
enthusiasts, mainly people who had had some kind of personal contact
either with the Sapperton craftsmen or with Waals or Edward, but the
revival of scholarly interest was yet to come, and Barnsley wanted to correct
some common misconceptions. He had been offered the opportunity in 1944
when John Farleigh had asked him to contribute a chapter to *Fifteen
Craftsmen on Their Crafts*,[3] but he had felt unequal to the task then, and Eric
Sharpe had taken it on, devoting his whole chapter to the story of Gimson
and the Barnsleys, with a slightly barbed reference to others who could tell
it better than he if they tried.

Barnsley's second aim was to write a book which would be useful to
teachers of woodwork in schools and colleges, a group with whom he had
much contact, because of his Loughborough work and his occasional
lectures elsewhere, and whom he believed to be essential for the continuation of the crafts.

The most difficult task he set himself was to deal with the problem of
'design' in a practical and down-to-earth fashion. His aim was to inspire
readers to think for themselves rather than persuade them to his own point
of view, though he did want to convince them of the importance of craft
workshops. These he considered to be even more important now technology
and scientific invention dominate the world. He was not a sentimental
backward-looker but genuinely marvelled at new industrial techniques,
such as the invention of 'float' glass by Pilkington's, which he described
with great enthusiasm to Vera Simpson in 1977.[4]

His notes for the design section of the book, ranging from abstract
concepts to particularities about arrises and cross-banding, make interesting
reading but perhaps indicate why he never got very far with it: 'Problem of
individual appreciation of beauty, problem of novelty, can we say there is
such a thing as good design? comparison of designs, ref. to G Russell Ltd,
beauty, design, to plan — arrange how a thing shall be made, experiment,
anchors for thought as background to work, purpose, materials, construction, fitness, proportion, harmony, examples of details based on fitness for
purpose & pleasure in use, overall dimension and shape, sliding sashes,
shutter front in place of doors, handles, examples of use of solidwood when
veneer is right treatment, examples of new materials and new design', and
so on.[5]

Through his client Arthur Mitchell he had some correspondence with
Tudor Edwards, a writer who suggested he might instead produce a popular
book of reminiscences about his life, and he approached Allen and Unwin in

1966 because they had asked him to write a book about design twenty years before. He picked up his notes again and again, but he found that he was unable to co-ordinate exactly what he wanted to express, and by 1968 he knew that he couldn't do it. 'For years I have wished to produce an adequate book about Gimson and the brothers Barnsley — only I could do what is required here, or what I think is required, but firstly I can't write, secondly I lack tenacity, thirdly I prefer hard physical labour, opportunities for which are constant and many here, fourthly I can rightly claim that I'm fairly fully occupied as it is. But, these are excuses. How do you do it?', he wrote to Fiona MacCarthy.[6]

As part of the same effort to put forward his views about the Arts and Crafts Movement, Barnsley also gave talks to groups of educationalists or craftspeople, preparing very carefully, writing out his ideas and memorizing the points so that he could speak without notes. If only he could express himself properly, he could convince his listeners of the importance of the place of the craftworker in society. Inevitably, he sometimes left things out or failed to phrase them as he had intended, came away feeling that he had failed, and often needed a session of heavy work in the garden to dispel his depression.

He also occasionally gave talks at colleges, though he never enjoyed these as much as his less formal work in the workshops at Loughborough. He made an annual visit to see the students' work at Redland College in Bristol and was amused when in 1969 a friend at Redland apologized for not having invited him for over eighteen months but explained that the previous year's students had insisted that they could learn nothing from someone over 60. 'Jolly refreshing was my reply, and my word, won't it give me a happy opening when I do go down next time'.[7]

On more than one occasion, he was invited to speak at Attingham, the country house near Shrewsbury owned by the National Trust, where his friend Sir George Trevelyan was Warden. Trevelyan said later that he simply organized courses about subjects that he wanted to know more about, and Attingham became the venue for meetings held by the Society of Designer-Craftsmen on subjects such as 'The Place of Crafts in our Time' and 'The Training of Craftsmen' in the 1960s.[8] An earlier gathering called 'Educating the Public' seems to have been typical and brought together about forty manufacturers and retailers to discuss how to improve design in the furniture trade. Talks were given by Gordon Russell and Paul Reilly of the Council of Industrial Design, David Pye, Alec Jessup of Harris Lebus Limited, Jack Pritchard of the Furniture Development Council, and Wyndham Goodden of the Scottish Committee of the C.O.I.D.[9]

One of Barnsley's talks, to the National Society for Art Education in 1966 was tape-recorded and a transcript survives in the Trust archives, revealing that he could be a little rambling in his argument but very persuasive. He quoted his favourite D. H. Lawrence poem, 'Things men have made with wakened hands, and put soft life into, are awake through years with transferred touch, and go on glowing for long years. And for this reason, some old things are lovely, warm still with the life of forgotten men who made them.' Then, defusing any possible offence by explaining his attitude to constructive criticism and 'people of quality', he launched into his central theme, the importance of making and the purpose of education to draw out the talents of pupils through practical work, rather than to impose ideas upon them. His subject was 'The Future of Fine Craftsmanship' so he spoke of the need to recognize craftwork as something warm and human in contrast to the undoubted but different qualities of machine products, and he described the position of his own workshop as an instructive case study. One lesson he took from his own story was that without the security of a regular income from Loughborough he might have put more effort into securing the future through such bodies as the Crafts Council and Crafts Centre, and that craftspeople must put their differences aside in order to change the general view of their work. Since he was talking to teachers he also mentioned the benefits of working within pleasant surroundings and the low standard of furniture and buildings in schools, and he returned to the main theme, quoting 'the late Dr. L. P. Jacks, that "every rise in the quality of the work which a man does is followed swiftly and inevitably by a rise in the quality of the man who does it." ' Every argument was put with a personal illustration and provocative comments were balanced by self-deprecating asides which in the transcript conjure up a vivid picture of the man talking.[10]

It was of some comfort to him that a revival of interest in Gimson and the Barnsleys occurred in the 1960s and he was able to make his corrections to the story in a stream of long letters, which he saw partly as a way of accumulating information until such time as it could be made into 'a more useful set of notes'.[11] For years he had been writing about the fundamental principles of the Arts and Crafts Movement, about the importance of Morris and the falsity of the myths which had grown up about Morris's attitude to machinery, seeing the question very differently from design historians of the period because he did not accept the tenets of the Modern Movement and was trying to live according to Morris's principles. He also wrote admiringly about C. R. Ashbee, as in a letter to George Trevelyan: 'Have you a copy of "Craftsmanship in Competitive Industry" by C R Ashbee? I dip into it from time to time and find it interesting. Mainly about the Guild of Handicraft and its problems at Chipping Campden. A man of great courage and of tenacity of purpose. I think you would find it worth reading. To me it's very sound and I am left with a regret that the Guild failed. The actual things they made were too much Art Nouveau for my liking, but the human social venture was of a fine quality.'[12]

This did not mean that he felt there was no room for criticism and he disagreed with contemporaries of his own who thought that all of their heroes' work was wonderful: 'This just will not do now-a-days, especially for the younger interested generation. They accept the greatness of a William Morris, but they do not, much, like his work. And there is so much of it that is not really greatly to warm one's heart. I myself, as I have so often said

62. Edward Barnsley photographed in 1976 at the desk with its beautiful outlook where he often sat very early in the morning. Here he wrote the long letters in which he put down his thoughts on the place of the crafts in society.

consider Morris a man head and shoulders above any of his colleagues, in the way of his simple, definite true beliefs, and his clear understanding of what socialism and communism are really about, especially if you word the beliefs differently and can get away from "isms". But, there is not the same wonder in his works, to my mind, and I believe we lose our case with the young by overstating it.'[13]

From the late 1960s he put his case to the wide variety of correspondents who contacted him. These ranged from a schoolboy embarking on an O-level project, to whom he sent a two-page letter closing with his cherished quotation from D. H. Lawrence; through the younger generation of design historians, such as Fiona MacCarthy, dealing with Gimson and the Barnsleys as a part of a wider survey; to his contemporary and cousin by marriage, Olga Barnsley, writing from Australia.[14] She was attempting to make sense of her early memories of Sapperton and her feeling that it had been a failure, by relating it to other attempts to live the 'good life', such as Eric Gill's community at Capel-y-ffin. Her four-page close-typed letter elicited a nine-page close-typed response, both documents illuminating considerably the motives, personalities, and achievements of the Gimson–Barnsley group, as well as Barnsley's view of Gill in a brief aside: 'I know too little of him to venture an opinion, but will just say that something seemed, and seems, to me, "not quite genuine"!'[15] In response to this letter Olga proposed to write a novel based on the story of the Sapperton group, to be entitled 'Never a Dark Corner' after Alice Barnsley's frequent lament over the house in Birmingham which she had to give up when the family went to live in the country. While Edward agreed with Olga about the beauty of Sapperton '"bathed in the warm glow of the setting sun, just like a Samuel Palmer", yes indeed', and he also had intimations of a hidden side of village life — 'there was the strife, the startling incests and fornications, the meannesses, ignorances and hating'[16] — he clearly thought she was being a bit over-dramatic about relations within the Gimson and Barnsley families, and their correspondence petered out.

His view expressed to Olga about the work of Gimson and the Barnsleys was that it 'never quite "flowered"',[17] but he was quick to defend them against 'that fellow Russell' and his 'damnable preface', when Gordon Russell wrote in the catalogue of the 1969 'Ernest Gimson' exhibition at Leicester Museum a piece which misunderstood the fundamental basis of Gimson's work, and by implication, Edward's too. 'As far as I'm concerned, he's "out". I enjoyed his autobiography, thought it a good job, though too much claiming for self, he's climbed up, a good deal, on the work and reputation borrowed from others, especially his brother R.D., and namesake Russell, manager of the firm, a very competant and charming man.'[18] His opinion of Russell was not consistent for in 1978 he wrote to Paul Reilly about trying to influence the Crafts Advisory Committee in a different direction and suggested that Reilly should get together with Russell, since 'Gordon had the position and experience to do more than EB.'[19] By contrast, he was full of praise for Sir George Trevelyan and his contribution to the Leicester catalogue, and for the generosity of spirit which shines through it.

The Leicester exhibition, organized by Lionel Lambourne to commemorate the fiftieth anniversary of Gimson's death, was the first large-scale and nationally publicized display of Gimson–Barnsley work since the days of the Arts and Crafts Exhibition Society, was attractively displayed, and gained a lot of attention.[20] Although Edward was, as always, qualified in his praise, since he thought some of Gimson's best pieces had been left out and there was too much of Waals, he considered it 'a very fine achievement indeed.'[21] Apart from the preface, he found errors of fact or interpretation in other parts of the catalogue and wrote screeds of corrections for museum files and for circulation to interested friends such as Humphrey Gimson. This became his standard practice when anyone wrote about Gimson and the Barnsleys, and his pages of notes picking up unfair inferences and small errors are very illuminating, though not always themselves accurate.

The attention generated by the exhibition, which included as examples of the 'Living Tradition' several items designed by Edward, resulted in an increased interest in the Froxfield workshop over the next few years, which was of course good for business and very welcome. Barnsley was approaching his fiftieth anniversary in business and was investigating the possibility of an exhibition at the Victoria and Albert Museum, without success. Like his father, he was never very good at publicity. He wanted appreciation and enjoyed praise but felt it was devalued if it had to be sought out. He was very tentative when he asked Sir George Trevelyan to consider writing an article about the workshop for *Country Life* in 1973, in spite of the fact that they were very old friends and enjoyed an understanding based on similar values. 'How stupid of me to write you about Gimson–Barnsley–Waals having special lives, as I've said above, you who know so much of it and have it in your very bones!', he wrote in 1973.[22] Although Barnsley provided notes and Trevelyan drafted an article, it seems not to have been published because Edward delayed in responding to the draft.[23] This was partly because Max Burrough, who had published pioneering articles on Gimson and the Barnsleys in *Connoisseur* in 1969, contributed one about Edward to the same magazine in 1973, in celebration of the anniversary.

John Norwood of the Hampshire County Museum Service had also visited in 1972, armed with a tape-recorder, and included Barnsley in a book on Hampshire craftsmen published in 1977; and the *Illustrated London News* printed an article about him in 1973.[24] Visitors coming for information were made welcome by Edward and Tania and were often invited to lunch, a good meal which usually finished with delicious fruit from the garden and home-made yogurt. The cottage was a revelation of what the Arts and Crafts Movement was about, with its oak table scrubbed white from years of use and the early Sidney Barnsley dresser, which Edward had inherited after his mother's death, providing shelf space for pots by Bernard Leach and Lucie Rie, one chosen by the potter for Edward and the other purchased as a second at the Crafts Centre. Edward was particularly keen on pottery and had a number of pieces by contemporaries as well as many lovely wares painted by his sister and a set by Alfred and Louise Powell which he had ordered when he got married. In later years he also occasionally bought other items at the Crafts Centre, an alabaster bowl by David Kindersley and various small sculptural figures. Much of the furniture in the cottage was by his father or from his own workshop, apart from an eighteenth-century long-case clock from his mother's family home, the rather ordinary desk at which he worked, and an easy chair made by a teacher at Lydney Art School.

As Edward was approached by more and more people for information about himself, he began to schematize the details he gave out, describing events in similar terms in letters to different people, emphasizing particular points and glossing over others, probably simply by force of repetition. Even when he elaborated on the basic facts it was usually on specific themes, such as Bedales, Gilbert and Sullivan, or the use of machine tools, and he said little on some topics, such as his year at the Central School and his work for the Crafts Centre, either because he felt they were of minor importance, or perhaps because he felt he had not achieved much. Eventually, the listing of events and influences in his life seems to have become like building up his own image almost as something to hang on to, like the quotations he was so fond of, from Plato, Wright and Lawrence. Of these, he said that he had 'for long held the view that memorising quotations is sound policy, and greatly assists in the planning of works. In so far that the quotation becomes, because it is in the memory and not sorted out on any particular occasion, a part of one's automatic actions, therefore likely to be spontanious and not a sort of applied principle when one's on the job'.[25]

In 1971 he was amused, but also a little mortified by a reference to himself as 'the grand old man of Designer Craftsmen', though some of his feelings were connected with the fact that the writer concerned clearly thought his work had peaked in the 1920s.[26] At an exhibition of the Devon Guild of Craftsmen in the early seventies it was evident to him that the furniture makers were unable to break away from the ideas of Gimson and the Barnsleys and that his own work had been influential.[27] He was also very gratified by the company he kept in a G.C.E. Woodwork exam question which asked for a description and sketch of a work by Charles Rennie Mackintosh, Edward Barnsley, William Morris, or Robert Adam.[28] He seems to have been increasingly conscious of his position as the elder statesman of the furniture crafts and began to refer to himself as 'old Barnsley', though in his letters he never lost his self-questioning.

Discussing Sir George Trevelyan's essay in the Leicester Museum Gimson exhibition catalogue, Barnsley wrote in 1972, 'Trevelyan is, in his writing, concentrating on furniture, and furniture of the small special group of which I am now the "unquestioned leader", and anybody less like a leader I am still to meet. But this matter of being something in the nature of a known person for known works in one's own lifetime, that is not altogether rare, of course, but it's not common, and I am sometimes asked vague questions about what it feels like. Well, really it doesn't feel like anything because that's not the way I feel.' There were times, he said, when he lay in bed wondering about whether it had all been worthwhile, and he continued:

> How few, how very few are fortunate to produce things that do remain, and that are constant reminders of facts. Those who produce in the higher arts & crafts, in those which pass but do not pass — music, poetry, drama, writings generally, and above all ideas — they are above the material, but they touch

comparatively few. Furniture can, and sometimes does, touch people very closely and leaves a something behind in their own lives and their own personalities, and in that way a happy design and a well made job plays a fairly high ranking part in human affairs. And an even greater, far greater importance lies in the actual making. There is, I think, something of extreme value in the human experiences of making a fine thing. Even more important, perhaps, than the results or effects of making non-material things. Perhaps, only perhaps, and I'm not at all sure what exactly I am trying to say. I do have a vague belief, unexpressible, that our placing the higher arts too high, we have caused a loss to human experiences and to human advance towards happiness in life. Our emphasis is, I fancy, unbalanced. When the majority of men were artists or craftsmen, or both, and the change is quite recent after all, life had values which have gone, and their going is a disaster. It is not, I think, unreasonable to answer the statement "but all people can't be craftsmen" by the reminder that historically most of them were at one time, and for century after century, and one can add that the world will not recover its balance and its poise and its values until most of them are once more.

He was not entirely pessimistic and thought it possible that computers would make it possible for people to achieve leisure and a knowledge of how to use it, 'and then the marvel of rediscovery that life is truly enjoyable, rightly creative, and that we are moving towards the light.' For himself, 'It always causes me disappointment and some shame that I have never faced up to anything in my life, hardly. Always run away, and the job has got me along in spite of myself!! You may be inclined to say, rubbish, but you would be wrong. This little admission gives some sort of balance and correction to the first part of my self congratulating letter.'[29]

Self-congratulating he was not, and while in person he remained affable and expansive in company, privately he became more introspective and devastatingly self-critical, writing, for instance, to George Trevelyan, 'I was never able to build up any proper fund of knowledge or of feeling, and have always had to fall back on things very near surfaces, and to try to "get away with" a certain modicum of charm, and on limited degrees of ideologies'.[30]

While he composed his long letters and pondered on the ultimate value of making furniture and whether he had added anything to 'the world' by his efforts, the workshop carried on as usual, and continued to cause anxiety. Clive Balcombe had left in 1968, after sixteen years and when Malcolm Clubley found that he could no longer manage on his wages after his marriage in the early 1970s, having proved his commitment by travelling twenty miles each way to work every day for twelve years or so, Barnsley felt he had reached crisis point. Not only was Clubley an excellent craftsman who had just made 'a faultless job' of a chair and prayer desk for the Archbishop of Canterbury, but Edward had started the year by making what he thought was a generous increase in wages 'as a friendly gesture to those who hold the firm together.'[31] If Clubley left, the staff would be down to two craftsmen, both in their fifties, a pupil, Michael Bowen, and Bert Upton, who

63. Malcolm Clubley and Bert Upton upholstering the seats of the Magdalen College chairs, 1971. Upton generally preferred new materials, methods, and tools to traditional ones.

like Barnsley was approaching his fiftieth anniversary in the business and did not want to go on for ever.

The temporary solution was an increase in Clubley's wages by between 20 and 25 per cent, travelling-money where needed, and a reduction in the working week from forty-four to forty hours.[32] Barnsley thought this had worked and wrote 'Upton, Taylor, Oskar Dawson and the youngest, Malcolm, are all doing wonderful work, and I think they are happy, and certainly the rates of pay are now more reasonable'.[33] Unfortunately it was not enough, and in 1973 Clubley left, eventually to set up his own workshop, which is still in business in Portsmouth. Coincidentally, an article by Patrick Reyntiens appeared in *Crafts* magazine in May of that year, describing the problems for craft workshops in making adequate pension arrangements and paying enough for a maker to afford a mortgage since 'some might say one of the prerequisites of a man's dignity today is to own a house.'[34] When Malcolm Clubley left the workshop his pay was £1 per week less than the £30 Reyntiens considered the minimum. Upton had been pressing for years to

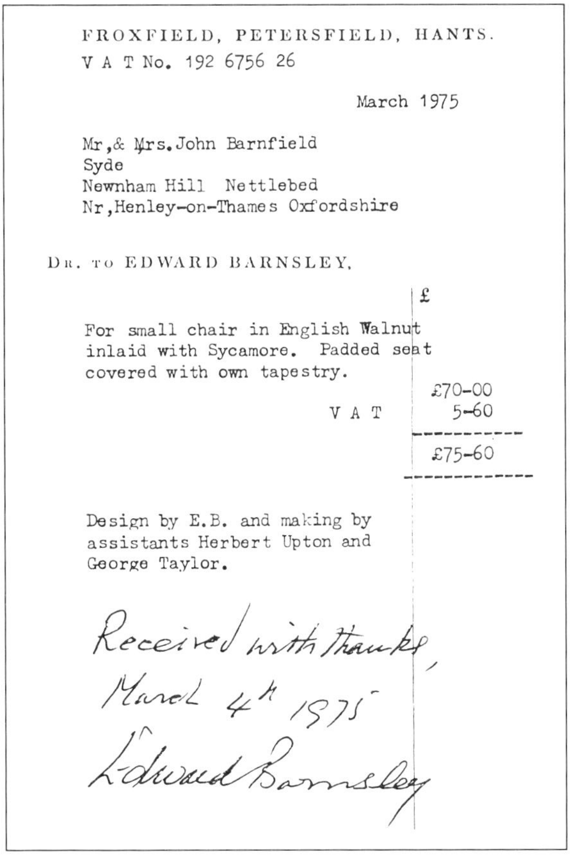

64. A bill of 1975 to Barnsley's long-standing clients, John and Rotha Barnfield, illustrating his normal practice of crediting the makers of a piece.

FROXFIELD, PETERSFIELD, HANTS.
V A T No. 192 6756 26

March 1975

Mr,& Mrs.John Barnfield
Syde
Newnham Hill Nettlebed
Nr,Henley-on-Thames Oxfordshire

DR. TO EDWARD BARNSLEY.

	£
For small chair in English Walnut inlaid with Sycamore. Padded seat covered with own tapestry.	
£70-00
V A T	5-60
	£75-60

Design by E.B. and making by assistants Herbert Upton and George Taylor.

Received with thanks,
March 4th 1975
Edward Barnsley

take on a new apprentice and probably Clubley's departure, along with the fact that the order book looked healthy,[35] helped to convince Edward that this was necessary, so in 1974 the workshop was joined by Mark Nicholas.

By now, Edward himself did very little making because, as he explained in 1968, 'My work lies in the design side, almost entirely, though I do work at the bench occasionally, though never on a major item of furniture because skill departs with lack of continuity and it is not satisfactory to start and stop at a job; the interruptions upset rhythms and quality of work!'[36] In the following year he wrote about how much he was enjoying making a cigar box in rosewood, a timber he had not used before, but when he was finishing it he cut by mistake through the lining and had to add a decorative feature to disguise the damage.[37] He had always had a tendency to precipitate action, and an affectionate friend described him as the kind of person who would cut off the branch of a tree while he was standing on it.[38] He had ruined several pieces of furniture by 'altering' them, apparently without a moment's thought. The most distressing (for a museum curator) of these alterations was the removal of the curved upright which originally supported the centre of the shelves of the dresser Sidney Barnsley had made for his own home, and which still stands in the cottage in Froxfield, but the truncated foot end of Barnsley's bed and the bookshelves summarily sawn in two are almost equally shocking.[39] Barnsley usually defended himself stoutly against comment about the dresser, on the grounds that it was a poor design and he had improved it, but he protested perhaps too much and occasionally admitted that he might have been wrong.[40]

He still revelled in physical labour and at 5 o'clock one morning in 1969 started digging a hole in the garden which became known to the family as 'Edward's folly'. He decided it would be nice for his grandchildren to have a swimming pool to play in, so without any consultation he began excavating on the slope below the cottage. When he had succeeded in making a hole 10 feet deep and 37 feet wide he asked advice from an engineer friend, who said it was in the wrong place and would cost about £3000 to make solid and watertight. It would also have to be reinforced before the winter because it was likely to collapse and cause subsidence in the cottage. So having laboured to dig it out, in the same year he had to install iron girders and build a vast wall, 37 feet by 10 feet high. Since the swimming pool was now seen to be totally impractical, he began to think again about his earlier notion of a garden room, and he later applied for and got planning permission.[41] His intention was to withdraw, hermit-like, to this room in his old age, but the scheme never came to fruition.

In character with his impetuosity and liking for heavy labour, he was also careless and unsentimental about tools. Bert Upton often had to true up the T-squares which Edward used as cutting edges at the drawing board and seemed puzzled at Barnsley's lack of care for the bench and tools he had inherited from his father.[42]

Edward had no illusions about his skills, and he tried often to explain to outsiders how the workshop worked. In writing about the perfection of making, he said:

> My chaps achieve it. I never or very seldom did. I try hard to prevent a myth developing around myself and the wonderful craftsmanship, all of which is the work of assistants. Nobody believes a word you say if it happens to be critical and yet the truth about oneself.
>
> My daughter in law has it correct, when she says "oh but grandad, we are all frauds". The idea round here is that I'm always extremely busy, always making lovely things etc etc, whereas the truth is that the busyer the workshop is, the less I have to do, especially with the advance of batch-production (about 95 chairs in process at present) because the designs are made and work goes on for months. And for some time I have done no work at the bench. A proper fraud in fact.[43]

He continued to feel uneasy about batch production, while appreciating both the quality of work and his own rather more secure income. On a design for a mirror of 1977 he recorded two years later that a batch of twelve had been made by Oskar Dawson and noted with apparent surprise that they had 'sold well at £345 each!'[44] By 1969 the workshop had eight powered tools, a planer, circular saws, band saw, mortise machine, spindle moulder, belt sander, and dimension saw.[45] 'We have recently completed 58 chairs as one batch', he wrote in 1971, 'and Upton has demonstrated his

65. Barnsley with parts of chairs made by batch production, 1977. His expression aptly indicates his equivocal feelings about this method of producing furniture.

66. The machine shop in 1971, when the Magdalen College chairs were in production. From left to right are Malcolm Clubley using the controversial spindle moulder, Oskar Dawson at the band saw, and Bert Upton planing.

phenominal ability in planning the machining, and making simple jigs for processes on the machines, with the result that we were able to produce our work at a cost very startlingly less than would have been the case in the earlier days.'[46] By clever use of the machines, Upton found that he could produce accurately cut parts and make up each chair of a large order for Magdalen College in twenty-nine hours. Further comments three years later indicate Barnsley's ambivalence about such advances:

> The adaptations of certain machines, or rather the devising of 'gigs' by foreman, to permit processes to be carried out, in which one day achieves as much production as two or more weeks 'by hand', frightens me a little. But 90 chairs? How could one ask anybody to go on week after week, months in fact, repetitively dealing with the hundreds of parts and joints? What is the real truth about this? What, exactly, is the loss of quality? It's something real enough but hardly to be defined. I suppose the word "art" is the one that's gone away.[47]

Art, and specifically the craftsman's art, retained its central role for Barnsley, though in the 1970s he felt completely excluded from the organized world of the crafts. He was pleased about news of government money for the crafts in 1971,[48] which resulted in the founding of the Crafts Advisory Committee, though concerned about the number of organizers who put sales as first priority to the detriment of quality; and at first he was enthusiastic about a proposed exhibition, to be called 'The Craftsman's Art', at the Victoria and Albert Museum, but soon became enraged at the way this was handled.

> Put quite shortly, the committee started launching a national exhibition of crafts, by putting out big ideas, giving impression that it was going to be a really ambitious national thing, a big step with government monetary backing. This was followed by the issue of grand entry forms, again giving impression that if six items were offered, subject to reasonable selection, but of fine quality, then they stood an excellent chance of being shown. In the event, there was no intention of a big show, no space for one, and as an example, the southern region advance selection was made at Southampton and about 140 people offered works, of which 24 went on for final selection in London, and six only were chosen. Consider for a moment the work of the disappointed makers, the trouble, the costs involved! There is a row on as you may imagine. One of the younger furniture makers was declined, all his works, and I have refused to show, as a protest against this sort of thing. I had prepared six items, one specially hastened on to get it ready, and then only one item was to be accepted. Mild personal umbrage, but my protest is general, and its gone upstairs to Sir Paul Reilley, Director of the Design Centre (which holds control of the general administration of the funds) and perhaps it will have a small effect. He is trying to butter me up, and persuade me to change my decision, and refers to me and Russell as two 'masters' who ought both to be represented. What can be the justification for including Russell who was never a craftsman, went away from early works into industrial production about 40 years ago, has been among the many industrial chaps to denigrate and play down craftsmen, and now that William Morris is respectable, and Gimson and the Barnsleys being in the news and salerooms, these damned chaps begin to claim they knew them and admired them. Blasted humbugs, but how CAN justification be claimed for inclusion of Russell when space is inadequate to show the works or the transparencies of present-day men at work?[49]

In the end, the assessors of the furniture section, John Makepeace and Sandy Mackilligin, rejected most of the items offered and filled the gaps with work by Royal College of Art students, two of which were actually made by the college craftsman rather than by the students themselves. Ironically, Alan Peters had been asked to write the section on furniture making for the catalogue though none of his work was shown.[50]

When Barnsley visited 'The Craftsman's Art' exhibition he had overcome his umbrage enough to be enthusiastic about it on meeting an acquaintance, but within days he wrote to qualify his approval. On his first visit he had been taken by the originality of the display, the inventive touches, lovely things seen here and there and new ways of making or arranging materials, but he found these impressions did not hold up on subsequent visits. He was then more struck by the 'mixing up of the first class with the mediocre, the genuine lasting quality things with those which (at least to me) appear as gimmicks ... The determination to be new and different at all costs.'[51] Too much space was given to the general part of the exhibition, he felt, and should have been used to display items turned away, and the quality of the photographs he thought shockingly low. So he went to console himself by looking at the eighteenth-century furniture in the other galleries, which immediately prompted him to question some of his new methods of construction.

'The Craftsman's Art' was well-received by the public and had 26,000 visitors in its first three weeks.[52] For such as Ann Hartree, who was inspired to set up the Prescote Gallery in 1975, it was a revelation of what the crafts could be, and it also led to the opening of the British Crafts Centre shop within the V&A in 1974.[53] Clearly Barnsley's views were out of tune with the spirit of the times, so it is not surprising that he and the Crafts Advisory Committee (from May 1979, the Crafts Council) had little contact over the next fifteen years or so. He nursed ideas of being able to persuade others of the importance of doing and making, as opposed to talking, but he was perhaps too much connected with his father's generation. His designs evolved slowly and had changed little over the past decade, and his work simply did not appeal to a younger generation which rejected the earnest image of the craft pioneers in favour of new materials, new colours, a lighter spirit, in much the same way as some of the post-war generation of craftspeople had done in response to Farleigh's criticism.

Along with increasing confidence in the value of crafts, and greater experiment with form and materials, especially by makers trained in art colleges, there came a more definite shift in attitudes in the craft world from the 1970s. Following Morris, Barnsley had spent his life trying to show that craftwork could be a part of normal everyday life and that craft and art were the same kind of activity, requiring a combination of practical and intellectual skills. He was thwarted in the end, as Morris had been, by the fact that a capitalist industrialized society would only tolerate such work at its margins, and by the entrenched attitude that real 'art' is an activity of higher intellectual and financial value than craft.

His aim was to show by example that it was possible to lead an artist-craftsman's life, as his father and Ernest Gimson had done, producing furniture in competition with larger manufacturers. It is doubtful if he could have achieved more by devoting his life to campaigning for political change, but it seems clear that such change would be necessary to enable large numbers of people to live as he would have liked. For Morris and Gimson and the Barnsleys, it must have seemed that it was not too late to show society a different direction to aim for, but in the late twentieth century, most craftspeople have to find another way of making it possible to earn a living from their work. For many, the best hope seems to lie not in changing attitudes to art as a special activity, but in allying craft to art and thus raising its status and saleability. Once mass-produced, factory-made goods are accepted as an inevitable and often desirable part of life, craftwork has to compete on different grounds by emphasizing its unique and special qualities.

Barnsley could not accept this shift and was increasingly more comfortable away from the world of contemporary crafts and involved instead with conservation bodies and museums. In 1970 he made a concerted effort to recruit members for the National Trust, with some success, and he joined the Friends of the Lake District and similar groups. He occasionally suggesting to friends that they might sponsor his walks: he would do the first 25 miles for nothing and they could pay 1d for the first mile, 2d for the second, and so on thereafter. [54]

In 1975 he was delighted that Cheltenham Art Gallery and Museum planned a commemorative exhibition of the work of the Barnsleys, which he himself had suggested in 1969 after the Gimson exhibition because he felt they had always been undervalued. This was largely because of the earlier death of Gimson and the production of the Gimson memorial book in 1924.[55] Edward offered both to write the catalogue introduction and to open the show. His introduction failed to materialize and was written instead by Mary Comino with a foreword by Nikolaus Pevsner, but the opening was a great success, 'a very cheerful happy sort of evening ... (Due no doubt, as you will immediately think, to my cheerful words!)'[56] The exhibition itself attracted so much attention that the catalogue had to be reprinted and the displays of the permanent collections of Gimson–Barnsley work were subsequently enlarged and rearranged in acknowledgement of public interest.

67. The opening of the 1976 'Good Citizen's Furniture' exhibition at Cheltenham. Left to right are David Addison, the Museum Director, Tania and Edward Barnsley, the Mayor of Cheltenham, and Mary Comino, its organizer.

68. Edward Barnsley at a favourite activity, 1980: a particularly fine
photograph of the eyebrows likened by John Arlott to 'combative prawns'.

The exhibition also resulted in quite a number of new commissions
amounting to one year's work, and this period seems to have been financially more secure than any other in Barnsley's working life.[57] The order
book was very satisfactory and soon included the prestigious Jubilee Cabinet
(pls 96-8), Edward was granted a Civil List Pension of £550 a year, 'in
recognition of your services to furniture design and craftsmanship',[58] he
acquired a new car, only two years old, and had several holidays in
Cornwall and the Lake District. He had recovered from a gardening accident
which happened in September 1973 when a sharp sickle slipped, causing a
deep wound to his left wrist, though he was left with a slight stiffness, which
everyone told him was his own fault for attempting manual work too soon
afterwards. He also recovered from the depression that followed this injury.

1976 was also significant because in this year Edward Barnsley made his
last piece of furniture with his own hands and from now on his work was
mainly confined to producing designs. Although he was now 76, he had not
given up on the future and he spent much time pursuing suitable timber,
which he still often bought through William Inman, who though retired
from Turner's, put himself to considerable trouble on Barnsley's behalf,
locating particular woods and arranging purchases.[59]

8. THE POST-WAR FURNITURE AND CLIENTS

*Reassessment and experiment in the late 1940s and 1950s –
changing shapes and methods – veneers and inlays – new timbers
– a lighter style – Arthur Mitchell and other clients – corporate
commissions – Barnsley's mature work – the Jubilee Cabinet –
Barnsley's place as a designer and craftsman*

Up to the end of the Second World War, most of Barnsley's furniture
followed the style of the Cotswold group, using the same type of materials,
construction, form, and decoration. He introduced some features of his own,
such as the crossing stretchers of a cabinet of 1934,[1] the rectangular
modernism of the doctors' desks (pls 29 and 30), and what he considered
later to be the aberration of the wardrobe with an Art Deco sunray (p. 69),
but these affected only a small proportion of his work. The black and white
inlay of Gimson–Barnsley work became finer and appeared only rarely, but
in general Edward Barnsley reached middle age without consciously questioning the basic concept of the work. And why should he, given that there

69. Walnut furniture for the Dean's room at St Mary's Hospital, Paddington,
1947. This suite, still distinctly 'Cotswold' in style, was made just before
Barnsley's designs began to lighten up to suit the post-war mood.

were several other independent cabinet-makers, such as Romney Green, Eric Sharpe, and Stanley Davies following in the same path, without the personal background and early formative experience at Sapperton? Indeed, the 'revolutionary' ideas of Utility furniture, which caused quite a stir in the trade when introduced, owed much to the Cotswold tradition, stylistically at least, so this type of design was not considered old-fashioned by this date, except by comparison with modernist tubular metal furniture, which was anyway not well received in Britain. Since many buyers of furniture still preferred antiques or approximations of antique styles, Barnsley designs were still considered too modern by most.

Edward Barnsley in the 1940s came to a period in which he diverged from the path trodden by his father and began to develop a style which was recognizably his own, still based on the principles of Cotswold work, but mixed with the influence of the lighter eighteenth-century furniture he admired. The seeds of this change can be seen in some of the plainer pieces of the 1930s, the veneered desks and faceted chests, such as one made in 1937 for the Hon. R. W. Morgan Grenville,[2] but in the 1940s Barnsley began to integrate the qualities of these into a consistent range of features. The recognized moment of change was the talk given by John Farleigh as a critique of the Arts and Crafts Exhibition Society Exhibition in 1944, appealing to the craftspeople to respond to the lighter spirit of the age, but the new developments were really already on their way and were brought about by a combination of factors. The financial pressure to use machine tools and Upton's enthusiasm and ability with these increased the range of techniques possible in the workshop and gave Barnsley a new freedom with his designs, while shortages of timber after the war resulted in the importation of new woods. Barnsley's need to think about design matters for his work at Loughborough, and his contact there with students also brought him more up to date, and he may have absorbed something from the ideas of one of his own pupils, Robert Townshend, who favoured what he called the classical as opposed to the gothic approach to woodwork.[3]

In the late 1940s and the following decade Barnsley went through a period of radical reassessment, experimenting with a number of new forms until by the early 1960s he had found a thoroughly personal style which he refined gradually over the next twenty years.

The major changes to Barnsley's furniture in the immediate post-war period were in the shape and form of the pieces. Most domestic furniture was made smaller and lighter than before and some elements which had been taken over from the Gimson–Barnsley style, such as solid stepped feet, were replaced by lighter features, in this case, tapering legs. Barnsley had used these since the 1920s but they now became the standard form of base on his pieces and were often combined with shaped apron sections, the curvaceous lines of which gave a slightly French flavour.

From around 1945 to 1960 was the period of greatest elaboration in both shape and decoration of his furniture, a time of experimentation with new ideas, of selection and rejection.

70 and 71. Two pieces of 1959, characteristic of the lighter style evolved in this decade. A console table of walnut inlaid with goatskin tooled by Roger Powell; and a cupboard in mahogany with ebony and sycamore inlay, its shape and decoration much influenced by eighteenth-century work.

Barnsley started to experiment with different shapes, and instead of varying the front plane by using facets, he began in about 1950 to design bow fronts, sometimes combining a rounded central section with angled sides. Making a bowed front is more complicated and time-consuming than flat facets, but Upton's success in accomplishing this by joining the solid timber in an invisible line with the handles, and his interest in adapting the tools and techniques to suit the designer's wishes, presumably encouraged Barnsley to go on to even more complex serpentine shapes, which were achieved through the use of laminated layers. By the late 1950s a favoured shape had serpentine sides and front with canted corners, often with a shaped moulding or reeded decoration down the corners, closer to Adam and Linnell than Gimson and Barnsley. In 1948 Barnsley had drawn an eighteenth-century mirror which seems to have been in the workshop for repairs, and the reeded columns of this may have provided the idea for much of the decoration on pieces of the fifties.[4] He also appears to have been influenced by Betty Joel's work of the 1930s.[5]

Laminations were also employed for chair backs, initially with results that were financially disastrous since the backs cracked in use and further work was required.[6] The experiment was tried in order to save money, but because of the nature of the design the grain of the timber had to be placed all in the same direction. Barnsley thought some special new adhesives would be very strong but they dried out and the laminations split down the joints, demonstrating perhaps that changes of method prompted by financial constraints need to be researched before use.

72. Oskar Dawson and Mark Nicholas using the veneer press, about 1980.

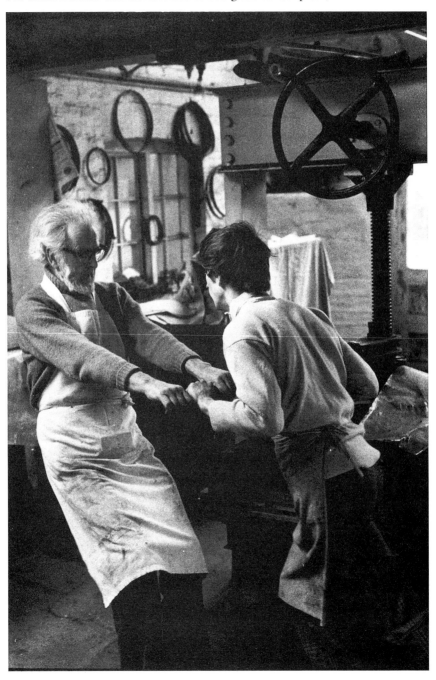

The frame and panel construction of Barnsley's early work was never entirely supplanted by flat veneered panels, but these were used increasingly and had a dramatic effect on the apparent and actual weight of the object. The visual effect of flat surfaces is more restful than that of panels, where changes of plane catch the eye and make the object seem more substantial, while the use of chipboard with veneer makes it possible to use thinner boards without risk of warping, thus making the piece physically lighter and more delicate in appearance. When fielded panels were used these were often shallower than before, and solid wood used for table tops and suchlike was also thinner in section.

Veneering was also used more often, partly in order to make pieces which would withstand the stresses imposed by the wider adoption of central heating, with its rapid temperature changes and lower relative humidity. Applying veneers was more expensive in terms of labour, but as good timber became harder to find it also seemed a better use of resources. According to William Inman, Barnsley started cutting his own veneers in the 1960s, getting about four or six from an inch board instead of the eleven per inch produced by the veneer merchants. He used thin bought veneers for the secondary parts of furniture and considered it impossible to achieve a properly finished surface on these without the use of filler.[7]

It was the acquisition of new machinery in the workshop that made possible the use of veneering on a large scale, and the same is true of other features adopted in the 1950s, such as the use of tambour fronts from about 1954. These occur on English furniture from the late eighteenth century and clearly can be cut entirely by hand, but in a small workshop they would be very expensive and although a few had been made at Froxfield before the war, they would not have been commercially viable until a reliable saw was

73. Sideboard with tambour doors, made for David Hellings in 1959. The delicately curved apron front was a feature of this period.

purchased.[8] Possible sources for the use of tambour doors may have been Betty Joel's furniture of the 1930s or Gordon Russell's book, *The Things We See: Furniture*, published in 1947, where Russell illustrated an American piece by Stonorov and von Moltke.[9] Cecil Gough at Loughborough advised Barnsley on how tambours should be made and practically wrote a manual for him.

Because they consist of narrow vertical strips of flat wood, tambours, like veneered panels, have the effect of lightening the appearance of the object when used in place of framed panels, and this theme was continued in the development of much lighter inlays, consisting of lines of a sixteenth of an inch in a single timber instead of the eighth-inch holly and ebony used by Gimson and Sidney Barnsley, and by Edward in his earliest work. He had questioned his father about this because he thought it unsuitable to use the same size of inlay on both large and small pieces, as Sidney Barnsley did simply because the lines were often cut using the circular saw, which only did one size. Edward himself had used little inlay in the 1930s. Now the thin line outlining drawers or flat planes or table edges became a hallmark of his work, consciously derived from Sheraton furniture, as he made clear in a letter where he referred to 'lovely streamlined engineering sorts of cabinets and boxes on stands — long tapering legs with the inlay usually of lines, beautifully emphasising the lines of the job itself. The start of the modern approach surely?'[10] Several woods were used but Barnsley preferred sycamore because the pale colour lightened the entire effect of the piece.

74. Side table in mahogany for Miss Elizabeth Watt, 1956, made in Barnsley's period of experimentation with shape and decoration derived from eighteenth-century furniture.

75. Metal handle by Frank Jordan on a chest of drawers of 1962 made by Barnsley himself as a late wedding present to his daughter, Karin. This detail shows the fine cogged dovetails at the corner as well as the effect of the pale sycamore inlay and ebony inset shape to which the handle is attached.

Inlay was also used along the lengths of the half-circular wooden handles adopted from the Cotswold style, making them appear thinner and more delicate, and lines on drawers were taken in graceful curves around metal and wooden handles, tying them into the overall design. The metal handles themselves, made by Biff Barker at Bedales or Frank Jordan, a teacher at Loughborough, also became lighter and thinner with more curve, and when he used the type of handles designed by Gimson, they were the small crescent-shaped silver handles which Gimson had put on the inner drawers of cabinets and desks, not the robust brass or steel drop-handles and plates seen on sideboards and chests of drawers.

Walnut, chestnut, and oak were still the most-used materials but new woods also made their appearance in the post-war period, partly because of shortages of native timber and the increased importation of exotic species, but also influenced by changing fashion. The 1925 Paris Exhibition had made rich, dark figured woods fashionable at the top end of the market but now some of the darker timbers, such as teak, were used by commercial furniture makers producing for a wider public. After the dullness of wartime and the wholesome plainness of Utility oak, customers seized on items made from rosewood and black bean because they were more dramatic and stimulating to the eye. Although Barnsley never designed anything as striking in its contrasts as Gordon Russell's 1950s furniture in rosewood with routed lines revealing a paler timber underneath, he did begin to use rosewood and black bean more frequently from about 1949. He also bought sapele, makore, and padauk. Black bean did not always give an exotic effect on its own, however, and Barnsley later criticized a bedroom suite of 1950 as 'alright' but pedestrian and lacking in interest.[11] The timber was very stable, had good colour and variation, but was unpleasant to work and was not much used in the sixties, though rosewood continued in favour.

76. Bedside table in mahogany with tooled leather panels by Peter Waters, Roger Powell's assistant, 1957. One of a pair made by Clive Balcombe in 157 hours for Mr and Mrs Dimitri Comino.

More contrast and pattern was provided on some pieces by the use of tooled leather panels, usually carried out in Roger Powell's workshop by Peter Waters, and Barnsley also designed pieces which incorporated ceramic tiles from the Crowan Pottery in Cornwall of Harry Davies, a contact from the Arts and Crafts Exhibition Society.

Before the war, Barnsley's work could be roughly divided, in Cotswold tradition, into plain, simple, and relatively cheap oak furniture which was left unpolished from the plane, and more elaborate 'cabinet-maker's work' in walnut and mahogany with decorative panels and beads. This division is a little arbitrary and there are examples of pieces in oak which are very similar to walnut items.[12] But usually oak was used as thicker timber and Barnsley preferred it 'left clean from the tool', ideally the plane, though a wide-bladed flat spokeshave was allowable if a scraper was necessary.[13] After Upton came back from the aircraft factory with new ideas and persuaded Barnsley to buy machine tools, this difference disappeared, and although pieces were still made in oak, there was no longer the same kind of contrast. Simple, undecorated oak pieces were made, but the thickness of the timber was now much the same as in other pieces, and the smoothness of the finish from the belt sander was uniform. On tables, this was further emphasized by the use of filler and spray cellulose varnish from about 1953,

77. Mark Nicholas in the spray bay, about 1980. Barnsley discovered the advantages of a cellulose finish in the 1950s, and though he never really liked, it the practical convenience for the client was paramount.

a treatment Barnsley never really wholeheartedly approved but which he acknowledged to be more practical than wax or oil.[14]

In terms of types of piece produced, the mixture was much as before, comprising a range of domestic items, an increasing number of larger commissions for boardroom tables and large sets of chairs, some prestigious work for churches and institutions, and prototypes and designs made for use by others.

Many of Barnsley's pre-war customers continued to order work from him and other members of their families often inherited their enthusiasm. Mrs Neale's daughters, Gonda Stamford and Barbara Holmes-Smith; Anthony Minoprio's son, John; and John and Rotha Barnfield's daughter, Jane; all commissioned pieces for their own houses after growing up surrounded by Barnsley furniture, and they continue to take an active interest in the workshop, some as Trustees and others as active supporters of the Trust's work.

After the death of Peter Waals, Barnsley gained the custom of Arthur Mitchell, who lived at Charlton Kings near Cheltenham in a large house which he filled with Cotswold furniture. Mitchell was Chairman of Mitchells and Butlers Brewery in Smethwick and may have come across Sidney Barnsley through Birmingham connections. In 1923 he asked Barnsley to design panelling for his house, The Glenfall, and this was made in Waals's workshop at Chalford since Sidney Barnsley could not deal with such a large job in his small shop.[15] During the later twenties and thirties Mitchell commissioned much more work from Waals, for his own family and occasionally for the brewery. At the period of the Depression he was among the few clients who made it possible for Waals to carry on his business and he was clearly a valuable connection for Edward.

The development of their association is in some ways typical of Barnsley's relations with clients, and in others unusual. There is an extensive correspondence between the two in the archive over the period 1952 to 1965 which documents the increasing friendship and respect of both parties, and it illustrates some general points about the relationship between client and maker.

Mitchell initially approached Barnsley for chairs for the Brewers' Society in 1939, a job which carried on over a long period, and he also commissioned a magnificent long-case clock in walnut. In 1953 he enquired about having a desk made for his daughter-in-law but then saw a Gimson piece at an auction sale and purchased this instead. At the same time he bought a Gimson table and sideboard[16] and asked Barnsley to overhaul the table and to design some new chairs to go with it. 'Please put your best craftsmen on this work' he wrote in June 1953, 'as I want the finest you can produce and am prepared to pay for it as such. I am glad you are doing this for me. One of my last endeavours is to have a dining suite the best ever your crafts have turned out & I will have the decoration of the room all done in conformity, including the windows and fittings.'[17] A sample chair was made and it was agreed that it should be sent to an exhibition in Chichester and then to the Crafts Centre in London where Mitchell could see it, and Edward prepared estimates for a set of twelve chairs, with and without the decorative details used on the sample. By November, Mitchell had paid for the first chair but decided against having a set made. Concerned that Edward would be disappointed, he asked him to design a display cabinet, to cost about £150-£200.[18] Barnsley responded that he would bring some photographs of earlier cabinets for Mitchell to see, and in January 1954 he sent a sketch of his proposed design, following this the next day with an alternative idea, both being refinements on a type of cabinet first seen in a drawing of 1951, probably for use at Loughborough.[19]

At this early stage of the design he was taking into account the nature of the objects that would be housed in the cabinet (which was intended for the glass collection of Mitchell's son, Lawrence) along with other factors such as lighting, background colour, visibility, and access to the shelves, and also the need for the piece to harmonize with other items in the house. Drawings for some other commissions make it clear that Barnsley considered the whole room — the location of windows, height of skirting board, position of wall-lights and so on — before finalizing his ideas for the work in hand, and when asked whether the client's personality influenced the design, he responded that it was more a question of the atmosphere of the room.[20]

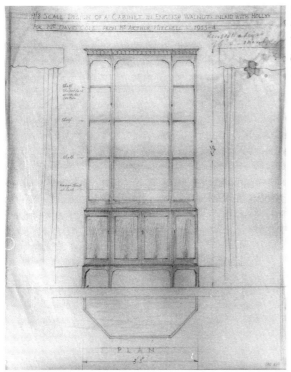

78. An early design for the cabinet commissioned by Arthur Mitchell for his daughter, Monica Cole, 1953-4.

When he sent the second version of the design, he was clearly becoming excited about the project, and said that he would probably make the cabinet even if Mitchell did not choose it, because he thought it would be a good exhibition piece. Mitchell and his son and daughter-in-law were impressed however and work proceeded. A two-page letter from Barnsley to Mitchell in March accompanied a scale-drawing and gave details of all the options. Barnsley was looking at the possibility of getting really fine walnut panels, which he said was now difficult, or using some delicate figured veneers on mahogany, and he was eager to try a decorative form of cornice 'as a chance to produce something that breaks away from the somewhat austere quality and simplicity that we have been compelled by financial considerations to produce since the war'. He proposed to have a sample length of this made before any decision was reached, but in a postscript had second thoughts and suggested that perhaps it was better to play safe and omit it. He estimated the price at between £190 and £245, the lower figure to include less decoration.[21]

Mitchell's next letter brought news which required drastic changes to be made to the design; his son was leaving England for the sake of his wife's health and the piece was now to be made for Mitchell's daughter, Mrs Davey Cole. He was clearly concerned about Barnsley's business and since the new piece was to be smaller and less costly, ordered at the same time a bed for his son-in-law. Barnsley's response, meanwhile, showed his ready sympathy for the disappointment Mitchell must be feeling about his son having to leave the family business.[22]

The cabinet was now to be smaller and was to suit a collection of jade. Mrs Cole was to be consulted about its design, and Mitchell was adamant that in materials and workmanship Barnsley was to aim for the best: 'I would like you to seek about until you have found the best solid walnut figured you can lay your hands on — no veneer, no three-ply, to be used in the work at all.'[23]

In his response to this, Edward expressed his gratitude for Mitchell's new order and some disappointment about the original design, which he hoped to be able to carry out at some later date. Mitchell's typically generous reply was an offer to stand sponsor for any loss if Edward wished to make the piece, for he was 'very sorry about the disappointment to you of being deprived of the opportunity of producing a work of craftsmanship that shall live as a great example of craftsmanship in the time you and I have the privilege of living in.'[24] Barnsley decided to keep the design and work on it now and again so that it would be available if a suitable client appeared or something was needed for exhibition at a slack period in the workshop, but a few months later, encouraged by Mitchell's generosity, he diffidently asked him for a loan to buy timber for a large order for college furniture. Mitchell's reply is not preserved, and his daughter had not heard of this request when asked in 1990, but presumed that her father would have granted it.

79. Walnut cabinet as finally made for Mrs Cole in 1955, described by Arthur Mitchell, who commissioned it, as 'one of the finest pieces of modern furniture I have ever seen'. The painted pottery is by Barnsley's sister Grace.

Work on the cabinet had not yet started in August when Barnsley wrote after a visit to The Glenfall and Mrs Cole's house, where he had looked at suitable positions for the piece. He was still keen to make it but was now concerned about whether Mitchell really wanted it or was making up for the loss of the original order. Reassurances received, he went on with the design; work did not actually start until May 1955 and the piece was completed in October.[25]

In shape it is tall with a display area divided into three horizontal bands by thin glazing bars, above a cupboard with two doors on a stand with a curved apron and short tapering legs. The serpentine front is fixed and access to the display area, with wide shelves fixed at the level of the glazing bars and narrower ones at the back, is through hinged doors at the side. Walnut was used and in accord with Mitchell's instructions, panels of exquisitely figured timber were found for the doors. The panels themselves are slightly convex and delicately hollowed at the edges, while the surrounding frame is outlined with a thin strip of lighter coloured inlay. George Taylor made the cabinet in 443 hours, about ten weeks' work, with Bert Upton contributing twenty-four hours, mainly in choosing timber and setting out. So happy was Edward with the piece that he had a label made for inside one of the doors, giving details of its making. He had occasionally

80. The simple stamp put on all furniture made after 1948.

signed his furniture by hand and since 1948 had routinely used a simple BARNSLEY stamp of the type used by cabinet-makers to mark their tools, since signed craftwork was eligible for relief from Purchase Tax, but this cabinet deserved special treatment. He also wrote to Mitchell saying 'I am more pleased with this piece than I have ever been with any piece that we have done before, and I have no words with which to give you my thanks for giving me the opportunity to produce such a piece.'[26]

Mitchell was delighted that Barnsley was satisfied because this meant that he had entered into the spirit of what Mitchell had wanted and produced his very best. Then he was happy to bear the full costs: 'I deal with you as I dealt with my very great friend Waals. I asked him to give me of his best & an approximate cost. I do not think a craftsman can work on other lines and so I do with you. Give me of your best and I will of course respond.'[27] Embarrassed as often before by the final price, Barnsley proposed to make allowance for the fact that it had been experimental and had already resulted in another order after it was put on display at the Crafts Centre in Hay Hill, but Mitchell brushed aside his concern and simply offered his thanks that Edward had made it possible for him to give his daughter such a wonderful work of art.[28] He considered it one of the best pieces of modern furniture he had seen. Although now in his eighties, he was still committed to the idea of modern work, despite the fact that many of his friends had been scandalized when he bought something as modern as the 1916 Gimson table.[29]

In the next few years he asked Barnsley to make several things for him, including panelling and doors for a smaller house he moved to at the end of his life and some furniture for Nina Griggs, widow of the artist whose etchings Mitchell avidly collected. He died in 1965 aged 92, after more than forty years of support for the best of craftsmanship. The cabinet is still in the possession of Mr and Mrs Cole and continues to give daily pleasure.

While Arthur Mitchell's dedication to the encouragement of fine craft was unusual, he was by no means unique among Barnsley's clients: there

81. Furniture commissioned by John and Rotha Barnfield between 1938 and 1962. From left to right are a chair of 1958; desk of 1955; lady's writing table of 1962; and a chest of drawers of 1938, all from Barnsley's workshop. The spinet is by Arnold Dolmetsch, 1961.

82. Cabinet in English walnut with ebony and sycamore inlay for Mrs Ida Neale, 1950. Made by Bert Upton in 1230 hours.

were many others who enjoyed a similar relationship, who were happy to pay for the superb quality of work in spite of problems with estimates, and who furnished their houses with the finest of Barnsley furniture as finances allowed. They were not all as wealthy as Mitchell, but they were generally established in their businesses or professions. Among his clients were architects, doctors, industrialists, insurance brokers, solicitors, and so on. They enjoyed the furniture and the sense of their own contribution to its creation, which is one of the pleasures of commissioning work rather than buying ready-made, and some have a sense of privilege that Barnsley enabled them to live with such quality. Perhaps, too, they were impressed by his intense seriousness and earnest attention to detail combined with his diffidence about his work. Mrs Neale, for instance, after protracted correspondence and meetings with Edward from September 1949, felt she had to write to him straight away when he sent her a new design because he had been so pessimistic about it. 'I like Everything about the design' she said, '& the suggestion of a slightly bowed front is just lovely. I like the base & I was hoping that I might have "carefully chosen grain" wherever possible. Don't forget the one side on entering the room is in full view too. Good Gracious. Silver handles & (some) ivory! Is it possible.'[30] This was the piece which was intended to cost £200 but finished at £275, causing embarrassment for both Barnsley and Mrs Neale.

Those who were willing to give Barnsley a fairly free hand and were able to absorb any extra costs, probably got the best of Edward's work and enjoyed the warmest friendships with him. The frequent difference between estimate and cost must have caused real problems for some clients, however, and probably few realized how tight was the margin between profit and loss. Very occasionally the client would reject the finished piece and Barnsley would be left with the problem of finding another buyer, a considerable hazard for the furniture maker working to commission.[31]

Barnsley's care for the minutiae of the commission added to the pleasure of the buyer both in choosing and receiving the work, for he was concerned that the piece must be right in tangible ways and also suitable in spirit. In 1968, when Janet Roscoe (née Gimson), an old friend, asked Barnsley for something to give as a presentation piece from a group of people, he gave her a list of items available for the price suggested, but proposed a mirror decorated with special lettering or monograms by Roger Powell. He would have liked to get rid of something already in stock, but he felt that 'You can't honour your friend unless you give her what honours all the 50-60 other people'. A mirror was made specially and proved to be a great success.[32]

83. Mirror in black bean with inlaid initials and signs of the zodiac in tooled leather by Peter Waters, 1958. These many-sided mirrors proved popular and quite a number were made in a variety of woods.

Not all items were made for specific clients and Barnsley made quite a number of sales through the Crafts Centre of Great Britain, mainly of mirrors and other similar small pieces made by batch production. These were usually versions of designs made for individual clients, sometimes with simplified decoration or different timbers, and clearly the design process was not the same, though the galleries had some influence by passing on visitors' comments and information on what woods were most in demand.

The types of piece made to Barnsley's design in the fifties, sixties, and seventies were much as before, though there were more very big items and larger numbers of chairs because the workshop was now equipped to deal with these. A few unusual items were made, such as the torchères in 1967 which are classical in spirit and appearance,[33] but on the whole the domestic furniture consisted of sideboards, cabinets, dining tables, and so on. As form followed function, some pieces such as beds, were designed to reflect new ways of living, and after the war these generally had flanking cupboards and a headboard instead of the head- and footboards of pre-war examples.

Most of the work was still made for domestic use but from the 1950s companies and colleges provided an increasing market. Some required items which were simply larger versions of domestic pieces. The Appleby Frodingham Steel Works commission of 1956 was one such, comprising a sideboard, serving table, two occasional tables, a 40-foot dining table made up of five separate sections, and forty-two chairs. The sideboard has a definite Regency flavour, with its bowed central section and a cupboard at each side, and the serving table with a tambour front is an early version of

84. Dining furniture for the Appleby Frodingham Steel Works in Scunthorpe, 1956, in African mahogany with ebony and holly inlay. The small sideboard with this set has a practical Formica sheet below a hinged top.

a type which Barnsley continued to produce and refine in the 1960s. Both are light and elegant, in contrast with the rather heavy chairs with solid upholstered backs, which are more like boardroom than dining room chairs. A letter about a similar commission some years later indicates how Barnsley approached the planning of a whole room. This was a boardroom in Park Lane for which the clients wanted a table and chairs to seat twelve, and a

85. Office furniture in Cuban mahogany made for David Eccles, a champion of the crafts, when Minister for Education in 1960. Photographed in 1971 when used by the Minister for the Arts at 38 Belgrave Square.

writing table or desk. Edward realized on seeing the room that it would look cramped with such a large table as a permanent feature. Learning that the full board of twelve only sat about twelve times a year, he designed the table for ten and planned a long sidetable-cum-writing desk to be placed against the wall, which could be moved to join up with the larger table for extra space when needed.[34]

Other clients, like the Minister of Education, David Eccles, whose office was furnished by the Barnsley workshop in 1960, required good-quality versions of office equipment such as a desk, in and out trays, chairs, bookcases and a cabinet in Cuba mahogany. The different tastes of changing ministers and officials resulted in some of this being put away in the 1970s causing problems within the status-ridden civil service system since it was wasted in store but could not be allocated to anyone too junior. It was, however, used by Paul Channon as Minister for the Arts, and when the Arts Minister's office moved out, the furniture remained in Elizabeth House, Waterloo, where it is now used by the Senior Chief Inspector of the Department of Education and Science. Apart from office furniture, the workshop received a number of commissions from the Ministry of Works and the Department of the Environment between 1954 and 1972, mainly for domestic pieces for embassies abroad. These were presumably the result of the Ministry's post-war policy of trying to improve the quality of design through its own purchasing.[35]

Some of the institutional commissions were for items on a much larger scale, such as dining tables for Nuffield College, Oxford in 1957. Magdalen College, Oxford, commissioned fifty-two common-room chairs in 1971, and at the request of the Bursar a series of photographs was taken during the making, providing an unusually complete record of the processes involved and the extent to which batch production was now used for such jobs.[36]

Other work for institutional clients was made by more traditional methods on a small scale but for a specialist purpose, and brought prestige to the workshop. One piece made in collaboration with Roger Powell, Sydney Cockerell, and William Gardner in 1946 was a cabinet containing six volumes on the exploration of Rhodesia, which was commissioned by the Southern Rhodesian government and presented to H.M. King George VI and H.M. Queen Elizabeth (pl. 42). Edward was very conscious of the publicity value of the occasional item made for royalty, and felt that it was good for the craftworker's image to carry out such commissions to show the general public that little-known people were able to do such fine work.[37] A similar piece involving a more complex design problem was a cabinet of 1954, made to hold the four volumes of the Book of Kells, newly rebound by Roger Powell, under slight pressure within drawers which could also be carried individually like attaché cases.

86. Oak screen at All Saints' Church, Steep, Hampshire, made by Bert Upton in 243 hours in 1954. The screen to the organ pipes is not by Barnsley.

Quite a number of commissions came from churches and cathedrals after the war, including chairs and a table made for Coventry Cathedral in 1947 (and more items later), an altar table and chairs for the Bishop's chapel at Portsmouth Cathedral in 1953, and several pieces for local churches at Froxfield and Steep.

87. Prototypes of chairs for use in the Senior Common Room at the University of the Gold Coast, Ghana, 1955.

An interesting commission for a foreign university came to the workshop through the architects Harrison, Barnes, and Hubbard. This project was to make designs and prototypes for furniture for the dons' rooms at the University of the Gold Coast in Ghana: the actual furniture was to be made in Africa. Twelve samples of different pieces were made in the workshop in 1955 'as evidence of quality so that designs in scale and full-size could be understood and carried out by native craftsmen.'[38] The detailed designs were sent with them in a scheme somewhat reminiscent of the furnishing of Loughborough College by the students. This process of designing for less skilled makers, who would not be able to ask for help from the designer as work progressed, may have had some influence on the later simplification of Barnsley's own design work. The finished work must have retained the Barnsley character, for clients told Edward of a visitor from Ghana who exclaimed with pleasure at seeing Ghanaian furniture in their London house and would not believe it to be by Barnsley until he was brought to see the workshop.[39]

A similar project in 1962, organized by Pearce Hubbard and Partners, was for designs for library furniture, tables, and chairs for the Sief Palace in Kuwait. The architect sent details of the colours and materials used in the building, the robes worn by the people using the room, and the traditional furniture of teak studded with brass. Teak was to be used with black leather upholstery for the chairs, and although the work was to be done by skilled craftsmen with the best tools, Barnsley was asked to keep the designs simple, though large and massive. Pearce Hubbard felt it necessary to remind him that it was to be 'Palatial, not Bourgeois or Suburban'.[40]

The nature of these two schemes was very similar to the work that Barnsley did for the Rural Industries Bureau from 1949 to about 1957. Certainly the range of pieces illustrated in the R.I.B.'s folder *Hand-Made Furniture Designs* (pls 50 and 51) caters for woodworkers of greatly varying expertise. Full-size working drawings were obtainable from the R.I.B. and these were almost identical to the designs used by Barnsley's craftsmen.

Barnsley now routinely made full-size drawings as well as those in eighth-scale, but the amount of information on them varies considerably. Some still left much for interpretation by the maker, while others gave very precise instructions, isometric drawings of secret lap dovetails, and details of the cut of the handles.

After experimenting through the 1950s with form and decoration, Barnsley simplified his designs in the sixties, retaining the proportions and many other features from his fifties work, but dispensing with the canted corners and elaborate mouldings. The basic form of the Appleby Frodingham serving table, for example, was re-used several times in the 1960s and 1970s but the reeding down the corners was removed and the top was usually flat rather than panelled. Often the later pieces were extensively decorated with inlaid lines but appear more simple because inlay is more restful to the eye than the three-dimensional effect of mouldings and beads.

88. Chest of drawers in walnut made for Anthony Minoprio in 1972. A refined and elegant piece typical of Barnsley's mature style.

89. Lady's writing table in walnut, 1961, with 'Cotswold-style' features.
90. Writing table in sapele, mahogany, and sycamore for Miss Towle, 1965, closer in style to commercial work of the 1960s.

Lightness and grace were the hallmarks of Barnsley's domestic furniture from the late fifties to the end of his career, except for those pieces such as desks, which by their nature demand *gravitas*. As in previous decades, his work varied considerably, and while with some designs he was happy to make very minor adjustments over long periods,[41] he was also on occasion capable of surprising modernity and awareness of fashion. A small writing table of 1965, for instance, is similar in proportion to a piece of 1961 which combines the influences of Sheraton and Cotswold style, but with its strip handles incorporated into the horizontal lines of the drawers, its contrasting blocks of colour, its clean lines and paired stretchers, it suggests the influence of Alan Peters or perhaps something seen at Heal's. This may have been the result of a request from the client, Miss Towle, or, like a set of chairs of 1973 (pl. 92), the idea may have come from seeing a photograph of a Danish design which inspired a new direction. Through Barnsley's career there was always a mainstream of work which continued and developed the Cotswold style and which often appeared old-fashioned to younger makers, but he also had an appreciation of other designers' work and this appears both in his occasional unusual designs and in his letters. In 1950, for instance, he wrote to a former pupil, Bob Townshend, commenting on production work by Milne, Spence, Russell, and Goodden and on the Scandinavian influence on them, from which he felt artist-craftsmen could learn.[42] He was, however, wary of too much influence from industrially made work because he felt there was little point in using hand skills to produce something which looked as if it were machine made, and he was critical of makers who did not see this incompatibility.[43]

91. Dining table of English walnut with sycamore and ebony inlay, 1972. The elegant curved stretcher made of thin laminated layers of wood is a development from the chamfered 'wishbone' stretchers of Cotswold work.

Since the late 1940s, Edward himself had been designing pieces in the contemporary spirit with much more slender, tapering, and splayed legs, and from around 1957-8 tables appeared with arching legs on solid bar feet, echoing the 'hay-rake' and 'wishbone' stretchers on Cotswold furniture, but now made of laminated sections of timber with pale lines at the joints. Graceful curved legs and stretchers also formed an essential part of the design on sideboards and smaller side tables, again made of laminated lengths, bent round a forma and glued together, and these pieces are among Barnsley's most elegant and successful designs. Such stretchers were also occasionally used on chairs, like three seats made for Devon County Hall in 1962 for presentation by John Day.[44] These throne-like chairs give a suitable impression of solidity combined with a lightness effected by the sinuous curve of the backs, though some years later Barnsley wrote: 'I've got to watch our curves carefully. Something firm and unpretentious is, sometimes, lost in the aiming for interesting overall curvilinear effects. Wood is wood, and there are times, I fancy when we abuse it. I may have told you of a remark that Stanley Davies made on these lines about a year ago, and I want to talk it out with him when I see him again.'[45]

Whether or not Barnsley and Davies reached a conclusion about this problem, which raises an echo of the English Arts and Crafts Movement's hearty disapproval of immoral and unseemly Art Nouveau, Barnsley designed a number of chairs in the sixties and seventies with gently curved back splats which show off the beauty of the chosen feathered veneer. This was not an entirely new departure, however, since the workshop had made for Charles Hawkins in the 1930s a set of walnut dining chairs and a

92. A dining chair in rosewood with sycamore inlay, the high back inspired by a Danish design seen at Heal's, 1973. A set of ten chairs was made by Bert Upton and Michael Bowen in 600 hours.

93. The Archbishop of Canterbury's armchair, of walnut and sycamore, 1971. The chair and a prayer desk and stool were made by Bert Upton and Malcolm Clubley in 473 hours, with carved shields by Oskar Dawson.

mahogany chair reminiscent of eighteenth-century design, all with solid curved back panels. A newer feature was the use of a taller back on chairs for Mrs Comino-James made in 1973, which Barnsley said were influenced by some Danish work at Heal's but which also follow from his work on ceremonial chairs for the Archbishop of Canterbury in 1971 and the Devon County Council in 1962.

Typical of Barnsley's consideration for practicality was his approach to the design of the Archbishop's chair, which he regarded as highly successful because function dictated 95 per cent of the form. He had an order for similar chairs for churches near Froxfield so he tried out his ideas on them first and took the results to Canterbury to see what they looked like in the larger setting.[46] The curve of the back of the seat was planned to suit the average human body in a relaxed position with the arms easily at rest on the arms of the chair and the mitre and other ceremonial attire looking well in relation to the height and width of the back. There was even a suggestion that the back was designed to support the body upright in a dignified and suitable position should the occupant fall asleep.[47] In contrast, Barnsley was unhappy about a set of chairs with beautifully shaped backs which had proved to be inordinately uncomfortable.[48]

A new feature on cabinet furniture, from about 1965, was the incorporation of wooden handles into the top edge of the drawer, giving a smoother appearance with minimal disruption of the grain of the wood on the drawer front. A similar handle had been used on a 1952 cabinet, but was let in as a separate piece and did not give the smooth continuous flow of later versions.[49] This move of the handle from the centre to the top resulted from the use of magnetic catches on the doors; Barnsley suddenly realized that if a magnet was fitted at the top of the door, the handle should also be at the top, and the handles of drawers needed to harmonize. Sometimes these handles were lobed and had decoration on the upper surface in a contrasting wood; often they were inlaid on the edge with a thin line of ebony or sycamore which carried on along and around the drawer to define its shape. After the death of Frank Jordan, who made metal handles for Barnsley for many years, wooden handles were almost always used.

While these handles owe their genesis to the Cotswold style they are the result of gradual developments by Barnsley over a period of forty years and are unlike anything designed by his father or Gimson. Other elements of his designs in the last twenty years of his life are much closer to the Cotswold work of his youth and include bands of chip-carved lozenge decoration, a renewed interest in frame and panel construction, and a conscious attempt

94. Writing cabinet in Indian rosewood with ebony and sycamore inlay and interior fittings of English walnut, 1968. Note the wooden handles incorporated into the tops of the drawers and the band of chip-carved decoration.

95. Drinks cabinet in English walnut with sycamore inlay, 1973, made for Mr and Mrs W. G. Jenkins by Malcolm Clubley in 317 hours. This was a piece which satisfied Barnsley's critical eye.

to do something which would compare directly with Sidney Barnsley's work. A drinks cabinet of 1973, with its solid-looking cupboard resting on an open stand, is redolent of a type of piece favoured by all the Arts and Crafts designers, while the Jubilee Cabinet of 1977 is a direct descendant of works by Sidney Barnsley and Ernest Gimson.

The Jubilee Cabinet was the result of a request from Lord Reilly for a special piece for display in a forthcoming exhibition at the British Crafts Centre in Earlham Street, organized to celebrate the Queen's Silver Jubilee. It was clear from the start that an item for a 'Masterpiece' exhibition should be a special one, and Barnsley was fortunate that one of his existing clients, Nigel Grimwood, became interested in the project and offered to buy the cabinet when it was finished, without limitation as to cost.

Barnsley was of the opinion that 'no-one in the history of furniture design and making has ever achieved a cabinet on stand in which both parts harmonise'[50] and his ambition was to show that it could be done. He had made an attempt in the early 1920s with a piece in which he had followed Sidney Barnsley in the design of the upper part and changed the lower section, but he had considered this unsuccessful.[51] He was pleased to have another opportunity, especially since the 'Good Citizen's Furniture' exhibition at Cheltenham included the burr oak desk by his father which had prompted the first try. That exhibition opened in November 1976 and the first draft of the Jubilee Cabinet design was made on Christmas Day of that year, so the connection between the two pieces is very clear.

96. This first sketch
design for the Jubilee
Cabinet, made on 25th
December 1976, was
rescued from the waste
paper basket by Professor
Kellgren, Tania's brother.
It illustrates Barnsley's
habit of adding later
notes to his drawings.

This first sketch shows the basic form of the cabinet as made but with a wishbone stretcher which was changed after much deliberation to a curving rail and then to a panelled shelf. The drawers were also changed slightly to suit the new stretcher. The upper part is rectangular with panels on all sides and a fall front which had to be re-made twice because it warped along the length, causing Barnsley to say that it had caused more trouble than any other piece ever made in the workshop.[52] The complex figure on the walnut panels, cut from a part of the tree where the branches fork, was inherently unstable and caused movement and twisting, which though slight was immediately noticeable. The eventual solution was to build up a frame with a core of marine ply faced with walnut and with a solid edging of walnut, which was not in the original design but was needed to cover the exposed plywood, and which provides a defining outline.

Such a solution would have been anathema to Gimson and Sidney Barnsley, though not to C. R. Ashbee who made a similar use of veneers on an ostensibly solid piece in a cabinet of 1902 by the Guild of Handicraft,[53] and the Jubilee Cabinet demonstrates how far the pursuit of perfection in the making had overtaken purist Arts and Crafts ideals about honesty of construction (Ashbee was never a purist because he was not a woodworker). That Edward had never entirely gone along with the purist line is shown by a bed he designed for Miss Watts in 1939, of yew turned in imitation of bamboo, and a desk for Dr Newall-Watson in 1976 with two deep drawers each fitted with two handles so that each looks like two drawers.[54] His difference of attitude is perhaps explained by the fact that Gimson and the Barnsleys had discovered the crafts for themselves through the study of old work and their understanding of techniques was absorbed gradually and then refined intellectually into a set of principles. These were accepted wholesale by Edward, but because he did not have to think about them deeply they did not have the same binding force as they had for the previous generation.

Similarly, although the body of the Jubilee Cabinet is panelled, it does not show off the construction like Cotswold furniture and there are none of the cogged dovetails, exposed through tenons, and dowels that would have been used by Gimson and Sidney Barnsley on such a piece. Edward Barnsley had largely given up using through tenons in the 1930s because he felt that the darker colour of the end grain was an unacceptable disturbance of the beauty of the wood. Decorative dovetails at the angles were useful in defining and emphasizing the shape, so these were often employed, though he thought that the joints should only be shown when they added to the design, and that they should be concealed if they interfered with qualities such as repose, which were of greater importance. Romney Green had put to him the argument that if the joints were concealed one could suppose them

97. The Jubilee Cabinet of 1977. Made in English walnut with ebony and holly inlay by Bert Upton and George Taylor, with assistance from Oskar Dawson and Mark Nicholas, in over 900 hours.

98. The interior of the Jubilee Cabinet: craftsmanship of precision and delicacy.

faulty, but Barnsley seized on this as an unwarrantable slur on the honesty of the craftsman, which should be taken for granted.[55]

Inside, the bureau is fitted with a small bowed cupboard and several drawers and pigeon holes within a framework made of eighth-inch oak. The drawers and doors are of walnut inlaid with a thin line of ebony and holly, diagonally striped, and fitted with small turned ivory handles made by Oskar Dawson.

Once the problems of construction were solved, Barnsley was completely satisfied with the craftsmanship of the piece, which was made by Upton and Taylor with assistance from Dawson and Nicholas. He was not so confident about his own contribution however, and in letters he alternated between being 'more than usually pleased with the whole thing', and 'it has failed in one special detail, the overall harmony or proportion of the thing'. Six months later he was planning the slight modifications he would make to the design if he had an opportunity to make another.[56]

As Barnsley said of the Jubilee piece 'the work of my craftsmen cannot be faulted; it is perfection'.[57] The standard of craftsmanship in the workshop at this time was of the highest order: the timber is carefully matched, joints fit perfectly, drawers glide easily into place with just the slightest resistance as they reach the back. Upton would allow no deviation from the goal of excellence. Occasionally there was a disaster, usually caused by an experiment with the unknown, as when the tables made for Courtauld's in 1964 crazed and blistered a few years later in the dryness of the building, but this was not a problem unique to Barnsley and in 1970 he described similar difficulties experienced by another furniture maker, Ernest Joyce, on an even larger scale.[58] In general the products of the workshop were designed for modern conditions and have survived extremely well.

99. Desk of English walnut with veneered panels of finely figured American walnut: home-grown walnut of top quality was becoming costly and hard to find. Made by Oskar Dawson in 885 hours in 1976. Barnsley considered this one of his more successful designs. It shows clearly the curved handles used often in his late work.

The Jubilee Cabinet was made of finely figured walnut which had been seasoning in Barnsley's timber sheds for decades and was chosen by Upton for its decorative qualities. This timber continued to be popular with clients but it was now very expensive and difficult to find, and a wide range of other woods was also employed. These included rosewood, oak, mahogany, cherry, teak, ash, iroko, padouk, and occasionally, pine, and by 1965, Barnsley estimated that the workshop used 80 per cent imported timber and only 20 per cent home-grown.[59]

Edward Barnsley's last designs were made in the early 1980s and in 1982 he handed over to his son Jon, who took over the design side (working very much within the limits of the Barnsley style) and some of the management of the business. In 1981 Edward wrote to Vera Simpson saying that the chest made for her would never be copied exactly but that it was possible in future that they would look through the designs and carry out similar pieces, though he hoped that this would not happen while he was still working.[60] In fact he himself had been doing this for years, and clients were occasionally disappointed to find that the piece they thought unique was one of a series,[61] but it was part of Barnsley's approach to design that small changes were of great significance, and for him made the difference between a piece which had 'come off' and one which was a failure. The idea of simply repeating an old design without considering how it could be improved was unthinkable, and many of his drawings are annotated with comments added later, and exclamations such as 'Heavy!!!' in reference to the base of a cabinet. His other notes on this cabinet include 'Bottom cupd. proportions right — but the top cupd. not so successful & position of handles too high & grain of wood rather restless.'[62]

In the event his fears were not realized, since old designs were used as the starting point but were changed by Jon Barnsley or by the craftsmen and apprentices to suit new clients and different tastes (see pls 106 and 107). Interestingly, much of the inspiration for the new pieces comes from the earliest work made in the workshop, such as a delicate two-tiered table for Charles Hawkins of 1929,[63] perhaps because of the increasing interest in Arts and Crafts furniture among collectors.

During his long career, Edward Barnsley's design work shows three very marked characteristics. His style grew out of his background and his place within the Cotswold group and although he moved away from this superficially, it always remained as a source of inspiration, a vocabulary of shapes and ideas to which he often returned. In addition, it gave him a respect for the restraints imposed by the nature of materials and tools. Then he was also aware of work by others, particularly commercial makers, and often made pieces which were directly inspired by something he had seen in a London showroom or the pages of a magazine, pieces which now seem a sideline on the development of his own style, but which must have contributed to his understanding of form and decoration. Finally, there is the continual development of his own original work: the experimentation in the 1950s with features inspired by eighteenth-century makers, and the emergence in the 1960s of his own authentic style, which he honed and polished for the next twenty years in his constant search for the design in which 'nothing can be added and nothing taken away'.[64]

It is too soon for a full evaluation of Barnsley's place as a twentieth-century designer. He was conscious that he was not a pioneer like his father and Gimson, who had constructed a new language which had a wide influence on manufacturers as well as on craftworkers, but he also knew that the value of the work, theirs and his own, was not simply a matter of style. In 1963 he wrote of his anxiety that his own ability 'to produce work of individual quality, in design, is very small indeed. But I do not let this worry me unduly, as a matter of fact, because the making of quality work, though obviously lacking in advanced thoughts, seems to me to be a worth while job, especially if the conditions of its making, and its own lasting qualities, and the pleasure to the eye of present day people, and (perhaps) to the eyes of those who come later, is its own justification.'[65] For him it was not enough to produce a design that was interesting: 'Interest is cerebral and everything is interesting, it's love and affection which are so rare and beyond price.'[66] He also found support in the words of Frank Lloyd Wright and was fond of quoting him: 'The innate harmony of an art object is established by certain truths which have stood the test of time. Whether the form is severely modern in concept or has classical design and structural overtones, basic precepts not fully comprehended will establish some work to have lasting beauty and acceptance, while other work may capture momentary spectacular attention, then fade into obscurity.'[67]

Edward Barnsley was usually behind the commercial firms in producing new ideas and did not see it as part of his role to invent new fashions, but among the craftsmen he was indubitably a leader. His work developed more than that of Eric Sharpe, Stanley Davies, Oliver Morel, Hugh Birkett, and other fine craftsmen who followed the Gimson–Barnsley tradition, and he influenced almost every maker of handmade furniture in Britain until the 1970s when new ideas about the crafts sprang up in the colleges and exhibition centres. Then the emphasis shifted to using new combinations of materials, brighter colours, new methods of construction, and light-hearted ideas, in marked contrast to Barnsley's approach of gradual refinement on the lines of fitness, proportion, and harmony. In the new climate, as the crafts became more closely allied to 'fine art', his work looked old-fashioned in comparison with other craftwork as well as with manufactured furniture. But the conservationist era of the 1980s and 1990s has brought a growing appreciation of the work of Gimson and the Barnsleys and a renewal of interest in the qualities and values it represents. Fitness for purpose and pleasure in use were Edward Barnsley's aims and his achievement.

9. THE EDUCATIONAL TRUST AND THE FUTURE

The formation of a Trust in 1980 − the first apprentices −
retirement of Bert Upton − exhibitions and recognition in the early
1980s − Barnsley's ill-health and death in 1987 − tributes −
the work of the Edward Barnsley Educational Trust − a continuing
tradition of fine furniture

In the late 1970s, a major problem looming into view was that Bert Upton wanted to ease off into retirement. He had been in charge of the workshop for so long that it was difficult to see how the firm could survive without him, since he knew the capabilities of all the staff, had long experience of interpreting the Guvnor's drawings, dreamt up endless possibilities for the machines, and had even persuaded the factory inspectors to look again at the regulations as they affected small workshops. Edward also had to think about the Barnsley workshop without Barnsley. His son, Jon, to his great pride, had an increasingly busy architectural practice and could not be expected to take over the firm, and though Edward had hopes that his grandson Peter might develop into a craftsman, he had already put him off by treating the matter too seriously, unable to think of woodwork as something one could do for fun.

By January 1979 Upton had begun to work half-time, and at his own suggestion, George Taylor, who was in his late fifties, was working only

100. Barnsley (right) and the workshop craftsmen in 1980: left to right are George Taylor, Mark Nicholas, and Oskar Dawson.

three days a week. Oskar Dawson was to follow suit in April, leaving only Mark Nicholas in the workshop full-time.[1] This arrangement seemed uneconomic to Edward because some years before he had calculated that overhead costs made it necessary to have five benches at work to keep the business going.[2] He was unhappy about the prospects of a future dependent on grants, but he was beginning to be persuaded that the only answer was for the workshop to be organized as an educational trust, an idea proposed some years before by two long-standing clients, Gerry Jenkins and Nigel Grimwood. A trust would keep alive the tradition of fine furniture making and training of cabinet-makers, and continue to provide income and involvement for Edward and Tania. Jon Barnsley was keen, partly because of a slight feeling of regret that he had not been much involved before, and Barnsley's daughter, Karin Antonini, was willing to help as Secretary to the Trust.

The first trustees' meeting was held in January 1979 and it was agreed that they should aim to raise about £150,000 to set the scheme going. Barnsley was to visit or write to clients to drum up support, a prospect which caused him some anxiety and embarrassment,[3] and it was hoped that

101. The first day of the Trust's apprenticeship scheme, January 1981:
Barnsley, Giles Garnham, Colin Eden-Eadon, and George Taylor.

enough money would be promised to enable the Trust to offer a really competitive salary for an experienced trainer and to give a golden handshake to each of the senior craftsmen on his retirement. The Trust obtained charitable status in 1980, help was promised from high places, and much work was done by trustees and family. By the end of 1980 only £28,000 had been raised, but it was decided nevertheless that this was enough to start with, and that the Trust should take on its first apprentices.

A number of young people had written over the previous few years asking to join the workshop, and they were now contacted and interviewed. Colin Eden-Eadon and Giles Garnham were taken on to start in January 1981 and Robert Lawrence in September. David Butcher, who had been in charge of woodwork at Bedales for some years, agreed to come to the workshop part-time to start off the training programme, with the idea that he would gradually give more hours to the work. He was to learn the special skills of the workshop from the senior craftsmen and supervise the apprentices, who were to study the practical side of the work with him, Taylor, Dawson, and Nicholas, and the design side with Barnsley.

In spite of its obvious attractions, Barnsley felt ambiguous about the trust idea. He had a strong sense of family continuity and liked to think that 'the firm' would live on, but he also yearned to ease off a little and had occasionally thought that perhaps he could carry on in a small way, making designs which could be executed by Mark Nicholas. He was impressed with the way Nicholas's work developed after Bert Upton retired in September 1979, and that he had found new and quicker methods of doing certain jobs.[4] However, once the Trust started in earnest and the first apprentices arrived, he was reconciled to the idea and also rather proud of it.

This did not relieve him of all responsibility, however: '1980. I'm not entirely without some anxiety for this year. For me it is a proverbial milestone, and though I talk too much about labour, and make claims that I will not allow sorrow to take much part in my future, it's extremely unwise to boast, as I know well, with all my talk about walking up the highest bit of England on my 85th year. Well, I will let the future deal with me as it will, and try not to be foolish.'[5]

After visiting the mysterious ancient stones of Men-an-Tol in Cornwall in 1975, Barnsley had vowed to view the world with more detachment, but the pessimist in him struggled with his good intentions and as always, won. Perhaps Bert Upton's heart attack in mid 1979 had reminded him of his own advancing years, or perhaps he was conscious of his fault in the row which soured their long association. Upton retired in September, and though he continued to work on upholstery at home, delivered to him by Tania, he refused to visit the workshop or to speak to Barnsley. He did not talk of the cause of the rift, but it seems that Barnsley had at first agreed to Upton's request that he should work at his bench on his own jobs for half of each day while keeping an eye on the workshop, and had then changed his mind. Edward said it was uneconomic and disruptive to stop and start jobs, and he clearly wanted Bert to work full-time without consideration for his health.

102. Jon and Edward Barnsley in the drawing office, 1983. Jon Barnsley continues to design for the Trust, within the Barnsley tradition.

The workshop was now run by the Trust, with most of the day-to-day administrative work undertaken by Tania Barnsley and Karin Antonini, so Edward spent his time designing furniture, looking occasionally at the work of the apprentices, and writing letters and notes. He also managed the walk to the top of Scafell Pike on his eightieth birthday.[6] His age attracted attention from the media and he was interviewed for 'Woman's Hour', and in the following two years for two television programmes. Fiona MacCarthy wrote a piece for *Crafts* magazine, for which, as usual he produced copious notes, and he was delighted when this was published in 1981. His letter of sincere thanks in his firm and clear handwriting[7] gives no hint of recent problems which he described to Vera Simpson a little later: 'So much has happened here, and I don't think I can tell you about a good deal of it. I think it was sometime in April that I fell into what I think would be called some form of nervous breakdown. Not for the first time either, from time to time in the past it has been "money" problems which began "it", but I don't quite know what it was this time, so I'll not go on. No confidence, no assurance, no courage, inabillity to face the workshop and the problems, incredible trouble to Tania, no that's enough and too much, and please write soon, but without mentioning this. I'm out of the muddle and determined to keep out.'[8]

Determined as he was, he had increasing problems of concentration and his letters became disjointed notes, composed over long periods of time. He had to give up driving because he no longer considered himself safe, though some would say he never had been: he admitted that he had 'always been liable to take thoughts off the job' when driving.[9] Of greater concern, in the

103. Tania Barnsley working out wages in 1983, as she had done since 1938. Behind her is the cabinet Edward gave her as a wedding gift (pl. 28).

winter of 1981 he was found wandering in the countryside in the snow, and the supervision of the workshop was left increasingly to Jon and Tania.

The Trust organized an exhibition at the Fine Art Society in New Bond Street and the Holburne Museum in Bath, with an excellent illustrated catalogue. The displays prompted articles in the woodworking magazines about the workshop and Edward was interviewed by Joan Bakewell for a television programme shown in February 1982. In 1982 he was also invited to give a lecture at the Royal Society of Arts, on the subject of 'Things Men Have Made'. John Makepeace introduced the talk, paying eloquent tribute to Barnsley's work and influence, but he was a somewhat unfortunate substitute for Lord Eccles, who was ill, given Edward's views on Makepeace's work. Though he had rousing things to say, Edward frequently forgot where he was in his speech and had to appeal to Tania for help, a circumstance which clearly made him anxious.

As time went on he became more vague and forgetful and increasingly distressed by his knowledge that his mental powers were failing. Eventually in 1986 it simply became impossible for him to be at home, for the familiarity of the surroundings was a constant reminder to him that he was not as he had been. He stayed for some time with his son and daughter-in-law, and then went to hospital in Portsmouth. Here his mind sank deeper into oblivion, betrayed by the strength of body in which he had always taken pride, giving up the struggle to face the world.[10] Occasionally he would enjoy a visit from an old friend such as Geoffrey Wicksteed or his favourite craftsman, George Taylor, but he hardly spoke and could no longer follow conversations. He died on 2 December 1987.

104. Edward Barnsley on Scafell Pike in 1975. It was when he was walking in his beloved Lake District that he felt most at ease with himself and the world.

A memorial meeting in the Lupton Hall at Bedales School on Saturday 16 April 1988 brought together several hundred of the wide range of people touched by Barnsley's life: family, friends, and neighbours, fellow makers, ex-students, clients, dealers, museum curators, and academics, together in the school hall and later in the library Edward had helped to build, to celebrate a long life. Loving tribute was paid by friends and contemporaries, such as Janet Roscoe, Gonda Stamford, and Roger Powell, who recalled the warmth and enthusiasm of his character. Sir George Trevelyan, whose own distinguished contribution to education and the cause of the crafts should be properly recorded, talked of their long friendship, and George Taylor of their long and fruitful working relationship. An extract from a radio interview was played and George Taylor recalled John Arlott's description of Barnsley's alarming bristling eyebrows as like 'predatory prawns'.[11] In more serious vein, there were readings from Edward's favourite poetry and prose about the importance of craftsmanship, and music played by his nieces, Sarah and Virginia Firnberg.

Unexpectedly, Edward's will specified that he wished his ashes to be placed in a simple oak casket from his own workshop and buried with his parents, in Sapperton churchyard, where his uncle and Ernest Gimson are also buried. Mark Nicholas made the box and the family went to Sapperton for a brief service, attended also by Nancie Jewson and Betty and Ernest Barnsley. An inscription was added to the slab of his parents' grave by Denis

McQuoid, a letter-cutter based at Slindon in West Sussex, who does lettering for the workshop. So Edward Barnsley's memorial is with his roots, in the place where he was born, rather than in the village where he lived most of his life.

But his real memorial is in the thousands of pieces of furniture which came out of the Froxfield workshop over sixty-four years, in the skills of hand and eye and brain transferred to younger makers, and in the continued existence of the Barnsley workshop as a training centre. One of his cherished quotations was from George Jack's book on *Wood Carving*: 'The fact is that it takes many generations of ardent minds to accomplish what at first each thinks himself capable of doing alone.'[12] The establishment of the Trust created the conditions under which his work could go on.

Under the Edward Barnsley Educational Trust the workshop has continued to provide a similar range of types of training but some changes have been necessary because of the ways in which education in general has changed. In the past, apprentices were usually the sons of skilled parents who realized the importance of skills and were prepared initially to subsidize low wages in order to gain better future prospects for their children. Few scholarships and grants were available and many children who would now gain places at college went to work in order to start earning. Since the raising of the school-leaving age, the increased provision of grants, and different attitudes to mobility, it has become more difficult to find local applicants who want to start apprenticeships straight from school.[13] The system always relied in part on the fact that apprentices would live at home, and wages for apprentices are too low to cover the high cost of renting in Hampshire. Those prepared to face the difficulties of trying to make a living from furniture making often feel that a college training along with many others of their own age is preferable to working in a remote country workshop and staying at home, and the Trust has had to recognize this. While preference is still given to local school-leavers, apprentices and trainees now come to the workshop with more previous experience than in the past. Often they have had some training at centres like the Highbury Technical College in Hampshire, various colleges in the Manchester area, Rycotewood, or the London College of Furniture, and allowances have to be made for different levels of experience. After a six-month trial period, trainees usually stay for three years and then a further two years by mutual agreement, working for experience. Those with more previous training arrange their time in the workshop according to the grants they are able to obtain and their productivity.

As in the past, each apprentice works only with hand tools for the first year if they have not already passed the relevant City and Guilds Courses before joining the workshop; in this case they can take day release courses. Handwork is a slow but rewarding experience according to most of them. Jobs are allocated according to experience and ability and each maker works on one piece from beginning to end, unless it is particularly complicated and requires two people. Shorter periods of training are provided by what are the

105. Colin Eden-Eadon, Mark Betterton, Chris Butler, George Taylor, Mark Nicholas, and Richard Elderton in the workshop in about 1985.

equivalent of pupilships, but there is no longer the same kind of division into those encouraged to think about design and those for whom it is assumed to be irrelevant. All received advice from David Medd (an architect who specializes in buildings and furniture for schools) and help with technical drawing from Jon Barnsley and the workshop manager.

Over the years the organization has changed and grown and in 1987 the workshop became a limited company, responsible for the training scheme and reimbursed for teaching time by the Trust. David Butcher's commitments at Bedales increased in 1982 and he was unable to continue, so Richard Elderton was appointed to the post of Workshop Manager in 1983, staying until 1990.

The death of Oskar Dawson in 1984, shortly before his retirement date, and the retirement of George Taylor in 1986, inevitably caused problems for the training programme, and the ratio of trained craftsmen to apprentices is a continuing cause for concern. Regular meetings of the workshop management group, comprising two Trustees, the accountant, the family, and Mark Nicholas, provide a forum for discussion, and changes to the management of the training scheme have been implemented when agreed. Considerable improvements have also been made to the premises, largely as a side-effect of the new status as an educational establishment, which both requires higher standards of facilities and attracts grants. Jon Barnsley has become more actively involved in the workshop and the craftsmen and apprentices are encouraged to introduce their own ideas for design, within the framework of the Barnsley style. The Educational Trust to date has trained eight apprentices and provided workshop experience for pupils from New Zealand, Japan, and Sweden, as well as Britain.

In the tradition of the workshop, financial problems constrain the organization and attempts are still being made to raise the money to buy the premises for the Trust, which, since 1987 has run both the educational venture and the furniture business. In 1992, the Trust has paid for about 80 per cent of the buildings-freehold of the workshop as well as for machines and tools, and is still appealing for the final £19,500 needed. It is considerably helped by donations like David Pye's recent generous gift of his hand-tools. Most of the day-to-day work is done by the family, for whom the Trust seemed the inevitable step, in much the way that Edward Barnsley took over Lupton's business in 1923. They cling to his ideals and some of his old-fashioned business methods, since there would be no point for them in doing it differently.

Despite its lack of adequate finances, the Trust has achieved a great deal in its first ten years. The archive of drawings and designs, which in Edward Barnsley's day was kept in a roof space where conditions were not ideal, has been preserved and catalogued. It is available for reference by the makers in the workshop as a starting point for new designs and for study by historians.

106. The Barnsley tradition continues under the Trust: chest of drawers in burr oak, English oak and bog oak, designed by Jon Barnsley, craftsman Richard Elderton, and apprentice Darren Harvey, and made by Harvey in 1986. The form of the feet reflects the work of Gimson and the Barnsleys.

107. Writing bureau in cherry, based on the Jubilee Cabinet (pl. 97), designed and made by apprentice Adam Gamble: a commission of 1991.

Edward's vast correspondence has also been sorted and boxed, providing documentary evidence of his own work and of ideas and associations in the wider field of design history in the twentieth century.

After the exhibitions organized by the Trust in London and Bath in 1982, it was thought desirable to go further north and enquiries were made in Manchester, where Edward had often exhibited with the Red Rose Guild. Stockport presented itself as an alternative and a fine display was put on in the Memorial Art Gallery in 1985, with a catalogue covering work from all periods of the workshop's existence. A smaller show went to the Pennybank Gallery in London in the following year, and a few years later the Area Museums Service for South East England (in 1987-8) toured an exhibition which visited a wide range of museums in the south and a few less expected venues, such as the I.B.M. offices in Winchester. Further shows were held in Farnham in 1989 and in the new gallery designed by Jon Barnsley for Bedales School in 1990. In the early 1990s, exhibitions are planned for Chichester, Farnham, and Cheltenham, giving the opportunity for a wide audience to see the standards of craft skill which can still be achieved in the twentieth century.

Thus the Trust continues the educational work of Edward Barnsley as a fundamental aim of its existence. Just as Edward used his income from teaching at Loughborough to underpin the business and his experience as a craftsman to inform his teaching at the college, so the Trust involves itself in a series of mutually dependent activities as part of the continuing struggle to keep the crafts alive. As Edward Barnsley wrote in 1942: 'How many are there of craftsmen, and who are they, wishing sincerely to work for the revitalizing of the crafts, and of making it possible for individuals in future to live the craftsman's life. I had thought I was playing some part in this, carrying on as a working craftsman, training men in the crafts and encouraging them to live as craftsmen, not just draw a wage as employees, lecturing to and training students, and so on. What else can one do?'[14]

NOTES

Most of my information about Edward Barnsley's life has come from him or his family, and the text has been checked by his daughter, Karin Antonini.

All letters, photographs, and other documents cited are in the archive of the Edward Barnsley Educational Trust unless otherwise specified. Barnsley's letters in the archive are generally stored in alphabetical order under the name of his correspondent. The archive number is given here only if the document is filed under another name. Roger Powell's letters, for instance, are in the Arts and Crafts Exhibition Society file which has the number A36.

When I started this work the archive was uncatalogued. I have attempted to double-check all references but have been unable to locate a few letters.

References to works listed in full in the bibliography are given here in a short form.

Abbreviations: Edward Barnsley is abbreviated to EB, the Edward Barnsley Educational Trust to EBET, Cheltenham Art Gallery and Museums to CAGM, and the Victoria and Albert Museum Archive of Art and Design to V&A AAD.

INTRODUCTION

1. J. Cole-Morgan (ed.), *Visiting Craft Workshops in the English Countryside*, Ashbourne 1992. This probably includes some firms which make reproductions. It is co-published by the Rural Development Commission and does not cover urban workshops. The equivalent directory published by the Council for Small Industries in Rural Areas in 1986 listed only about eighty furniture workshops.
2. Derrick 1945 p. 138.

1. BARNSLEY'S BACKGROUND AND EARLY LIFE

1. Information from *Against the Grain*, film made for the Arts Council by Margaret Dickinson and Jan Marsh, 1983.
2. S. A. Gimson, *Random Recollections of the Leicester Secular Society*, Part 1, March 1932,

unpublished account in the Leicestershire Record Office, 10D68/18.
3. Leicestershire Record Office, DE1763.
4. R. Weir Schultz and S. H. Barnsley, *The Monastery of Saint Luke of Stiris, in Phocis, and the Dependent Monastery of Saint Nicholas in the Fields, near Skripou, in Boeotia*, London 1901.
5. The delicately painted trailing flowers on the roof beams were executed by Sidney Barnsley himself because he could find no-one else to do the work: EB-F. MacCarthy, notes of interview September 1980. Similar decoration on chests and cabinets was later carried out for him by Alfred and Louise Powell.
6. Photo 43/48 is signed and dated 1892 by Sidney Barnsley and may have been one he showed at the 1893 Arts and Crafts Exhibition Society.
7. EB-O. Barnsley 25.11.68.
8. EB-B. G. Burrough 22.1.81.
9. Though Gimson's reported comment on Ashbee, that Gimson preferred 'work not words', is quoted in Crawford p. 404, and EB often expressed a similar view., e.g. EB-I.Cleaver 12.6.69.
10. CAGM has Gimson's collection of press cuttings about the post-war housing situation, 1941.225.104. His letter to Sydney Cockerell about the workshop in 1918 is quoted in Comino p. 189.
11. EB-O. Barnsley 25.11.68.
12. EB-M. Comino 7.12.77.
13. EB-G. Trevelyan 28.3.73.
14. EB-O. Barnsley 25.11.68.
15. EB-O. Powell 14.12.82.
16. EB-O. Barnsley 25.11.68.
17. EB-O. Barnsley 25.11.68.
18. S. Barnsley-P. Webb 1.5.1904.
19. S. Barnsley-EB 25.8.26.
20. EB-B. G. Burrough 5.7.76. The names of the assistants are not given.
21. L. Morley-J. Gimson 9.9.1894, B21/1.
22. EB-O. Barnsley 25.11.68.
23. O. Barnsley-EB 12.9.68; EB-O. Barnsley 25.11.68.
24. S. Barnsley - Florence (Morley?) 30.12. 1900.

25. G. Davies-EB undated D7/13.

26. E. Barnsley-Lord Bathurst 12.3.01, 9.5.01; G. Davies-EB undated D7/13.

27. *Blind Man's Gate*, transcript of a radio interview with Ernest Smith by Philip Donnellan, uncatalogued, p. 32.

28. Photos 41/1, 41/4.

29. EB-O. Barnsley 25.11.68. Grace also felt alone and wrote in about 1973 that she thought this was because the nurse she had as a baby was replaced when Edward was born by a third cousin, who was not kind to Grace and brought out in her an impulse to self-sacrifice, which caused her to give up things she wanted when she believed, often wrongly, that others wanted them more. G. Davies-EB undated D7/13.

30. EB-O. Barnsley 25.11.68.

31. EB-O. Barnsley 25.11.68.

32. Jewson (3rd edn) p. 86; G. Davies-EB undated D7/13.

33. See Edward Gardiner's account in Carruthers 1978 pp. 54-9.

34. Herbert Barnsley's negatives are at CAGM.

35. EB-O. Barnsley 25.11.68 suggests that Ernest Barnsley did something in connection with business of which Gimson did not approve, and that the two Mrs Barnsleys had made it plain to Emily Gimson that she was not good enough for Gimson. She, in turn, looked down on the Barnsleys as tradespeople, according to Grace Barnsley: G. Davies-EB undated D7/13.

36. EB-B. G. Burrough 5.12.69.

37. Jewson (3rd edn) p. 40.

38. EB-G. Trevelyan 28.3.73, 8.4.74.

39. EB-O. Barnsley 25.11.68; EB-G. Trev-elyan 1.1.76.

40. S. Barnsley-P. Webb 1.5.04.

41. EB-F. MacCarthy 21.10.80.

42. Malcolm Powell taught science, mathematics, woodwork, archaeology, and singing according to *Bedales School Roll*.

43. Badley p.105.

44. Marsh pp. 216-17.

45. Stewart p. 465.

46. Marsh p. 215.

47. Stewart p. 435.

48. Rothenstein pp. 20, 24-5.

49. F. Partridge, *Julia: A Portrait by Herself & Frances Partridge*, London 1983 pp. 87-8.

50. Rothenstein pp. 20-9, 22.

51. EB-F. MacCarthy 3.11.80.

52. MP21, 'As Head Boy his energy, sound judgement, and unfailing cheerfulness has been of the utmost value to the School, and he has shown himself a most loyal and efficient leader'. S. Barnsley-EB 7.12.17.

53. MP6/4, lecture to Loughborough students 14.7.38.

54. EB-O. Powell 30.11.71.

55. M. C. Lupton - A. Carruthers 31.10.89; *Bedales School Roll*.

56. *Bedales School Roll*.

57. C. Kelly, *Geoffrey Henry Lupton (1882-1949) and others*, unpublished thesis Portsmouth Polytechnic 1976 p. 11. Uncatalogued.

58. Prints of the photographs are in Bedales School Library and possibly result from a pupil's hobby; Tania Barnsley suggests that they may have been taken by Mark Taylor. EB-H. Irwin 15.8.72.

59. This should be Sapperton.

60. See Edward Gardiner's account in Carruthers 1978 p. 58.

61. EB-? 4.12.80 MP9/12.

62. F. V. Burridge, *L.C.C. Central School of Arts and Crafts, its Aim and Organisation. Report by Principal*, 1913 p. 10, quoted in Backemeyer and Gronberg p. 23.

63. See C. Spooner, 'House and Church Furniture', in T. Raffles Davison (ed.), *The Arts Connected With Building*, London 1909 pp. 153-68.

64. EB-B. G. Burrough 22.3.73.

65. EB-? 4.12.80 MP9/12.

66. EB-G. Trevelyan 8.4.74.

67. EB-B. G. Burrough 11-12.81.

68. Quoted by kind permission of William Inman. The incident took place in about 1946.

2. THE WORKSHOP AND BUSINESS PRE-WAR

1. A series of job record books gives details of items made, clients' names, makers' names, hours spent, costs, and so on.

2. EB-J. Arnold 22.7.69.

3. M. C. Lupton-A. Carruthers 31.10.89.

4. EB-F. MacCarthy 25.8.65; Peters 1984 p. 23.

5. S. Barnsley-EB 14.3.26 mentions that the saw is ready when EB wants it; S. Barnsley-EB 26.6.26 that he proposes to send the bench by rail.

6. See Carruthers 1984. EB may have been mistaken about the dresser being Sidney Barnsley's last work since a sideboard made

for Mrs Edge, now in CAGM, 1962.100, was invoiced in 1924 and does not appear to have been made at Froxfield.

7. A dresser and sideboard made for Smith are in Leicestershire Museums, 114.1974, 74.1975.

8. S. Barnsley-EB 27.5.26, 26.6.26, 20.8.26, 25.8.26.

9. H. Thomas, *As It Was and World Without End*, London 1972 p. 115.

10. S. Barnsley-EB 8.9.26, 11.9.26.

11. Information from Herbert Upton.

12. Owen Scrubey was apprenticed to Waals in 1921 and worked unpaid for the first three months to see if he was suitable. He then received 5/- per week for the next twelve months, after which time the pay went up gradually. Apprentice wages in EB's workshop were £11/0/6 in the first year, at Waals's, £9/15/-. The wages were roughly the same as for similar jobs and probably about 1d more per hour than an ordinary carpenter received. Information from Owen Scrubey 12.8.86, in files at CAGM. Cecil Gough was apprenticed at Gordon Russell in 1924 and was paid 5/- per week, increasing so that eventually he earned 1/- per hour: information from Cecil Gough 18.2.90. Max Burrough was apprenticed in 1928 and received 7/6d per week for the first year and an annual rise of 2/6d until at the age of 20 he earned 17/6d per week: B. G. Burrough, 'Then', in *The Woodworker*, vol. 88 no. 1089 Aug.1984 p. 542. T. R. Dennis's story appears in J. Burnett (ed.), *Useful Toil: Autobiographies of Working People from the 1820s to the 1920s*, Harmondsworth 1977 p. 347.

13. P. Kirkham, 'The London Furniture Trade 1700-1870', in *Journal of the Furniture History Society* vol. 24 1988 p. 52; P. Kirkham, R. Mace and J. Porter, *Furnishing the World: The East London Furniture Trade 1830-1980*, London 1987 p. 3.

14. Jewson (2nd edn) p. x.

15. H. B. Grimsditch, 'The British Government Pavilion and Basilica at Wembley', in *The Studio*, vol. 88 1924 p. 27.

16. *The Cabinet Maker and Complete House Furnisher*, 4 July 1925 p. 3. *The Journal of Decorative Art*, September 1925 p. 306, described the British Pavilion as awful but claimed that the contents could compare with those of any other country. *The Studio* seems to have mentioned it only in passing

but dealt at length with work from Poland, Sweden, Denmark, Austria, and the host country in vol. 90 p. 154.

17. M. C. Lupton-A. Carruthers 31.10.89.

18. See Gimson's job record book in CAGM, 1941.225.121, pp. 83-4, 87.

19. EB-H. Irwin 15.8.72.

20. EB-O. Barnsley 25.11.68.

21. EB-C. Wood 27.6.63.

22. Documents relating to Sidney Barnsley's estate were found only recently and are uncatalogued.

23. S. Barnsley-EB 14.3.26.

24. S. Barnsley-EB 20.8.26.

25. The prototype chair is at CAGM, 1970.47. Weir Schultz had changed to Weir Schultz Weir during the First World War to spare his wife the insults she received because of the Germanic name.

26. Badley pp. 226-7.

27. EB-G. Trevelyan 8.4.74.

28. EB-G. Trevelyan 8.4.74.

29. EB-O. Powell 30.11.71. Tania Barnsley thinks that any disapproval was only because of confusion between her and her younger sister.

30. EB-B. G. Burrough tape recording; EB-O. Powell 30.11.71.

31. Peters 1984 p. 32.

32. The job record book in CAGM, 1941.225.121, shows 164 commissions, of which 64 were for stock. It is very difficult to make any definite statements about this because the book only covers the period 1914-19 when the business was affected by the war, and there are no earlier job books surviving. Items in stock in 1919 which were shown in a 1907-8 exhibition include a cabinet in CAGM and two boxes and a cabinet in Leicestershire Museums. Nevertheless, in a letter of 1918, quoted in Comino p. 189, Gimson was optimistic about post-war business.

33. Crawford p. 145.

34. EB's client book provides an alphabetical list of main clients and a miscellaneous list of more casual purchasers.

35. P. Waals - (C. V. or H. W.?) Goddard 15.5.30 in the files of Leicestershire Museums shows that this was a common problem. Waals was concerned that his estimate had been exceeded but hoped that Goddard would find the prices to be on the same basis as other items made for him.

36. The prices of plain walnut desks provide

a rough comparison. One designed by EB for Nina Kellgren in 1932 cost £40/13/- (p. 29). One by Waals of 1930 was £38 (Carruthers 1978 p. 38). Russell's 1938-9 catalogue included a desk at £35 (CAGM, Fairclough Collection). Heal's 1937 catalogue illustrated one at £29/10/- (CAGM, Max Burrough Collection). I am grateful to Graham Leake for allowing me to read his unpublished thesis, *Gordon Russell: 'Decent Furniture for Ordinary People'*, City of Birmingham Polytechnic 1983. This shows that Russell's prices were competitive in relation to commercial manufacturing companies and also indicates the difficulty in making comparisons.

37. J. Maslin-A. Carruthers 4.1.90.

38. EB-V. Simpson 7.4.65.

39. S. Barnsley-EB 16.4.26 and information from Anthony Davies, Grace Barnsley's son.

40. W. R. Lethaby, *Form in Civilization*, London 1922 p. 35. Rogers 1930, p. 2.

41. Gloag (3rd edn) pp. 152-60.

42. H. Mayhew, *London Labour and the London Poor*, London 1851-2 (repr. 1967) p. 223. Board of Trade p. 143. Ray Leigh lecture at CAGM in 1986.

43. Branson and Heinemann p. 158, suggest that the upper classes with incomes over £250 per annum were less hit by the Depression than those with lower incomes. Consumption expenditure fell by about 9-11% among those with incomes over £250 per annum 1929-33, probably less than the fall in prices. The current recession seems to confirm, however, that the purchase of large household items is postponed at such times, since large retailers and small craft businesses alike report a drop in orders.

44. EB-B. G. Burrough 30.4.81. Baynes pp. 12, 35, 50. Information from Cecil Gough, who was laid off when Gordon Russell closed down for a fortnight in 1933. There was no unemployment benefit or holding pay so he had to find another job.

45. EB-B. G. Burrough 29.3.79.

46. Information from Owen Scrubey 12.8.86, in files at CAGM. Information from Mary Greensted.

47. Correspondence between EB, Lucy Barnsley, Grace Davies, and Gilbert C. Morley of Dennes and Company, Solicitor, was found recently and has been added to the EBET archive but is not yet catalogued.

48. He had received a loan of £1172/18/- according to a probate document, uncatalogued.

49. EB-O. Barnsley 25.11.68. EB-G. Davies, EB-G. C. Morley, uncatalogued, see n. 47.

50. Correspondence of October 1943, uncatalogued, see n. 47.

51. EB-O. Barnsley 25.11.68.

52. V&A AAD 1/60-1980, Committee minutes, 16.2.26.

53. EB-I. Neale 31.10.28.

54. V&A AAD 1/61-1980.

55. EB-I. Neale 27.11.31.

56. EB-I. Neale 30.11.31.

57. 15.5.30. 'The considerable order we have just completed for you has been a great help to me at the present difficult time. I feel much obliged to you'. See n. 35.

58. EB-G. C. Morley, uncatalogued, see n. 47.

59. EB-L. Barnsley 23.9.35.

60. EB-L. Barnsley 23.9.35.

61. D. Kelly-EB 4.10.85.

62. MP6/3, lecture to the National Society for Art Education 15.4.66.

63. Stewart p. 152.

64. Edward Barnsley Memorial Meeting 16.4.88, typed transcript p. 11, uncatalogued.

65. The 50-hour week was unusual in the furniture trade by 1920 when hours of journeymen in major cities were between 44 and 47 according to the Department of Employment and Productivity, *British Labour Statistics: Historical Abstract 1886-1968*, London 1971 table 5.

66. Townshend p. 53. Alan Peters says that the makers no longer drew their own full-size details when he started in 1949. Information also from Oliver Morel and Joe Maslin.

67. I am indebted to Rod Herdman for his clear explanation of this complex business. The accounts, cash books, wage records and job books all contain relevant information.

68. Board of Trade pp. 33, 145-6.

69. S. W. Davies-EB 20.7.42.

70. EB-H. Gimson 10.10.69

71. C. Kelly, *Geoffrey Henry Lupton (1882-1949) and others*, thesis Portsmouth Polytechnic 1976 p. 11. Uncatalogued.

72. Comments from Herbert Upton and George Taylor.

73. Information from Owen Scrubey, Cecil

Gough, and Max Burrough.

74. 1938 salary and expenses, £151; 1940 £333; 1942 £243; 1944 £245. For a part-time post this seem to have been generous since it is only a little less than Bert Upton received as foreman in 1945.

75. James pp. 8-9.

76. J. Maslin-A. Carruthers 4.1.90.

77. D. Porter-A. Carruthers 12.6.92, points out that it was uncertain if the college would survive at all.

78. Information from Cecil Gough; J. Maslin-A. Carruthers 4.1.90.

79. Jones p. 5.

80. MP6/5, MP6/4, lectures 28.4.38, 14.7.38.

81. MP6/5.

82. This is a rather obscure incident. Bray returned to the workshop after the war but according to George Taylor, never forgave Barnsley for demoting him.

3. EARLY FURNITURE AND CLIENTS

1. Design Bed 8.

2. EB-? 10.1.80 mentions first piece at 7 years old, Unidentified file; Norwood p. 123 says 5 years old.

3. EB-? 4.12.80 MP9/12.

4. Information from Max Burrough.

5. CAGM 1962.100.

6. Illustrated in Powell *et al.* p. 25.

7. The price was low in comparison with £16/10/- for oak bookshelves made in Waals's workshop in 1920 for W. A. Evans, see Carruthers 1978 p. 47.

8. EB-B. G. Burrough tape recording; EB-B. G. Burrough 25.11.69.

9. S. Barnsley-EB 20.8.26 refers to some of these problems.

10. Leicestershire Museums, 114.1974, illustrated in Carruthers 1978 p. 33.

11. EB-Frank ? 17.5.74, Unidentified file. See also EB-B. G. Burrough 20.10.71. According to the first job book, this piece was made in 1926.

12. S. Barnsley-EB 25.8.26.

13. EB-B. G. Burrough tape recording.

14. Illustrated in Powell *et al.* p. 28.

15. EB-G. Trevelyan 8.4.74.

16. H. Upton-P. Laughton in conversation 5.6.85, Oral History Project file. Curiously, the two desks by Barnsley were veneered while a similar piece designed by R. D. Russell and now at CAGM 1984.143, looks like a veneered piece but is of solid timber.

17. EB-A. Mitchell 11.3.54.

18. EB-C. Wood 27.6.63.

19. J. Maslin-A. Carruthers 4.1.90. EB-B. G. Burrough tape recording refers to the fact that his pieces invariably conformed to the *vesica piscis* and that the height of tall pieces, such as chests of drawers, could be determined as H = diagonal of square of base.

20. Jones pp. 5-6, Proposition 9.

21. Rogers 1932 p. 50.

22. J. Maslin-A. Carruthers 4.1.90.

23. Information from Oliver Morel.

24. EB-B. G. Burrough 2.3.82.

25. Design Cab 30 of 1932 is a good example. Such pieces were made for Charles Hawkins and Timothy and Enid Houghton.

26. S. Barnsley-EB 7.12.17.

27. Information from Rosemary Mulholland, daughter of Charles Hawkins.

28. CAGM 1947.147. EB made his comment to Mary Comino.

29. The cabinet cost something between £200 and £275. The client book gives one figure and letters from EB the other.

30. It would be interesting to look at the numbers of architectural commissions in relation to domestic work and the time spent on each type but I have not had time to analyse this. The figures are very variable: for instance in 1923, 38 jobs were all domestic; in 1924, of 53 jobs 12 were architectural; in 1935, of 77 jobs 2 were architectural.

31. This was how Weir Schultz worked with Gimson.

32. Gimson's job book, CAGM 1941.225. 121. Waals's ledger, Gloucestershire Record Office D2876.

33. V&A W.125-1978. Comment by F. Levson from V&A file. Illustrated in Arts Council p. 84. There is a design in the Royal Institute of British Architects Drawings Collection.

34. Designs Bed 4, 5.

35. There are several Russell catalogues in CAGM, Fairclough Collection.

36. It is difficult to compare costs because the Russell catalogues state that prices for school furniture vary according to number ordered and changes in cost of materials. See *A Catalogue of Furniture for Schools*, CAGM, Fairclough Collection.

4. THE WAR YEARS AND AFTER

1. EB-C. H. St John Hornby 21.3.40.
2. Stewart p. 444.
3. R. Powell-EB 7.10.42 A36/16. Roger Powell's letters are quoted by kind permission of his family, Ann Donnelly, David Powell, and Jill Thompson-Lewis.
4. EB-R. Powell 5.2.44 A36/?; information from Gonda Stamford.
5. Information from Cecil Gough.
6. For H. H. Martyn see J. Whitaker, *The Best*, privately published 1985.
7. EB-E. Whittall 11.8.44 A36/92.
8. See Geffrye Museum, *Utility Furniture and Fashion 1941-1951*, London 1974, for details of the wartime regulations.
9. H. Norris-EB 18.8.42 A36/8, 23.9.42 A36/10.
10. EB-H. Norris 30.9.42 A36/12, 30.9.43 A36/39.
11. Farleigh 1945 pp. 44-51; B. Leach, *Beyond East and West: Memoirs, Portraits & Essays*, London 1978 p. 219.
12. V&A AAD 1/62-1980.
13. EB-B. G. Burrough 22.3.73.
14. MP6/5 lecture 28.4.38.
15. Gimson's letters in CAGM, Max Burrough Collection.
16. *Crafts: The Red Rose Guild Magazine*, no. 1 1948 p. 3.
17. Quoted by F. MacCarthy, *Eric Gill*, London 1989 p. 274.
18. J. Myerson, *Gordon Russell: Designer of Furniture 1892-1992*, London 1992 p. 122.
19. EB-C. Wood 17.4.63.
20. EB-I. Cleaver 12.6.69.
21. A. Huxley, *Antic Hay*, London 1923, 1948 edn pp. 100, 112, 'It was a pity she couldn't afford to change the furniture. She saw now that it wouldn't do at all. She would go and tell Aunt Aggie about the dreadful middle-classness of her Art and Craftiness.'
22. J. Collins, *The Omega Workshops*, London 1983 pp. 6-7, 30-1.
23. Sweet p. 16.
24. Branson and Heinemann pp. 1-2, 42, 241.
25. E. Maclagan-C. Sempill 19.1.42, quoted by Howes p. 68.
26. Sweet p. 15.
27. R. Powell-EB 7.4.42 A36/3.
28. 62 members were in favour of the changes from a response of 82 out of the membership of 150, EB-R. Powell 1.11.42 A36/?
29. London 1932.
30. R. Powell-EB 30.9.42 A36/13.
31. EB-J. Farleigh 2.10.42 A36/14.
32. J. Farleigh-Arts and Crafts Exhibition Society members, 7.12.42 A36/28.
33. R. Powell-EB 27.10.42 A36/17.
34. Noel White 1988 pp. 69-71.
35. Noel White 1988 pp. 58-60. M. Pilkington-EB 6.2.44 A36/56.
36. R. Powell-EB 5.1.43 A36/30.
37. EB-R. Powell 14.2.44 A36/60.
38. EB-H. Norris 7.2.44 A36/58; H. Norris-EB 12.2.44 A36/61.
39. V&A AAD 1/64-1980, Report of President, May 1945.
40. J. Farleigh-Arts and Crafts Exhibition Society members, 11.11.44 A36/100.
41. V&A AAD 1/64-1980, Reports of 21.10.44, 17.3.45, 2.3.46.
42. R. Powell-EB 5.1.43 A36/30 responds to an idea from EB but EB's earlier letter is not in the file. Other relevant letters EB-R. Powell 1.7.44 A36/76, 22.7.44 A36/83.
43. EB-R. Powell 22.7.44 A36/83.
44. J. Farleigh-Arts and Crafts Exhibition Society members 7.8.45 A36/107.
45. R. Powell-EB 23.7.45 A36/?
46. Noel White 1989 pp. 207-14.
47. Crafts Centre of Great Britain leaflet of 1946 in CAGM, Max Burrough Collection.
48. Noel White 1989 p. 210.
49. A. Hudson-E. Sharpe letter of 1950 at Abbot Hall Museum, Kendal.
50. Farleigh 1950 p. 53.
51. Alan Peters also had good orders via the Crafts Centre when he set up in about 1962, but Stanley Davies said in 1955 that he had received only one small commission through the Centre and had sold nothing there since 1952, S. W. Davies-EB 18.4.55.

5. NEW DIRECTIONS IN THE WORK-SHOP

1. EB-F. MacCarthy 25.8.65.
2. Surprisingly, there is no correspondence file about this in the EBET archive.
3. Information from Mary Greensted (née Comino).
4. In conversation with Penny Laughton, Bert Upton said he accepted a drop in wages from £15 to £3 per week, Oral History Project file. The wages book shows he re-

ceived £5/10/- per week at Barnsley's just after the war so it may be that he meant he took a drop to a third.

5. EB-M. Pilkington 1.10.45 R7/46. This survey by the R.R.G. on the state of the crafts was probably used for the 1946 Board of Trade Report on furniture.

6. Barnsley did not sell anything through British Handicrafts Export until 1949 when he sold an oak lectern, walnut chairs and table, and rosewood mirror for £359/18/-.

7. Probably Barnet, Murray, and Osmond.

8. Robert Townshend was the ex-service-man. The other two were presumably David Powell and Peter Hensman.

9. Russell 1968 p. 223.

10. Information from Hugh Birkett.

11. Loughborough salary reduced from £223/5/4 in 1945 to £20/7/8 in 1946, nil in 1947 and £109/9/1 in 1948.

12. Oral History Project file.

13. Board of Trade p. 131.

14. EB-D. Pye 12.12.51.

15. EB-I. Cleaver 12.6.69.

16. EB-I. Cleaver 14.12.1971. See also EB-F. Ockenden 24.11.71.

17. Bert Upton made a chair like this and Harry Davoll made one that is now at Rodmarton.

18. W. R. Lethaby, 'Cabinet making', in A. H. Mackmurdo (ed.), *Plain Handicrafts*, London 1892 (repr. as *Simple Furniture*, Dryad Leaflet no. 5, Leicester 1922) pp. 3-5.

19. EB-B. G. Burrough 22.11.81.

20. EB-? undated part letter in Unidentified file.

21. S. Barnsley-P. Webb 1.5.1904.

22. EB-J. Arnold 22.7.69.

23. M. Cardew, *A Pioneer Potter: An Autobiography*, London 1988 p. 32.

24. Jewson (3rd edn) p. 30.

25. E. Gimson-W. R. Lethaby 10.5.1916, 18.4.1916, CAGM, Max Burrough Collection.

26. R. H. Hordern, 'Furniture and Furnishings 1880-1955', in *The Cabinet Maker*, July 1955 pp. 69-70, states that great improvements to woodworking machinery took place in the decade 1920-30.

27. Information from Godfrey Beaton, Mike McGrath, Alan Peters, George Taylor and others.

28. EB-V. Simpson 7.4.65.

29. EB-I. Cleaver 12.6.69.

30. EB-I. Cleaver 12.6.69.

31. EB-L. Lambourne 30.4.73.

32. Tania Barnsley thinks Upton was wrong and that EB did know exactly how pieces were to be made.

33. H. Upton-P. Laughton conversation, Oral History Project file.

34. In contrast, Alan Peters himself makes the pieces in which some design or constructional problem needs solving and his assistant, Keith Newton, makes the things when these difficulties have been resolved and what is needed is his extra technical skill. It appears that Barnsley was not interested in the minute detail of how things were made and left this much more to his foreman.

35. Planing appears as a chargeable cost in the job book in 1951.

36. EB-Wilton Curb Company 1955 deals with problems of the veneer press. EB-B. G. Burrough tape recording, describes the solution.

37. MP18, annotated leaflet about the sale, 18 February-2 April 1956.

38. Oral History Project file.

39. Peters 1984 p. 26.

40. EB-G. Peters 29.1.49.

41. Peters 1984 p. 26.

42. EB-B. G. Burrough tape recording.

43. EB-V. Simpson 24.6.74. EB often said that after the war the workshop could produce a chair in 29 hours, a considerable reduction in time. I hoped to be able to make detailed comparisons of the time saved by using machine tools, but have found that the variations in size, style, and timber has made this impossible in the time available to me.

44. D. N. Chester-EB 16.7.57 N27/23.

45. N27/71-82.

46. H. Upton-P. Laughton in conversation believed the reduction in staff was caused by greater efficiency through the use of power tools, Oral History Project file. EB-D. Leach 26.8.68 said work had been short for past 6-8 months but the order book was now full.

47. S. W. Davies-EB 18.4.55.

48. EB-V. Simpson 7.4.65.

49. Information from Arnold Pentelow.

50. Derrick 1950 p. 64.

51. Information from A. Pentelow.

52. R.I.B. Report 1950-52.

53. R40/23-28.

54. R.I.B. salary and expenses 1949 £291/

5/8; 1950 £18/18/-; 1951 £569/15/- ; 1952 £255/13/-; 1953 and 1954 £120/ 16/-; 1955 £225/16/-; 1956 £55/1/6; 1957 £38.

55. *R.I.B. Report* 1954-55.

56. R40/255. An extensive tour by EB to visit 18 craftsmen in 1951 took in Cambridge, Leicester, Loughborough, Chalford, Daneway, Cirencester, and Cheltenham, where Barnsley gave a talk at the Exhibition of Cotswold Craftsmanship at the Montpellier Rotunda.

57. EB-S. W. Davies 27.3.55; S. W. Davies-EB 18.4.55.

58. R. Fyson-EB 25.2.61 N27/85.

59. EB-B. G. Burrough 18.11.81.

60. I have seen two items made to Barnsley's R.I.B. designs, one by Owen Scrubey, who trained in Waals's workshop, and one by a doctor who did woodwork as a hobby.

61. EB-E. W. Parkhouse 14.2.57 R40/182.

62. *R.I.B. Reports* 1950-2, 1953-4.

63. EB-W. Inman 20.8.73.

64. W. Mallinson-EB 20.10.54 W41/1-29.

65. For example, EB-B. G. Burrough 19.7.79.

66. Oral History Project file.

67. Early cashbooks show payments to magazines. EB-V. Simpson 7.4.65 mentions the idea of advertising.

68. EB-V. Simpson 7.4.65.

69. EB-B. G. Burrough 18.4.73; transcript of *Blind Man's Gate*, Ernest Smith and Philip Donnellan radio interview, uncatalogued.

70. EB-J. Barnsley 8.11.58.

71. EB-J. Barnsley 17.1.59.

72. Transcript of S. Barnsley-P. Webb, undated part letter B97/1. Jon Barnsley, however, says that his grandfather was as frugal with the firewood as with everything else, so for him this does not conjure up visions of a roaring blaze.

73. EB-J. Barnsley 11.4.61.

74. Plans dated 3.6.61-15.2.62.

6. THE WIDER WORLD OF THE CRAFTS

1. EB-C. Wood 2.10.63. The official accounts show a profit in 1965 of £1027, though the cash book shows a debit in this year.

2. EB-V. Simpson 7.4.65; correspondence with Courtauld's.

3. EB-V. Simpson 4.11.69.

4. Information from Godfrey Beaton, John Purdy, Ken Rosewarne and others.

5. Crowther Report 1959, Newsom Report 1963.

6. D. Porter-A. Carruthers June 1992.

7. Among the older ones were Joe Maslin and Cecil Gough.

8. James pp. 16-17, and comments from Arthur Dearden, John Purdy, Ken Rose-warne, John Warburton.

9. Nuttgens p. 59. Quoted by kind permission of Patrick Nuttgens.

10. MP6/3 lecture 15.4.66.

11. EB-V. Simpson 13.10.69. Alan Peters, who went through the traditional training and then taught, agrees with this; Don Porter, with long experience in teaching, disagrees.

12. James p. 27.

13. Carruthers 1978 p. 14.

14. Patrick Nuttgens in his book of 1988 seemed optimistic about a change of view. Don Porter is less so, and feels that the National Curriculum since 1988 has ruined C.D.T. since it does not allow time for the making of things children have designed.

15. EB-O. Barnsley 25.11.68.

16. S. W. Davies-EB 18.4.55.

17. EB-V. Simpson 7.4.65. If we take £500 as EB's average, comparison with figures in G. Routh, *Occupation and Pay in Great Britain 1906-79*, London and Basingstoke 1980, pp. 70, 92, 101, suggests this relates most closely to the salaries of Civil Service laboratory assistants, clerks, and skilled workers such as carpenters and bricklayers. It is unlikely, however, that Barnsley included in his figure the benefit of rent-free accommodation and the expenses which can be claimed from a business.

18. EB-O. Barnsley 25.11.68.

19. EB-O. Barnsley 25.11.68.

20. EB-B. G. Burrough 8.1.82.

21. EB-O. Barnsley 25.11.68.

22. MP6/3 lecture to National Society for Art Education 15.4.66, mentions overheads of £150-£170 per week and the need to sell furniture to the value of £180-£200. EB-O. Powell 20.5.67.

23. EB-B. G. Burrough 26.1.70; EB-V. Simpson 4.11.69.

24. Information from George Taylor. Ernest Smith said that Gimson also did this and would sooner lose his profits on a job by putting a little extra work in to make it better; if the maker had given an estimate

of time this could be a bit aggravating: transcript of *Blind Man's Gate*, Ernest Smith and Philip Donnellan radio interview p. 58, uncatalogued.

25. There seem to have been no paid holidays before the war and in the mid 1950s the craftsmen had only 1 week paid holiday, H. Upton-P. Laughton, Oral History Project file. EB-O. Barnsley 25.11.68. EB-I. Cleaver 14.12.71.

26. EB-V. Simpson 7.4.65.

27. EB-C. Wood 1.5.64.

28. EB-S. Pocock 21.11.62 C81/35, 30.11. 61 C81/22.

29. V&A AAD 1/67-1980 Minutes. D. Kindersley-S. Pocock 22.6.61, D. Kindersley's archive.

30. C81/23. Signed DK/RN but RN was probably David Kindersley's secretary rather than a collaborator.

31. A37/6. See Sweet p. 12.

32. C81/2.

33. EB-JF 12.3.61. There must have been a file now lost.

34. V&A AAD 1/67-1980 Minutes 26.1.62. By 13.4.62, £1,200 had been received. Minutes 7.9.61.

35. He resigned from the Council of the Arts and Crafts Exhibition Society on 2.6.62 because of 'other commitments'.

36. The report was suggested to Crofton Gane as a useful way of helping the crafts by Arnold Pentelow of the R.I.B. Gane chose Wood, presumably from contact in the South West since Gane was from Bristol. Information from A. Pentelow. C. Wood-EB 19.3.63.

37. EB-C. Wood 23.6.63.

38. EB-C. Wood 12.4.63, 17.6.63.

39. EB-C. Wood 17.6.63.

40. EB-C. Wood 25.9.63.

41. EB-C. Wood 25.9.63.

42. EB-C. Wood 21.1.64, 25.9.63.

43. EB-C. Wood 2.10.63. According to Joel p. 52, average attendance at the Design Centre in 1968 was 3000 per day.

44. EB-C. Wood 3.11.63.

45. EB-C. Wood 22.11.63.

46. V&A AAD 1/67-1980 Minutes 13. 12.63.

47. C. Wood-EB 18.1.64.

48. EB-C. Wood 21.1.64.

49. EB-C. Wood 21.1.64.

50. C. Wood-EB 23.1.64. V&A AAD 1/67-1980 Minutes 15.11.63.

51. V&A AAD 1/67-1980 Minutes 31.1.64,

24.4.62, 1.2.64.

52. EB-C. Wood 19.5.64 C81/63. CAGM, Max Burrough Collection 1986.1243.

53. Wood had already retired so may have been in a hurry to get the Crafts Council started because of his age. He died in 1974.

54. Report by Chairman of Crafts Centre to Crafts Council of Great Britain, 29.10.64 C81/67, and reports to Crafts Centre Council, 25.9.64, 21.10.64 V&A AAD 1/67-1980.

55. It is not clear if any of these letters were sent or if they are just drafts; EB's letter to *The Times* was not published if it was sent. EB-D. Kindersley dated 9.11.2965 (*sic*), K19/1; EB-*The Times* in response to an article published on 13.11.64, C81/71; EB-Secretary of Crafts Centre 1.12.64 C81/73. See also F. MacCarthy, 'Crafts Conflict', in *The Guardian* 26.11.64 C82/29.

56. Crafts Centre of Great Britain Newsletter, 20 November 1965, CAGM, Max Burrough Collection 1986.1243.

57. Joel p. 63.

58. *Introduction to British Craftsmanship*, Crafts Council of Great Britain exhibition leaflet 1970 in possession of Alan Peters. Comment from Alan Peters.

59. EB-D. Leach 23.3.67.

60. EB-V. Simpson 7.4.65.

61. EB-O. Morel 30.11.67.

62. EB-W. Elloway 19.12.67. According to the report of the Chairman of the Crafts Centre of 1964, an exhibition for under thirties was held there in that year, David Kindersley's archive.

63. EB-D. Leach 18.9.68.

64. Crafts Advisory Committee p. 14.

65. Reilly p. 83.

7. RENEWED INTEREST IN THE ARTS AND CRAFTS

1. EB-I. Cleaver 11.2.72.

2. EB-M. Gimson 21.10.59.

3. J. Farleigh-EB 20.3.44.

4. EB-V. Simpson 2.8.77.

5. MP7

6. EB-F. MacCarthy 14.9.68.

7. EB-V. Simpson 13.10.69.

8. V&A AAD 1/35 1980.

9. *The Cabinet-Maker and Complete House Furnisher* 11.3.1950, pp. 931-8.

10. MP6/3 lecture 15.4.66.

11. EB-I. Cleaver 11.2.72.

12. EB-G. Trevelyan 18.12.72.

13. EB-I. Cleaver 11.2.72.

14. EB-P. Hurst 8.10.68. EB-F. MacCarthy 25.8.65. O. Barnsley-EB 12.9.68.

15. EB-O. Barnsley 25.11.68.

16. EB-O. Barnsley 25.11.68.

17. EB-O. Barnsley 25.11.68.

18. EB-V. Simpson 4.11.69.

19. EB-P. Reilly 22.5.78.

20. The Exhibition of Cotswold Craftsmanship at the Montpellier Rotunda in Cheltenham in 1952 seems to have been regarded as of only local interest.

21. EB-V. Simpson 13.10.69.

22. EB-G. Trevelyan 22.5.73.

23. EB-G. Trevelyan 13.12.73.

24. Norwood pp. 123-9. Robertshaw.

25. EB-G. Trevelyan 2.4.73.

26. EB-I. Cleaver 14.9-11.71.

27. EB-B. G. Burrough 18.1.7?.

28. EB-B. G. Burrough 18.6.72.

29. EB-? 17.8.72, Unidentified file.

30. EB-G. Trevelyan 18.12.72

31. EB-I. Cleaver 14.12.71. EB-W. Inman 11.1.71.

32. EB-I. Cleaver 14.12.71.

33. Undated part letter in Unidentified file.

34. P. Reyntiens, 'What sort of life?', in *Crafts* no. 2 May 1973, pp. 30-3.

35. EB-G. Trevelyan 28.3.73, EB-D. Leach 9.7.73.

36. EB-P. Hurst 8.10.68.

37. EB-V. Simpson 4.11.69.

38. Comment of Gonda Stamford.

39. Bookshelves belonged to Lady Sylvia Legge, notes in Oral History Project file.

40. EB-F. MacCarthy 13.3.71.

41. EB-V. Simpson 2.8.77.

42. Information from Herbert Upton.

43. EB-G. Trevelyan 8.4.74.

44. Design Mir 36.

45. EB-Mr Arnold 22.7.69; EB-Wadkin Ltd 31.10.68.

46. EB-I. Cleaver 14.12.71.

47. EB-G. Trevelyan 8.4.74.

48. EB-I. Cleaver 14.12.71.

49. EB-V. Simpson 21.2.73.

50. Alan Peters was the maker mentioned in EB's letter.

51. EB-L. Lambourne 30.4.73.

52. *Crafts* no. 2 May 1973, pp. 40-1.

53. Information from Ann Hartree. Crafts Advisory Committee p. 1.

54. W. Inman-EB 16.1.71 shows that Inman realized the hidden possibilities of doubling to 4d for the third rather than going to 3d as the victim might expect from the letter.

55. EB-B. G. Burrough 29.3.79 mentions a conversation he had with his father when he asked how Sidney Barnsley felt about not being credited in the book for his share in the work and he replied 'Oh you can't help that'. According to a memorial volume about Dorothy Walker privately printed about 1963, Norman Jewson was the editor of the Gimson book, which makes it more strange that the Barnsleys were hardly mentioned, since he was married to one of Ernest's daughters.

56. EB-W. Inman 1.12.76.

57. EB-G. Beaton 10.3.77.

58. C. V. Peterson, 10 Downing Street - EB 4.2.77 uncatalogued.

59. EB-W. Inman 23.12.70.

8. THE POST-WAR FURNITURE AND CLIENTS

1. Powell *et al.* p. 35, no. 24.

2. Powell *et al.* p. 36, no. 26.

3. Robert Townshend comments in Oral History Project file.

4. Drawing Mir 14.

5. See for comparison, Joel pls. 78-80.

6. EB-V. Simpson 4.11.69.

7. W. Inman-A. Carruthers 23.5.92. By slicing, up to 140 veneers per inch can be obtained. EB-E. Rodker 11.4.63.

8. Information from George Taylor.

9. For example of Joel corner cupboard designed by Alister Maynard in 1934 see Joel 1969 pl. 56. Russell 1947 p. 62.

10. EB-B. G. Burrough 3.11.69. This letter also mentions EB's uncertainty about whether this derives from Sheraton or Hepplewhite.

11. EB-B. G. Burrough 20.10.71.

12. Powell *et al.* p. 35, no. 24.

13. EB-E. Rodker 11.4.63.

14. EB-E. Rodker 11.4.63.

15. Waals's ledger, Gloucestershire Record Office D2876.

16. Now in CAGM 1971 43-44.

17. A. Mitchell-EB 9.6.53.

18. A. Mitchell-EB 9.11.53.

19. EB-A. Mitchell 28.1.54, 29.1.54; Design Cab 158.

20. For example see Design Cab 230.

21. EB-A. Mitchell 11.3.54.

22. A. Mitchell-EB 23.3.54; EB-A. Mitchell 25.3.54.

23. A. Mitchell-EB 23.3.54.
24. A. Mitchell-EB 30.3.54.
25. Design Cab 180, 181.
26. EB-A. Mitchell 14.10.55.
27. A. Mitchell-EB 28.10.55.
28. A. Mitchell-EB 11.5.56.
29. Information from Mrs Cole.
30. I. Neale-EB Good Friday 1950.
31. EB-C. Wood 3.11.63 mentions a mahogany bedroom suite rejected by a client. This had to be written off in the accounts as a bad debt.
32. EB-J. Roscoe 27.2.68; J. Roscoe-EB 27.9.68.
33. Powell *et al.* p. 55, no. 72.
34. EB-V. Simpson 13.10.69.
35. Russell 1968 p. 232.
36. Photos 33/57-9, 8/32-47.
37. EB-C. Wood 27.6.63.
38. EB-F. MacCarthy 25.8.65.
39. K. Antonini-A. Carruthers 11.7.92.
40. P. Hubbard-EB 25.3.62.
41. For instance, EB-A. Hartree 17.5.79 mentions that he was making mirrors designed in the 1950s.
42. EB-R. Townshend 18.7.50.
43. EB-A. Knight 21.4.60.
44. Powell *et al.* p. 51, no. 64.
45. Undated part letter in Unidentified file.
46. EB-H. Hammond 21.9.70.
47. EB-B. G. Burrough 23.9.70; EB-H. Hammond 21.9.70.
48. EB-B. G. Burrough 6.2.74.
49. Illustrated in Burrough 1981 (2) p. 75.
50. EB-G. Beaton 26.7.77.
51. EB-G. Beaton 1.8.77, 29.9.77.
52. EB-G. Beaton 26.7.77.
53. CAGM 1982 194.
54. Design Bed 28.
55. Undated part letter in Unidentified file.
56. EB-G. Beaton 1.8.77, 29.9.77; EB-B. G. Burrough 15.3.78.
57. Powell *et al.* p. 64.
58. EB-B. G. Burrough ?.11.70.
59. EB-Mr Parkes 7.4.65.
60. EB-V. Simpson 16.11.81.
61. Comment from Gonda Stamford.
62. Design Cab 274.
63. Powell *et al.* p. 30, no. 15.
64. EB-B. G. Burrough 25.3.77.
65. EB-C. Wood 17.4.63.
66. EB-B. G. Burrough 18.11.81.
67. EB-B. G. Burrough 1.11.78.

9. THE EDUCATIONAL TRUST AND THE FUTURE

1. EB-W. Inman 20.1.79.
2. EB-B. G. Burrough 27.8.76.
3. EB-B. G. Burrough 22.3.79.
4. EB-B. G. Burrough 12.11.79, 30.4.81.
5. Notes by EB, Unidentified file.
6. Prof. J. H. Kellgren, Edward Barnsley Memorial Meeting 16.4.88, typed transcript p. 9, uncatalogued.
7. EB-F. MacCarthy 7.1.81.
8. EB-V. Simpson 16.1.81.
9. Gonda Stamford said his driving was an adventure, Edward Barnsley Memorial Meeting 16.4.88, typed transcript p. 7, uncatalogued; EB-V. Simpson 16.11.81.
10. Alzheimer's disease was the diagnosis.
11. Arlott, p. 17, wrote 'combative prawns' but George Taylor recalled a more alliterative version.
12. George Jack, *Wood Carving*, London 1903 pp. 108-9. Quoted EB-BGB 22.1.81.
13. See similar argument by Stuart Devlin, a silversmith in *Crafts* no. 2 May 1973, p. 14.
14. EB-H. Norris 3.9.42.

SELECT BIBLIOGRAPHY

Arlott, John, 'An artist craftsman in Hampshire', in *Hampshire*, Feb. 1968, pp. 16-17.

Arts Council of Great Britain, *Thirties: British Art and Design Before the War* (exhibition catalogue), London 1979.

Aslet, Clive, *The Last Country Houses*, New Haven and London 1982.

Backemeyer, Sylvia, and Gronberg, Theresa, *W. R. Lethaby 1857-1931: Architecture, Design and Education* (exhibition catalogue), London 1984.

Badley, J. H., *Memories and Reflections*, London 1955.

Baynes, Ken and Kate, *Gordon Russell*, London 1981.

Bedales Society, Brown, Paul (ed.), *Bedales School Roll*, Steep 1962.

Board of Trade, *Working Party Report: Furniture*, London 1946.

Bradshaw, A. E., *Handmade Woodwork of the Twentieth Century*, London 1962.

Branson, Noreen, and Heinemann, Margot, *Britain in the Nineteen Thirties*, London 1971.

Burrough, B. G., 'Edward Barnsley', in *Connoisseur*, Dec. 1973, pp. 250-5.

Burrough, B. G., 'Bedales Library East Hampshire, England', in *Working Wood*, vol. 3 no. 2 1981, pp. 35-7.

Burrough, B. G., 'Made to stand the test of time', in *Antique Collector*, vol. 52 no. 7 July 1981, pp. 74-7.

Carruthers, Annette, *Ernest Gimson and the Cotswold Group of Craftsmen* (museum catalogue), Leicester 1978.

Carruthers, Annette, *Gimson and Barnsley: A catalogue of drawings by Ernest Gimson, Sidney Barnsley and other designers of the Arts and Crafts Movement* (museum catalogue), Cheltenham 1984.

Cheltenham Art Gallery and Museum, *'Good Citizen's Furniture'* (exhibition catalogue), Cheltenham 1976.

Cleaver, Idris G., 'The Edward Barnsley Educational Trust', in *Woodworker*, Aug. 1980, pp. 509-12.

Comino, Mary, *Gimson and the Barnsleys: 'Wonderful furniture of a commonplace kind'*, London 1980 (reprinted under name Greensted, Gloucester 1991).

Crafts Advisory Committee, *The Craftsman's Art* (exhibition catalogue), London 1973.

Crafts Advisory Committee, *The Work of the Crafts Advisory Committee 1971-1974*, London 1974.

Crawford, Alan, *C. R. Ashbee: Architect, Designer & Romantic Socialist*, New Haven and London 1985.

Derrick, Freda, *Country Craftsmen*, London 1945.

Derrick, Freda, *A Trinity of Craftsmen*, London 1950.

Farleigh, John (ed.), *Fifteen Craftsmen on their Crafts*, London 1945.

Farleigh, John, 'The Arts and Crafts Exhibition Society', in *The Studio*, vol. 130 1945, pp. 137-47.

Farleigh, John (ed.), *The Creative Craftsman*, London 1950.

Farleigh, John, 'The Crafts Centre of Great Britain', in *The Studio*, vol. 140 1950, pp. 52-3.

Gloag, John, *English Furniture*, London 1934 (2nd edn 1944, 3rd edn 1948).

Hemsley, John, and Peters, Alan, 'The Great Craftsman', in *Woodworker*, March 1988, pp. 204-6.

Houston, John (ed.), *Craft Classics Since the 1940s*, London 1988.

Howes, Justin, 'Documents of the Craft Revival I', in *Craft History One*, Bath 1988, pp. 65-72.

Hughes, Luke, 'The Edward Barnsley Workshop Today: Its Origins and Development' (exhibition review), in *Crafts*, no. 92 May/June1988, pp. 53-4.

James, G. T. (ed), *Handicraft to Creative Design: Loughborough 1930-1980*, Loughborough 1980.

Jewson, Norman, *By Chance I Did Rove*, privately published 1951 (2nd edn The Roundwood Press 1973, 3rd edn Gryffon Publications 1986).

Joel, David, *Furniture Design Set Free*, London 1969 (revised version of *The Adventure of British Furniture*, London 1953).

Jones, Owen, *The Grammar of Ornament*, London 1856 (reprint Studio Editions 1986).

Leicester Museum, *Ernest Gimson* (exhibition catalogue), Leicester 1969.

Lethaby, W. R., Powell, A. H., and Griggs, F. L., *Ernest Gimson, His Life & Work*, Stratford-upon-Avon 1924.

Liepmann, Kate, *Apprenticeship: An Enquiry into its Adequacy under Modern Conditions*, London 1960.

Lowenstein, Harold, 'Edward Barnsley: The grand old man of English furniture design', in *Fine Woodworking*, no. 16 May-June 1979, pp. 38-44.

Lowenstein, Harold, 'Edward Barnsley, craftsman', in *The Countryman*, Autumn 1980, pp. 46-51.

Lucas, John, 'Reminiscences of Edward Barnsley's Workshop', in *Woodworking Crafts*, no. 21 Nov. 1986-Jan. 1987, pp. 34-8.

MacCarthy, Fiona, 'Arts & Crafts & Bedales', in *Crafts*, no. 48 Jan/Feb 1981, pp. 26-33.

Marsh, Jan, *Back to the Land*, London 1982.

Noel White, James, 'The Unexpected Phoenix I: The Sutherland Tea Set', in *Craft History One*, Bath 1988, pp. 49-64.

Noel White, James, 'The First Crafts Centre of Great Britain: Bargaining for a Time Bomb', in *Journal of Design History*, vol. 2 nos. 2 & 3 1989, pp. 207-14.

Norbury, Betty, *British Craftsmanship in Wood*, London 1990.

Norwood, John, *Craftsmen at Work*, London 1977.

Nuttgens, Patrick, *What Should We Teach and How Should We Teach It? Aims and Purpose of Higher Education*, Aldershot 1988.

Peters, Alan, *Cabinetmaking: The Professional Approach*, London 1984.

Peters, Alan, 'Unsung Hero', in *Crafts*, no. 76 Sep./Oct. 1985, pp. 38-9.

Powell, Roger, Burrough, B. G., and Trevelyan, Sir George, *Edward Barnsley: Sixty Years of Furniture Design and Cabinet Making*, The Edward Barnsley Educational Trust, Froxfield 1982.

Pye, David, *The Nature and Art of Workmanship*, Cambridge 1968 (paperback edition 1978).

Reilly, Paul, *An Eye on Design*, London 1987.

Robertshaw, Ursula, 'Tradition in furniture making', in *The Illustrated London News*, June 1973, pp. 89-92.

Rogers, John C., *Modern English Furniture*, London 1930.

Rogers, John C., *Furniture & Furnishing*, London 1932.

Rothenstein, John, *Summer's Lease: Autobiography 1901-1938*, London 1965.

Russell, Gordon, *The Things We See: Furniture*, West Drayton 1947.

Russell, Gordon, *Designer's Trade*, London 1968.

Stewart, W. A. C., *Progressives and Radicals in English Education 1750-1970*, London 1972.

Stockport Museums and Art Gallery Service, *Fitness for Purpose and Pleasure in Use: Furniture from the Edward Barnsley Workshop 1922 to the Present Day* (exhibition catalogue), Stockport 1985.

Sweet, Meg, 'From Combined Arts to Designer Craftsmen: The Archives of the Arts and Crafts Exhibition Society', in *Craft History One*, Bath 1988, pp. 8-19.

Syson, Les, 'With The Grain', in *Woodworking Crafts*, no.18 Feb.-Apr. 1986, pp. 12-15.

Townshend, Robert, 'Hand Made Furniture', in *The Gift Buyer International*, March 1969, pp. 53-4.

Ward, Colin, 'Edward Barnsley' (exhibition review), in *Crafts*, no. 56 May/June 1982, p. 53.

Williams, W. M., *The Country Craftsman*, London 1958.

INDEX